Tradition of the Law and Law of the Tradition

Recent Titles in
Contributions in Criminology and Penology

Innovative Approaches in the Treatment of Drug Abuse: Program Models and Strategies
James A. Inciardi, Frank M. Tims, and Bennett W. Fletcher, editors

Coca and Cocaine: An Andean Perspective
Felipe E. Mac Gregor, editor

Police Under Pressure: Resolving Disputes
Robert Coulson

Punishing Criminals: Developing Community-Based Intermediate Sanctions
Malcolm Davies

Crack and the Evolution of Anti-Drug Policy
Steven R. Belenko

In Defense of Prisons
Richard A. Wright

Police in Contradiction: The Evolution of the Police Function in Society
Cyril D. Robinson, Richard Scaglion, with J. Michael Olivero

Drug Abuse Treatment: The Implementation of Innovative Approaches
Bennett W. Fletcher, James A. Inciardi, and Arthur M. Horton

State Police in the United States: A Socio-Historical Analysis
H. Kenneth Bechtel

Academic Politics and the History of Criminal Justice Education
Frank Morn

Crime History and Histories of Crime: Studies in the Historiography of Crime and Criminal Justice in Modern History
Clive Emsley and Louis A. Knafla, editors

The Effectiveness of Innovative Approaches in the Treatment of Drug Abuse
Frank M. Tims, James A. Inciardi, Bennett W. Fletcher, and Arthur MacNeill Horton, Jr., editors

Tradition of the Law and Law of the Tradition

Law, State, and Social Control in China

XIN REN

Contributions in Criminology and Penology, Number 50
Marvin Wolfgang, Series Adviser

GREENWOOD PRESS
Westport, Connecticut • London

Library of Congress Cataloging-in-Publication Data

Ren, Xin.
Tradition of the law and law of the tradition : law, State, and social control in China / Xin Ren.
p. cm.—(Contributions in criminology and penology, ISSN 0732-4464 ; 50)
Includes bibliographical references and index.
ISBN 0-313-29096-2 (alk. paper)
1. Criminal justice, Administration of—Social aspects—China. 2. Law—Social aspects—China. 3. Law—China—Moral and ethical aspects. 4. China—Social life and customs. 5. Social control. I. Series.
KNQ1572.R46 1997
340'.115—dc20 96-20676

British Library Cataloguing in Publication Data is available.

Library of Congress Catalog Card Number: 96-20676
ISBN: 0-313-29096-2
ISSN: 0732-4464

First published in 1997

Greenwood Press, 88 Post Road West, Westport, CT 06881
An imprint of Greenwood Publishing Group, Inc.

Printed in the United States of America

The paper used in this book complies with the Permanent Paper Standard issued by the National Information Standards Organization (Z39.48-1984).

10 9 8 7 6 5 4 3 2 1

Copyright Acknowledgment

The author and the publisher gratefully acknowledge permission for use of the following material:

"Appendix 7: A Brief Chinese Chronology," in *Chinese-English Dictionary* (Revised Edition), p. 1430. Beijing: Foreign Language Teaching and Research Press, 1995.

To my parents and
Sijin and Valerie
for their love, encouragement, and understanding

Contents

Foreword

CONFUCIANISM AND communism may not seem to have much in common, but in contemporary China there is a remarkably new conversion of these concepts into compatibility. The values of *Li* laid against the maxims of Marxism are found to be fertile ground for political ideology and even a thriving twentieth-century morality.

Crime, criminality, and punishment are universal terms that occupied the earliest writings of Western civilization, as in Sumerian literature that Professor Samuel Kramer brought to our attention. As a young man, Confucius (550–479 B.C.) was given the first nonhereditary post as Minister of Crime in the government of Lu. Crime is part of civilization, whether Western or Eastern.

Xin Ren has brought Chinese concepts of philosophy and law and of past and present cultures of Confucian and communist thought about deviance and crime into contemporary focus. There is at once both a blending and a bleeding opposition of these mighty concepts. I have scrupulously studied the criminal code of China since 1979 and in it I have found elements of Confucianism and elements of the traditional Marx-Lenin-Mao philosophy.

Life is precious and, therefore, crime is anathema both to Confucianism and to communism. The current criminal law is intertwined with old philosophical prescriptions and prohibitions of behavior. Confucian emphasis on the morality of the leadership as exemplary for the whole society is merged with the Legalists (*Fa jia*) in the calculus of contemporary Chinese Communism. This volume by Xin Ren has analyzed and laid these mergers clearly before us.

The author was one of my most brilliant students—a shining example for those who follow her. I am pleased to be part of her biography.

Marvin Wolfgang
University of Pennsylvania

Preface

UNDERSTANDING SOCIAL control in Chinese society has been as difficult for legal and social science scholars as actually establishing social control has been for China's leaders. But the attempt is still worth making, because of the increasing importance of China's role in the world's economic, political, and social affairs. Although China is, by no means, a Westernized democratic society yet, its recent programs to mondernize its economy, law, and legal system have raised enormous practical and intellectual curiosity about whether China is indeed heading in the direction of political democracy and economic privatization, which are deeply rooted in Western civilization and its legal tradition. It is this book's contention that in order to understand China's social control model today we need to know China's legal tradition and the role of the country's law in the past. Although the Westernization of law in China had begun long before Chinese Communists appealed to the former Soviet Union in formulating their social control model in 1949, the historical review of the Chinese legal tradition in this book centered around the legal traditions that were based on the Confucian teaching of an imperial moral code. It is not this book's intention to examine the changes of law under the Guomindang regime either during the period before the communist revolution (1911–1949) or during the postrevolutionary period (1949–present) in Taiwan.

For its political and ideological appeal to Marxism-Leninism, China continues to be characterized as a communist country. It may have been true that the Chinese approach to social control very much resembles that of the former Soviet Union. But it is not this book's attempt to conduct an analysis of the similarity and difference between Chinese Communists and Soviet Communists in controlling their respective societies. This book is intended to establish the historical and ideological connection between the imperial traditional notions of law and the Communist revolutionary agenda in ordering Chinese society.

In the world no other society has ever maintained such rich records of its own doings in such a meticulous manner as has China for such a long period of time—over three thousand years. Archaeological discovery in recent decades proved that China indigenously developed and administered its codified law as far back as 300 B.C. The rich and colorful history of Chinese law provides an enormous insight in understanding the echoes of traditional notions of the role of law and the state in ordering present-day Chinese society under Communist rule. This book is intended to fill some of the gaps in understanding the tradition of Chinese imperial law and Communist law from a historical and ideological perspective.

Writing this book was a long and difficult task that not only encountered the difficult question of the role of law and the state in China's social control model but also had to overcome the substantive and semantic differences in interpreting the classical and contemporary legal documentation and literature in Western and Chinese collections. While I was working on this book, many people kindly and enthusiastically offered their encouragement, advice, commentary, and criticism. My foremost thanks go to my advisor and mentor, Dr. Marvin E. Wolfgang. Through the years of my studies with him, Dr. Wolfgang has provided me with the intellectual inspiration, endless encouragement, and scholarly insight to help me form my ideas into a book. Without his encouragement, this book would have been impossible.

My appreciation also goes to my mentors, Dr. Maria Łos, Dr. W. Allyn Rickett, and an anonymous reviewer of my early manuscript. The book has greatly benefited from their valuable advice, suggestions, and criticism. For editorial assistance, my dear friend Selma Pastor deserves special thanks.

I must also acknowledge the enormous help I received from my Chinese friends and colleagues. I am especially grateful for the assistance I received from many Chinese colleagues and friends such as Dr. Zhengli Lee, an emeritus professor at Beijing University, who provided me with hundreds of legal publications, books, and references in time to help me overcome the meager availability of modern Chinese legal literature in the United States. Without their help, my work would have been much less comprehensive.

Finally, a tremendous share of the credit for the finished product belongs to Sijin and Valerie for their continuous encouragement and support, both emotionally and morally, throughout some of the most difficult of times. They have shared with me the joys, sadness, and anxiety in every aspect of developing and writing this book.

Editorial Notes on Pinyin Transliteration

THE PINYIN system, introduced to China in the 1950s, has become the official romanization system in the People's Republic of China. It has since been adopted by the United Nations and other international agencies and is widely used in scholarly and news publications, where it has supplanted the older Wade-Giles system. In noting this change, this author uses the pinyin system throughout the text.

The adoption of the pinyin system in this book is based on its official recognition by both China and the United States. In January 1979, the Chinese government adopted pinyin as the exclusive system for the transliteration of Chinese names and places in Western languages. In July of the same year, the United States Board on Geographic Names compiled a list of pinyin to compare with Wade-Giles spelling. Although some spellings are identical in the two systems, the pinyin system is distinguishable from the Wade-Giles system. For instance, in the pinyin system, China's capital is spelled "Beijing," as opposed to "Peking" in the Wade-Giles system.

In the text, for purposes of consistency, most Chinese names and places are spelled in pinyin. The switchover to this system certainly poses difficulty with respect to the well-known names that have long been familiar to Western readers. To minimize the confusion, some names spelled in pinyin are accompanied by their older Wade-Giles spelling in parentheses—for example, Sun Zhongshan (Sun Yat-sen). As an accommodation, a pinyin/Wade-Giles conversion table is included here to clarify any confusion. In circumstances where the longstanding conventional Chinese names are familiar to Western readers, the text retains the conventional spelling. For example, the text employs "Confucius" rather than the pinyin equivalent, "Kongzi."

The rules for transliterating Chinese book titles, as applied in the bibliography, were set by the *Journal for Asian Studies*, under which only the first word of the book title and proper names are capitalized and the transliterated title is set off in italics following the English translation of book titles. To ease the difficulties in pronunciation raised in the transliteration of Chinese titles to pinyin, hyphens are used in the pinyin transcriptions to distinguish each Chinese letter.

Pinyin to Wade-Giles

Pinyin	*Wade-Giles*	*Pinyin*	*Wade-Giles*	*Pinyin*	*Wade-Giles*
a	a	ce	ts'e	da	ta
ai	ai	cen	ts'en	dai	tai
an	an	ceng	ts'eng	dan	tan
ang	ang	cha	ch'a	dang	tang
ao	ao	chai	ch'ai	dao	tao
		chan	ch'an	de	te
ba	pa	chang	ch'ang	deng	teng
bai	pai	che	ch'e	di	ti
ban	pan	chen	ch'en	dian	tien
bang	pang	cheng	ch'eng	diao	tiao
bao	pao	chi	ch'ih	die	tieh
bei	pei	ching	ch'ung	ding	ting
ben	pen	chou	ch'ou	diu	tiu
beng	peng	chu	ch'u	dou	tou
bi	pi	chua	ch'ua	du	tu
bian	pien	chuai	ch'uai	duan	tuan
biao	piao	chuan	ch'uan	dui	tui
bie	pieh	chuang	ch'uang	dun	tun
bin	pin	chui	ch'ui	duo	to
bing	ping	chun	ch'un		
bo	po	chuo	ch'o	e	o
bou	pou	ci	ts'u	en	en
bu	pu	cong	ts'ung	er	erh
		cou	ts'ou		
ca	ts'a	cu	ts'u	fa	fa
cai	ts'ai	cuan	ts'uan	fan	fan
can	ts'an	cui	ts'ui	fang	fang
cang	ts'ang	cun	ts'un	fei	fei
cao	ts'ao	cuo	ts'o	fen	fen

Pinyin to Wade-Giles *(continued)*

Pinyin	*Wade-Giles*	*Pinyin*	*Wade-Giles*	*Pinyin*	*Wade-Giles*
feng	feng	hong	hung	ken	k’en
fo	fo	hou	hou	keng	k’eng
fou	fou	hu	hu	kong	k’ung
fu	fu	hua	hua	kou	k’ou
		huai	huai	ku	k’u
ga	ka	huan	huan	kua	k’ua
gai	kai	huang	huang	kuai	k’uai
gan	kan	hui	hui	kuan	k’uan
gang	kang	hun	hun	kuang	k’uang
gao	kao	huo	huo	kui	k’uei
ge	ko			kun	k’un
gei	kei	ji	chi	kuo	k’uo
gen	ken	jia	chia		
geng	keng	jian	chien	la	la
gong	kung	jiang	chiang	lai	lai
gou	kou	jiao	chiao	lan	lan
gu	ku	jie	chieh	lang	lang
gua	kua	jin	chin	lao	lao
guai	kuai	jing	ching	le	le
guan	kuan	jiong	chiung	lei	lei
gui	kuei	jiu	chiu	leng	leng
gun	kun	ju	chü	li	li
guo	kuo	juan	chüan	lia	lia
		chao	ch’ao	lian	lien
ha	ha	jun	chün	liang	liang
hai	hai			liao	liao
han	han	ka	k’a	lie	lieh
hang	hang	kai	k’ai	lin	lin
hao	hao	kan	k’an	ling	ling
he	ho	kang	k’ang	liu	liu
hei	hei	kao	k’ao	long	lung
hen	hen	ke	k’o	dong	tung
heng	heng	kei	k’ei	lou	lou

Pinyin to Wade-Giles *(continued)*

Pinyin	*Wade-Giles*	*Pinyin*	*Wade-Giles*	*Pinyin*	*Wade-Giles*
lu	lu	nen	nen	pin	p’in
lü	lü	neng	neng	ping	p’ing
luan	luan	ni	ni	po	p’o
lüan	lüan	nian	nien	pou	p’ou
lüe	lüeh	niang	niang	pu	p’u
lun	lun	niao	niao		
luo	lo	guang	kuang	qi	ch’i
		nie	nieh	qia	ch’ia
ma	ma	nin	nin	qian	ch’ien
mai	mai	ning	ning	qiang	ch’iang
man	man	niu	niu	qiao	ch’iao
mang	mang	nong	nung	qie	ch’ieh
mao	mao	nou	nou	qin	ch’in
mei	mei	nu	nu	qing	ch’ing
men	men	nü	nü	jue	chüeh
meng	meng	nuan	nuan	qiong	ch’iung
mi	mi	nüe	nüeh	qiu	ch’iu
mian	mien	nuo	no	qu	ch’ü
miao	miao			quan	chüan
mie	mieh	ou	ou	que	chüeh
min	min			qun	chün
ming	ming	pa	p’a		
miu	miu	pai	p’ai	ran	jan
mo	mo	pan	p’an	rang	jang
mou	mou	pang	p’ang	rao	jao
mu	mu	pao	p’ao	re	je
		pei	p’ei	ren	jen
na	na	pen	p’en	reng	jeng
nai	nai	peng	p’eng	ri	jih
nan	nan	pi	p’i	rong	jung
nang	nang	pian	p’ien	rou	jou
nao	nao	piao	p’iao	ru	ju
nei	nei	pie	p’ieh	ruan	juan

Pinyin to Wade-Giles *(continued)*

Pinyin	*Wade-Giles*	*Pinyin*	*Wade-Giles*	*Pinyin*	*Wade-Giles*
rui	jui	suan	suan	wu	wu
run	jun	sui	sui		
ruo	jo	sun	sun	xi	hsi
		suo	so	xia	hsia
sa	sa			xian	hsien
sai	sai	ta	t’a	xiang	hsiang
san	san	tai	t’ai	xiao	hsiao
sang	sang	tan	t’an	xie	hsieh
sao	sao	tang	t’ang	xin	hsin
se	se	tao	t’ao	xing	hsing
sen	sen	te	t’e	xiong	hsiung
seng	seng	teng	t’eng	xiu	hsiu
sha	sha	ti	t’i	xu	hsü
shai	shai	tian	t’ien	xuan	hsüan
shan	shan	tiao	t’iao	xue	hsüeh
shang	shang	tie	t’ieh	xun	hsün
shao	shao	ting	t’ing		
she	she	tong	t’ung	ya	ya
shen	shen	tou	t’ou	yai	yai
sheng	sheng	tu	t’u	yan	yen
shi	shih	tuan	t’uan	yang	yang
shou	shou	tui	t’ui	yao	yao
shu	shu	tun	t’un	ye	yeh
shua	shua	tuo	t’o	yi	i
shuai	shuai			yin	yin
shuan	shuan	wa	wa	ying	ying
shui	shui	wai	wai	yong	yung
shun	shun	wan	wan	you	yu
shuo	shuo	wang	wang	yu	yü
si	ssu	wei	wei	yuan	yüan
song	sung	wen	wen	yue	yüeh
sou	sou	weng	weng	yun	yün
su	su	wo	wo		

Pinyin to Wade-Giles *(continued)*

Pinyin	*Wade-Giles*	*Pinyin*	*Wade-Giles*	*Pinyin*	*Wade-Giles*
za	tsa	zhang	chang	zhuang	chuang
zai	tsai	zhao	chao	zhui	chui
zan	tsan	zhe	che	zhun	chun
zang	tsang	zhen	chen	zhuo	cho
zao	tsao	zheng	cheng	zi	tzu
ze	tse	zhi	chih	zong	tsung
zei	tsei	zhong	chung	zou	tsou
zen	tsen	zhou	chou	zu	tsu
zeng	tseng	zhu	chu	zuan	tsuan
zha	cha	zhua	chua	zui	tsui
zhai	chai	zhuai	chuai	zun	tsun
zhan	chan	zhuan	chuan	zuo	tso

Source: People's Republic of China: Administrative Atlas, pp. 46–47. Washington, DC: CIA, 1975.

Abbreviations

CCP	Chinese Communist Party
DIC	Disciplinary Inspection Committee
GMD	Guomindang (Nationalist Party or Kuomintang)
MPC	Ministry of Public Security
PLA	People's Liberation Army
PRC	People's Republic of China

Tradition of the Law and Law of the Tradition

INTRODUCTION

Law, State, and Social Control in China: Marxism or Confucianism?

UNDERSTANDING THE penetration of law and social control in Chinese society has been as difficult for scholars in the fields of legal and social studies as actually establishing social control has been for China's leaders. It has been noticed by many scholars in comparative legal studies that the Chinese leaders' ideological and political appeal to the Soviet Marxist orthodoxy does not always explain their behavior in ruling China's politics or predict their radical shift in ordering its social conducts.[1] Nor do the modernization of China's bureaucratic institutions and the Westernization of China's system of law provide a clear clue on who actually wields the "scepter" in governing China.[2] Established government institutions and the stipulated rule of law may have been changed, in a way, at such a fascinating pace and magnitude. However, the distribution and penetration of the state's power into the social fabric are far more subtle and complicated than understanding institutional reorganization and legislative stipulation. Over the centuries, China's rulers, regardless of their philosophical belief and political appeal, have displayed a consistent commitment to a model with the state's strong will in controlling and ordering Chinese society. Under this model, the state not only plays an active role in enforcing law and upholding order against undesirable human conducts but also aggressively penetrates into every thread of the social fabric, such as the family, kin, guild, trade union, school, and other social institutions. To the Chinese rulers, the ultimate goal of social control in Chinese society is far beyond the conventionally understood threshold—controlling human conduct. To the state officials, the task of social control unmistakably means both behavioral conformity and thought uniformity. Regardless of its political shortfalls, such a model has been carried on for generations by Chinese rulers and thus forms a unique inherent feature of the legal tradition that predisposes China's propensity in the contemporary legalization process.

ISSUES IN THE STUDY OF LAW AND THE LEGAL SYSTEM IN CHINA

Along with China's rapid transition from a centrally controlled national economy to a market-oriented economic model and the nation's growing involvement in international affairs, interest in studying China's law, its legal system, and its model of social control has dramatically increased in its importance. In recent history, we have witnessed an unprecedented willingness and enthusiastic commitment to the modernization of Chinese law and the Chinese legal system from both the West and the East. Although it remains a debatable issue in comparative legal studies whether the modernization of law in a non-Western nation such as China is equivalent to the notion of Westernization of law, China's rapid change toward the formalization of law and the legal system has provided an unprecedented opportunity in the study of Chinese law and society. Excited with China's economic reform, many Western observers are watching whether China is going to succumb to the influence of the Western model of law—which often means the separation of law from other political institutions, a professional class of jurists, an independent judiciary, a system of due process, a principle of presumed innocence, and the right to competent legal representation—and eventually to abandon its anti-individualism and nondemocratic legal tradition.

Certainly, the materialization and institutionalization of such a legalization process in China have been enormous and fascinating in recent years. From 1978 to 1992, China has promulgated more than two thousand laws, statutes, amendments, and decrees, exceeding the total number of laws enacted in its first three decades under Communist rule. To create a new class of legal professionals, hundreds of universities in China have resumed legal educational curricula since 1987 and sent their elite students abroad to study Western law and the Western legal system.[3] Public security officials, procurators, judges, and legal counsels are carefully selected to fill the judicial posts that hold important legal ramifications for any modern bureaucratic machinery.[4] Litigation pursued by ordinary citizens, plaintiffs, or grievant parties against government officials, corporations, or wrongdoers in seeking for remediable reliefs, compensation, or penalties through formally structured judicial proceedings is no longer a scarce phenomenon to Chinese people. While Western observers enthusiastically applaud China's unprecedented progress toward the "legalization" and formalization of its law and legal system,[5] they also dread China's stubbornness in ruthlessly crushing the political opposition who dare to challenge the paramount power of the Communist Party in China.

Apparently, China's economic openness and privatization have not changed its authoritarian tradition and lack of democratic voice in state-commanded social control efforts. What is even more puzzling to Western observers is that though China might have created what can be called laws, they are often sidestepped by the governmental officials.[6] There have been institutions that are called public security, people's procurate, and people's courts, but they seem to have no independent role in resolving the disputes brought before them. There have been defense counsels appointed or hired by the accused, but they have very limited access to the power and privilege that their Western counterparts can enjoy in defending their clients' innocence beyond a reasonable doubt.[7] There has been a constitution that guarantees the rights of free speech, press, and assembly, but its insistence on individuals' obligation to the state and the Communist Party often leaves little room for individuals to exercise their rights.[8] Obviously, many of our questions regarding Chinese law and social control may not be answered soley on the basis of a study of the rule of law; we also need to examine the culture, custom, tradition, and people's attitude toward law and authorities.

China, like other ancient cultures, has a longstanding *sui generis* legal tradition, and it indigenously developed a vast bureaucratic machinery for social control based on the philosophical teaching of Confucian moral codes (*Li*) that was endorsed by Chinese imperial rulers for more than two millennia. Due to the moralistic nature of Chinese imperial law, many comparative legal scholars believe that China has not been and cannot be, by Western legal standards, a "law-oriented" society despite the archaeological evidence that codified law existed in China as early as 300 B.C.[9] While what makes a society a law-oriented one remains an arguable question in comparative legal studies, scholars have agreed that law is a system of standardized norms that regulates human conduct, that is deliberately established for the purpose of social control, and that is interpreted and enforced by formal public (or political) authority rather than by custom. According to this definition, China might have had its first law, called *Xiaxing* or *Yuxing*, under the Xia Dynasty (1700–1600 B.C.). As opposed to the religious orientation in the Western legal tradition, the secular and atheistical origin of Chinese law that emphasizes man's, especially the ruler's, capability in administering law further alienates China from being considered as a law-oriented society by the Western legal scholars.

Further, what constitutes a Westernization of law in a non-Western society like China remains a debatable issue in the comparative study of Chinese law and society. Evidently, the process of China's Westernization of law had begun long before this recent economic reform. The Western legal influence on Chinese law began in the eighteenth century.[10] In the following century, the systematic replication of Western law began to emerge during the Qing Dynasty and continued to develop through the first half of this century.[11] Nevertheless, the Western influence on Chinese law obviously was not limited to the civil law and common law traditions. As a matter of fact, the current modernization of law in China emerged as a hybrid of the Chinese imperial legal tradition, Western law, and Soviet socialist law. Chinese law has been actuated at least as much by Soviet socialist law as it has been influenced by Anglo-American and European Continental laws.[12] Despite an unsettled debate over what makes socialist law socialist,[13] the legality of the Communist Party's ruling power over the legislative and judicial processes, the domination of Marxist ideology in legal education and the training of jurists, and the protection of the interests, status, and priviledge of the Communist Party in the administration of justice are profoundly accentuated as the common features of socialist law.[14] For purely ideological reasons, China was even categorized as one of the "older countries"[15] that received the socialist law founded by the Soviet jurists who were equipped with the teaching of Karl Marx, Friedrich Engels, and Vladimir

Lenin, even though China did not undertake the full-scale formalization of its law until the early 1980s.[16]

Speaking the similarities between Soviet socialist law and Chinese law, it takes little investigation to find the assimilation of former Soviet socialist law into Chinese law, not so much in terms of the procedural rules but primarily in terms of the ideological foundation of law. From the early Chinese Soviet Republic era (1930–34) to the initial promulgation of law in the 1950s to the recent modernization of law, China has endured the *socialization* of the Marxist socialist legal tradition. Despite the political and ideological battles between the former Soviet and Chinese Communist Parties since the 1950s, the Soviet law and legal system provided not only the platform for the architecture of the Chinese socialist system of law but also the professional training that enabled China to adopt the Soviet socialist model of law during the 1950s. William Butler points out that it would be inappropriate to treat China as a *sui generis* legal system after the socialization of the Soviet law and legal system has been taking place in China for more than four decades.[17]

To prove China's kinship in the family of socialist legal systems, however, still does not explain why the administration of law in China differs so substantially from the system in the former Soviet Union. For example, the Chinese legal system is typically characterized as having the vast participation of the political party in the actual dispensation of justice, an informality of law and the legal process, and strong moral characteristics in legal education and training as well as in the administration of adjudication, while the former Soviet Union maintained a much more formalized rule of law and judicial procedure. Simple recognition of the hybridized nature of Chinese law may not explain why these two systems are similar in some aspects but differ in others and why they may appear to be the same in their written form but different in practice. Much research has been conducted in an attempt to explain the similarities rather than the differences of these two socialist models of law.

Furthermore, legal scholars—both socialist and Western— often treat socialist law with benign neglect, taking it as a fact that "the architects of socialist law derive inspiration not only from the foreign non-Marxian legal system but also from the pre-revolutionary laws of the respective countries."[18] Those in the socialist camp have often attempted to sever the umbilical cord that links the new socialist system with the inequitable past so that "socialist law will sound historically a great future but without a past."[19] At the same time, ideological resentment against communism has also led Western scholars to quickly dismiss the importance of any possible historical connection of socialist law with its prerevolutionary past.

Law, however, in any socialist country bears the birthmark of the country's own history, culture, and tradition. This heritage is sometimes a force more powerful than the rules of law themselves in foretelling the consequences of law and in dictating people's thinking about the role of law and legal authority. This legal culture, according to Merryman, is the internal logic by which one can understand law and social control in a society. This internal logic determines what elements of a foreign legal tradition can be assimilated into Chinese legal culture and subsequently transformed into social reality in Chinese society. The current Westernization of Chinese law did not emerge from the *sui generis* law of Confucianism; it is, instead, a rather carefully selected assimilation of Chinese imperial legal tradition and Soviet socialist legal tradition. It is Chinese law, but it is also Chinese socialist law. To illustrate law of the tradition and tradition of the law in Chinese society, this book centralizes its discussion not on the comparison between Soviet and Chinese socialist law but on the linkage between China's socialist present and its pre-revolutionary past.

CONCEPTUALIZATION OF SOCIAL CONTROL

The term "social control" is often as difficult to define as a concept as it is to apply in criminological research. Theorists in sociology, psychology, and anthropology often speak of social control as an individual-centered mechanism to produce either social deviance or conformity, while historians and radical political scientists view it primarily as either a coercive apparatus of the state or a punitive hidden agenda in all state-sponsored social policies. Criminologists, too, have devoted much of their attention to individual-centered socialization in various social institutions—such as the family, school, peer group, or work crew—to form social conformity or otherwise produce social deviance.[20] When these internalized social constraints fail to produce adequate social conformity, an external control, such as an official sanction, steps in to control people's behavior.

Internalized control forces—such as tangible material rewards and benefits or intangible social acceptance or approval, and negative restraints through social disapproval, humiliation, ridicule, and fear—and external agents of social suppression—such as criminal penalties—are often said to neutrally reinforce each other to balance the conflict between individual freedom and societal order. Logically, the ultimate goal of social control under this model would be restraining individual behavior within minimal social standards. Whether individuals will acquiesce to or agree with those social standards in their minds and whether society should inculcate individuals to conform with minimal standardized behaviors under planned social programs are not as important as concerns about how to ensure that individuals behave within the legally allowed boundaries.

Certainly, the highly valued individualism in the Western cultural tradition at least freed men's mental faculties even though they must still reasonably obey legal rules in their acts. They act according to rules not so much because they agree with the rules but because of the potential penalties attached to disobedience. Therefore, social conformity no longer means conformity to socially accepted standards of right and wrong, but only obedience to legally enforced rules. Coincidently, the role of the state as the agent of external control is limited only to controlling the behavior of individuals under the law. Whether an individual should internalize a morally accepted standard of behavior and how individual socialization should be supervised are left largely to the family, school, or church to decide. Weakness in or even the disappearance of internalized conformity among individuals or, in other words, heavy reliance on external control is not only costly to human society but also dehumanizing.[21]

Contrary to this individualistic model of external social control, China may represent an example in another extreme—the socialistic-internalized model of social control. Compared with the state's role in social control in Western culture, the state in China certainly plays a much broader and more powerful role than its Western counterparts. The most important distinction, perhaps, is the efforts of the Chinese state to control both the behavior and the minds of the people. Social conformity in the Chinese vocabulary is not limited to behavioral conformity with the rule of law but always moralistically identifies with the officially endorsed beliefs of social standards and behavioral norms. Perhaps it goes against the free-will notion of the classical theory of criminology or perhaps it is socialist totalitarianism. Whatever it is, the Chinese tradition of so-called "greatest unity" has always attempted to achieve ultimate uniformity of both mind and act within Chinese society.

Perhaps Migdal's notion of two models of society-state relations can shed some light on this distinctive role of the state in non-Western societies. According to Migdal, basic society-state relations can be seen in two different models, that is, "society with a weak state"—such as industrialized countries in the West because of the strong will of the people as recognized by the law—and "society with a strong state"—such as China and others in primarily non-Western nations where the state has played quite a different role in ordering society.[22] Unfortunately, little research has been conducted on the different roles of the state in augmenting social control mechanisms, due, on the one hand, to the formidable cultural and linguistic barriers in a comparative study of non-Western legal traditions and, on the other hand, to political prejudice against the tradition of anti-individualism in the Chinese system of law.

Furthermore, some recent studies have also shed light on possible alternative variables of social control, in addition to traditional factors such as the family, school, church, and peer group, with a consideration of cultural and historical values and conditions in particular social settings. For instance, studies on different crime rates in rural and urban areas have suggested that the traditional social bond theory seems to be powerless in explaining lower crime rates among rural populations because rural youth commit to social bonding no more than do their urban counterparts.[23] Comparative studies in other cultures, too, have challenged the traditional approach—such as examining the relationship between a malfunctioning family and delinquency—in predicting social deviance.[24] These findings seem to suggest that additional variables in the social control mechanism—such as the state's role and the goal of social control—in different cultures or social settings may, indeed, hold theoretical validity although they have been ignored by the traditional approach of social control theory.

METHODOLOGICAL ISSUES IN STUDYING CHINESE LAW

In comparative studies, it is always important to distinguish the relevant from the irrelevant so as to produce an analysis that is both accurate in its depiction of societal reality and of significance to other scholars interested in the study of law and social control. Unfortunately, comparative studies of the Chinese system of law have not yet established a clear theoretical pigeonhole, legal presuppositions, and a reliable legal vocabulary for sorting out its relevance from its irrelevance.[25] For instance, in discussing the individual's right to privacy, we must first justify the conceptual relevance of privacy, which is at the heart of Western civilization but has literally no legal status in Chinese traditional law. To overcome this inadequate theoretical groundwork, an exegetical approach that focuses on an analysis of Chinese written statutes—with references from the Western legal categories of presupposition and terminology—has often been applied to determine how these statutes might be interpreted in Chinese society.[26] Although this approach is often successful, especially when the Chinese statutes are written in the Western legal formation, its conclusion can, in fact, be erroneous.

The Chinese language is another formidable obstacle in establishing reliable and accurate categories of legal propositions for a sound comparative study.[27] A lack of training in Chinese legal history and classical literature undoubtedly has hampered scholars in comprehending the codified statutes and legal literature compiled through two millennia of history. The particularly formidable difficulties in the style and vocabulary of the Chinese legal literature—such as the equivocal meaning of a legal term, the synonymous meanings of multiple terms, and the lack of equivalent and appropriate words in Western languages to translate a legal concept precisely[28] have frequently resulted in the distortion of the relevance and significance of Chinese law in the administration of justice and social control. Instead of analyzing the codified statutes, some scholars have approached the Chinese legal literature from another dimension, that is, by examining the structure and process of justice administration in Chinese society so as to compare them with Western society.[29] Nevertheless, the structure and process might demonstrate a great deal of similarity—such as business arbitration, dispute resolution, and mediation—but might also potentially serve different purposes of social control. The social outcome of implementing a codified law is often determined not by the form and language used in the statute or process that executes law but by the people's attitudes, expectations, and value systems regarding what ought to be restrained and what otherwise ought to be rewarded or compromised.

Too many assumed conceptual categories and theoretical presuppositions have been used so often within the paradigm of thought known as "legal culture" in Chinese society. Too many speculations on what is relevant or irrelevant and what is significant or insignificant in the study of the Chinese system of law have been accepted as factual. Even Chinese legal scholars themselves have offered little help in sorting out the relevancies from the irrelevancies, mainly because of the meager size of the professional jurist class in China's past and present. These voids in the theory and research methodology resulted primarily from two historical and political practices. First, law and the legal system in China have been traditionally regarded as utilitarian tools of the state to accomplish political goals; hence, they are worthless for study on intellectual and aesthetic grounds.[30] Second, a critical examination of law and the state's role in social control was vigorously prohibited by the authorities for fear of its potential in weakening the state's power of control.

Because of the meager research in this area, scholars are constantly puzzled by the reality of China's administration of justice, especially when the authorities constantly sidestep the law they themselves enacted. It leads one to wonder what is the practical purpose for China of formalizing laws if the state authority has no intention to implement these laws. By addressing these questions and by establishing a theoretically compatible and culturally relevant reference system for studying the Chinese system of law and social control, this book hopes to provide a conceptual framework for understanding some of the most important premises of the state's role in the administration of justice in modern Chinese society on cultural and historical grounds. Although many of the methodological difficulties mentioned above must be overcome in the future with enormous effort, this study identifies some important political and legal concepts relevant for comparative studies of non-Western traditions of law. Concepts such as ruling by law versus ruling by man, political power versus judicial independence, equal rights in Chinese culture, individual rights versus obligations, legal guilt versus factual shame, and behavioral control versus mind control will be examined in a social context through their historical passage into the current socialist society. It is this author's hope that these examinations will lead to an understanding of how the state's strong will in controlling both the behavior and minds of the people to achieve social conformity has obstructed China's formalization of law.

Many legal studies that deal with Chinese law are limited by the dearth of primary sources on the evolution of Chinese law and the legal system in either the English or the Chinese language. The growing legal literature on China focuses primarily on (1) the introduction or translation of the laws, statutes, and amendments promulgated since the economic reform of the 1980s and (2) descriptive narratives of social control mechanisms in Chinese society. Interest in the study of Mao Zedong's political and ideological influences on law and social control, which underlie China's socialist practice of law and current legal reform, remains scarce. This is probably associated with a misperception and ignorance of the early formation of the socialist control mechanisms from 1949 to 1979. Despite the existence of codified laws and a legal system in China, that era has been regarded as a socialist totalitarian period and was largely a time of lawlessness. Thus, anything that could be called law by Western standards is considered a very recent event in China. Only a handful of scholars have demonstrated research interest in Mao's ideological influence on social control and the function of law in socialist China.[31]

A second problem related, but not limited, to the scarcity of research on Mao Zedong's ideological influence on social control is the inadequate index and unstandardized data available abroad. Although mountainous volumes of legal documents and records have been a remarkable feature of Chinese legal history, these data were often badly produced and poorly indexed both because of meager interest among Chinese intellectuals in conducting legal research on intellectual and inspirational grounds and because of formidable difficulties in translating accurately and meaningfully the style and vocabulary used in the Chinese legal literature. Therefore, despite my command of the Chinese language and classical literature, the objective analysis of those data and documents in their historical context remains a difficult task in this study.

In addition, the Chinese authorities' highly guarded secrecy surrounding crime data and the administration of criminal justice further undermined the possibility of objective study. The authorities have long treated crimes and criminal justice data as classified information that cannot be made available to either the public or academic researchers.[32] Therefore, the government often views a research inquiry for criminal justice information as politically suspicious and socially detrimental to the consolidation of the state's power in ordering society. Even those data now accessible to researchers are most often fragmentary and equivocal despite the efforts of a handful of scholars in recent years to classify, categorize, and index them.[33] This political censorship certainly creates tremendous difficulties for obtaining primary sources of information to critically examine the state's role in interference with adjudication and in interaction with the public in ordering social conformity. Official censorship most certainly proves to be a major setback for an objective study.

To minimize these drawbacks, mainly secondary data sources will be used in this study, with careful comparisons to the scattered official data available. To concentrate on the analysis of convergency and divergence of Confucianism, Maoism, and Chinese Communism in reinforcing the role of the state, law, and social control in China, this study will not extend its discussion to the Westernization of law and the legal system during the Republic era from 1911 to 1949. Although the similarity and difference between these politically different Chinese societies may provide further evidence on the direction of legal reform influenced by the Chinese legal tradition, it is not the intention of this book to examine convergency and divergence of social control in these two politically different Chinese societies. My research emphasis as well as the method of presentation is historical only to the degree essential for a better understanding of the present development of law and social control in socialist China.

Despite these limitations and difficulties, this study explores the theoretical relevance and significance of those legal concepts in the social control process with a comparison between the Chinese traditional model of social conformity and the socialist model of political suppression. It is hoped that these qualities are represented coherently so that this author's interpretive and conceptualized synthesis will offer a valid and novel basis for future comparative studies between traditional and contemporary Chinese legal cultures, between Eastern and Western legal traditions, and perhaps between European and non-European Marxist states.

EMPHASIS OF THIS BOOK

In light of the cultural and historical dimension in social control studies, examination of the state's role in officially planned and carefully programmed responses to "crime" or "deviance" in the People's Republic of China (PRC) and analysis of the state-commanded operation of the law machine in ordering Chinese society are central to this work. To understand the influence of legal culture in present Chinese society, the book takes a two-part approach. The first part of this book provides a historical and ideological overview of the Chinese imperial legal tradition—primarily the law of Confucian morality that not only provided a basis for the selective integration of Soviet socialist law and the Chinese legal tradition but also dictated the selective process of the syncretism[34]—and the rule of punishment formed under the imperial legal tradition. Instead of following the chronological evolution of Chinese legal tradition, the discussion in this part centers on the substantive quality of Chinese traditional law, the role of state authority, and the organic basis of Chinese law in family infrastructure. Essentially, these qualities of China's *sui generis* legal tradition provide the necessary moralistic lubricant to soothe the socialization process of Chinese law under the Communist regime.[35]

Chapter 1 emphasizes the essential features of the Chinese legal tradition and the imperial system of law. Unlike in the common law and civil law traditions, traditional China was, by and large, a secular society in which no religion had ever successfully achieved a status as had Christianity in Europe, Islam in the Middle East nations, and Buddhism in Far East Asia. Chinese imperial law was indigenously developed from the secular philosophies of social morality, namely Legalism and Confucianism. Dictated by this secularity of the origin of Chinese law, the Chinese system of law had an organic basis, familism, in society. The patriarchal relationship and behavioral norms within the extended family or clan were not only reflected in the power structure of officialdom but also formed the basic foundation and standards for social conformity. The fundamental values of familism, such as the authority and reverence associated with seniority, the absolute and unconditional duty of filial piety, and the superior status of group welfare over individual interest, were an integral part of imperial law and served as guiding principles for the criminal penalty system.

In addition to the influence of Confucianism in the codification and application of Chinese imperial law, the contribution of the Legalists to the development of law in imperial China will also be outlined in Chapter 1. Historically, the contribution of Legalism in the formalization of Chinese law and the legal system has always been overshadowed by the domination of Confucianism in the Chinese official orthodoxy. Even when it was the subject of legal studies, Legalism was often portrayed as an advocate of brutal and ruthless suppression. The literature on Legalism has traditionally ignored the fact that Legalist scholars such as Zi Chan,[36] Lord Shang, and Li Si were the earliest Chinese jurisprudents who introduced the concept of law to China and constructed China's first imperial legal system, which successfully helped Qin Shihuang (246–208 B.C.) conquer China in 221 B.C. Thus, the Chinese legal tradition is not limited to the influence of Confucianism but is a combination of both philosophies. Even today's legalization process is the continuation of the long struggle between Legalism—rule by law or "rule under the law"—and Confucianism—rule by man or "rule above the law."

In addition to the general characteristics of the Chinese legal tradition, their exemplification in China's imperial system of punishment will be explored as well. Chapter 2 focuses on the legal rule and moral justification of punishment established under the imperial law. The use of a familism-oriented reward and penalty system against political heterodoxy, violations of filial piety, and common crimes will be outlined in this chapter.

The second part of this book comprises four chapters that are primarily designed to illustrate historical echoes of the legal tradition in socialist China through a discussion of judicial independence and the Communist Party, equal rights and class division, counterrevolutionary crime, and voluntary confession in Chinese law. Chapter 3 will focus on the central propositions of Maoism on the role of the Communist Party and the function of the state in the administration of justice. Mao, no doubt, was a Marxist believer, but he formed his radically revolutionary ideology within the Chinese traditional thinking on power, authority, the ruling and the ruled, and the role of law. Although his attitude toward Confucian humanitarianism was scornful,[37] Mao was by no means a serious iconoclast. In fact, he was an ardent admirer of Legalism, especially its belief in the iron power of the state and the rigorously repressive function of law and the legal system. The influence of Chinese traditional values predisposed Mao in the process of selective adoption of Marxism-Leninism. Mao and his party's zealous advocacy and exercise of the state's power in all societal affairs were best exemplified through the history of legalization in the PRC. In accordance with this belief, the term "judicial independence" was redefined to meet the "state society model." The interrelationship between the ruling status of the Chinese Communist Party, the Party elite, and the judicial personnel in the monopoly of the power of legislation, judicial review, and the administration of criminal justice will form most of the discussion in Chapter 3.

In addition to constitutionalizing the state's political power over the judiciary, Mao also set the general tone for whose and which conducts should be the priorities of social control in the PRC through the implementation of his class line. Although equal rights before the law have been constitutionally guaranteed since 1954, equal rights were never meant to be interpreted as equal treatment. Contrary to the Western notion of equality before the law, which is based primarily on an individual's citizenship in a given society, equality in China was intercepted by the coercive division of political class lines, namely, the division between the "people" class and the adversary class. In practice, whose and which conducts were subject to penal sanction and control were not based on the nature of the conduct or the harmful impact on society but were predetermined by an individual's political membership in a given class. Therefore, the application of equal rights along class lines inevitably resulted in differential treatment before the law. An examination of the inherent convergence between this differential treatment before the law in the PRC and the Confucian hierarchical tradition will be illustrated further in Chapter 4.

In the characterization of China's state society model in social control, nothing provides as much insight as the area of so-called political crime, that is, the controversy surrounding counterrevolutionary crime. Like its predecessors, the Chinese government has regarded counterrevolutionary crime as the most detrimental and vicious crime against the socialist state and thus subject to the most severe legal sanctions. Chapter 5 explores the significance and relevance of counterrevolutionary crime in serving the purposes of both behavioral control and mind conformity. Diverging from most Western commentators' approach to this controversy, under which counterrevolutionary crimes were criticized mainly from a political aspect, Chapter 5 will approach the issue from a legal and historical perspective. To do so, the chronology of counterrevolutionary crime in Chinese law will be reviewed in detail.

Despite recent developments in the formalization of law, the statutory definition and scope of counterrevolutionary crime have not changed significantly. This persistence not only reflects the Maoist notion of the proletariat democratic dictatorship but is also backed up by China's traditional practice against those who dare to challenge the state's authority. After all, controlling counterrevolutionary crime is not just the political suppression of socialist enemies but also the Chinese traditional way of repressing free thinking that runs counter to the political ideology endorsed by the state authorities. By examining counterrevolutionary crime in Chinese law, we will be able to understand both the cultural and historical grounds for the state government's intention to control both the behaviors and the minds of the people. It is fairly accurate to say that the treatment of political or ideological dissidents is the best indicator of the level of social control and the acceptance of democracy in a given society. The Chinese government today is no different from its predecessors in how it treats free-spirited or independent-thinking individuals.

To further understand the state's penetration into controlling the minds of its people, Chapter 6 will address the issue of voluntariness in Chinese law and the adjudicatory process. Practices such as voluntary surrender and self-confession under the current penal law are central themes of this chapter. In an adversarial system of law, such as that found in the United States, the establishment of legal guilt, which centers on the admission or proof of the commission of a crime through due process, is the ultimate goal in reaching a legal conclusion so that the appropriate degree of punishment can be determined. Under this system, whether the individual agrees with the legal conclusion is, for the most part, irrelevant to the process.[38] This situation is due primarily to the fact that such a system is designed only to control those conducts that have exceeded the boundary of law. But for the Chinese, finding factual guilt, which insists on the offender's either voluntary or coerced admission of the crime and repentance of the crime, is an almost indispensable element for concluding criminal cases before the courts.

There is no doubt that the voluntary admission of crime and guilt is self-incriminatory in nature and potentially infringes upon an innocent individual's rights to a legal defense under the Western concept of due process. However, the criticism surrounding voluntariness in China's system of adjudication is actually more than just a procedural consideration. While Westerners view voluntary surrender and confession as a means of helping the state to secure the favorable conclusion of a criminal case, the Chinese regard this as an essential part of the efforts to achieve the ultimate goal of social uniformity through either voluntary or coerced thought conformity. By the same token, judicial officers in China—in addition to their legal responsibilities to the state—are also morally obligated to secure a defendant's self-induced repentance for his misdeeds. Evidently, voluntary surrender and confession are not only encouraged and insisted on at the pretrial and trial stages but are also continuously administered beyond the point of conviction and are often practiced in correctional institutions. Whether one calls it brainwashing or thought reform, moral cultivation about right and wrong is an important component of the administration of justice, a way to change both an offender's behavior and heart. Therefore, to Westerners it is a means; to the Chinese it is an end of justice. The symbolic meaning of voluntary surrender and confession, that is, an offender turns himself in to the authorities as evidence of his initiative to return to social conformity, is also worth a discussion.

To conclude, the state authority in China has played much greater and broader roles in the social control process. China's low crime rates and effectiveness in maintaining high social conformity may be partially explained by the conventional variables in social control theory, such as the individual containment of social norms, and family, school, and community coherence. Nonetheless, we certainly can not overlook the proactive role played by the state authority in manipulating those conventional variables either by reinforcing their traditional functions or by redirecting their impacts on individuals. It may be difficult at this point to measure different impacts of the state on planned and programmed control policies to maintain social conformity or the control of social deviance, there exists a "state model" versus a "stateless model" of social control.

It is still debatable whether China can completely Westernize its law and its system of social control, considering the enormous impacts of longstanding legal traditions among the Chinese people and society. The socialist revolution was not the sole reason that China adopted Marxist ideology and socialist authoritarianism to control the social order. The Chinese tradition of bonding individuals to the family, community, and state has enabled the Communist government to continue its traditional role in legislation, justice administration, and social control in China. Ideological identification with Marxist socialism did not necessarily lead China to the same path of social control as it did in the former Soviet Union. By the same token, opening the Chinese market to the world economy today may or may not lead the Chinese to Westernize their law and legal system. There is no doubt that the society's desire for modernization will reshape the law and social control mechanisms in China; but the legal culture and traditions will continue to provide much influence in shaping the foundations of the modernization and in dictating the direction and magnitude of the modernization process.

NOTES

1. For instance, the collapse of the Soviet Union and its abandonment of Marxist ideology have not altered China's leaders' stubbornness in adhering to Marxist orthodoxy.

2. Unlike in the former Soviet Union or, perhaps, other countries, a person's position in the bureaucratic hierarchy does not always indicate his power in the system or his obligation to the people. Instead, the Chinese traditional attitude toward authority, seniority, and political superiors and their admiration for the wisdom of a person determine who should guard the throne. This may explain why Deng Xiaoping is still regarded as having the final

say in all crucial decision making in the government even though he no longer holds any official position within the governmental bureaucracy.

3. Cohen, 1980, pp. 1533–39.

4. Goodman, 1980, pp. 13–19.

5. "Concepts of Law in the Chinese Anti-Crime Campaign," 1985, p. 1891, and Schatz and Silkenat, 1980, pp. 13–14.

6. Goossen, 1989; Hansen, 1980; and Hipkin, 1981.

7. V. H. Li, 1978; Reynolds, 1980; and Woo, 1989, addressed issues of due process in the Chinese legal system.

8. Fiss, 1989, and Seymour, 1980, provide a detailed discussion on China's constitutional law.

9. See Hulsewé, 1985; Morris, 1973, p. v; and Ni et al., 1987, pp. 26–33, for early codified laws in China.

10. See Hsu, 1990, for the history of the Western influence on China's political, economic, and social affairs. For the Western influence on Chinese legal reform before the Republic revolution of 1911, see Bodde, 1973.

11. See Hong-Lie Yang, 1990, pp. 868–1028, for the early replication of Western laws from the Qing Dynasty through the middle of this century. Berman, Cohen, and Russell, 1970 and 1982; Ginsburg, 1970; and Kun, 1934 also detailed the Western influence of Marxist-Socialist law on Chinese legal reform during the early twentieth century. The Western influence includes civil, common, and soviet socialist law.

12. See Glendon, Gordon, and Osakwe, 1982, pp. 267–68, for a discussion on the assimilation between socialist law and Western legal traditions.

13. As Glendon et al., 1982, pp. 270–72, point out, for many years students of comparative law have openly debated the issue of whether the socialist legal system deserves to be placed in a separate chamber in the house of law, alongside the other two major legal systems of the modern world, that is, common law and civil law. With regard to the fundamental question of whether socialist law is sufficiently different from the civil system so as to be segregated from the latter, two opinions have emerged among legal scholars: (1) socialist law is distinct enough in its peculiarities to be granted an independent status vis-à-vis the other two major legal traditions; and (2) socialist law is not radically different from civil law and, therefore, it shall not be separated from the civil law family.

Recently, three schools of thought have debated this topic. The first school believes that socialist law is absolutely distinctive from the two major forms of Western law—common law and civil law— because of the unique social, economic, and political features of socialist law, which are typical only of socialist states. The second school emphasizes the pseudoreligious aspects of socialist law. The third school—by nature one of integrated thought—examines three dimensions of socialist law: a conceptual-formalistic category; a historical, political, economic, and social category; and a pseudoreligious category.

14. W. Butler, 1980, p. 11, suggested that the socialist state normally contains the following features: (1) a state structure built on the people's power, with the working class at its head and the Communist Party as its vanguard; (2) state ownership of the instruments and means of production; (3) defense of the country against the inroads of imperialism; and (4) the ultimate goal of achieving communism.

15. Ibid.

16. Although the term *socialism* has multiple meanings in political science that are often linked to European parliamentary democracy, the term *socialist system of law*, as used throughout this book, refers only to the communist system of law.

17. W. Butler, 1980, p. 11.

18. Glendon, Gordon, and Osakwe, 1982, p. 258.

19. Ibid.

20. According to social control theories, two aspects of control mechanism—personal control agents such as the psychological notion of self-concept and esteem and social control agents such as personal attachment to social organizations—are essential for explaining individual adherence to the rule of law and social norms. These theories primarily view social control from two dimensions that either control undesirable social behavior of individuals or reshape individualistically centered social groups such as family, school, and peer groups.

For theoretical and empirical studies on social control theories, see the following—on the conception of the containment theory: Reckless, 1961 and 1967; Reckless, Dinitz, and Kay, 1957; and Reckless, Dinitz, and Murry, 1956; on the assessment of self-concept: Schwartz and Stryker, 1970; Schwartz and Tangri, 1965; and Wells, 1978; on the delinquent disposition theory: Kaplan, 1980; Kaplan, Martin, and Johnson, 1986; and Rosenberg, Schooler, and Schoenbach, 1989; on the conceptualization of the social bond theory: Hirschi, 1969; on religion and social control: Glueck and Glueck, 1950; Nye, 1958; and Stark and Doyle, 1982; on the family and delinquency: Hasskell and Yablonski, 1982; and Platt, 1977, among others; and on school performance and crime: Jesen and Rojek, 1980; Kruttschnitt, Heath, and Ward, 1986; and Liska and Reed, 1985.

21. The United States is a good example of how heavily a society relies on external forces to control people's behavior because of the absence of an internalized control of power among individuals. This may also explain why most sociological studies on social control focus on social deviance rather than social conformity—perhaps because social conformity is culturally incompatible with the American spirit of individualism that seeks the ultimate freedom of the individual. See Jan, 1983, for a comparison of deterrence as a social control agent in the United States and China.

22. Migdal's theory (1988) is concerned primarily with society-state relations and state capabilities in social control in the Middle East. His theory was inspired, in part, by the French sociologist Pierre Birnbaum's (1985) notions of "state society" and "stateless society."

23. See Lyerly and Skipper, 1981.

24. Rahav's study (1976) tested the validity of the traditional concept of delinquent behavior and family dysfunction in Israel. He discovered that the two seemed to be unrelated in that society.

25. "Concepts of Law in the Chinese Anti-Crime Campaign," 1985, p. 1892. As this article pointed out, the predetermined relevance of judicial independence in the West normally does not require justification when we discuss the judge's role in the legal disposition of a case. Other American jurists have also suggested that the task of conceptual categorization is especially important because scholars today are overwhelmed by the mass of data from China that is the primary source for studying Chinese law. In fact, this enormous body of written statutes, legal documents, and reports of judicial cases has existed in China for two millennia. The formidable difficulties in style and legal vocabulary and the lack of training in Chinese culture and history often minimized Western scholars' accessibility to these valuable sources (Bodde, 1973, p. 4).

26. "Concepts of Law in the Chinese Anti-Crime Campaign," 1985, p. 1895.

27. Bodde, 1973, p. 6.

28. See Bloom, 1981, and Bodde, 1962, on the Chinese culture and language. See also Laws and Regulations of the People's Republic of China, 1982, vol. 1, p. iv, for examples of the equivocality of Chinese legal terms and language. For instance, *renfan* and *fanren* sometimes refer synonymously to "criminal"; sometimes they are different concepts, as when *renfan* refers to a "culprit" and *fanren* means a "criminal."

29. Bhatia and Chung, eds., 1974; Bonnichon, 1958; and Chiu, 1982b and 1985, pp. 143–60.

30. Bodde, 1973, p. 3.

31. Leng, 1977, pp. 356–73.

32. The Department of Public Security (DPS) of the PRC is responsible for compiling crime and criminal justice statistics with assistance from the National Bureau of Statistics. The final reports are classified information, and availability is restricted to criminal justice system personnel with certain ranks. In 1985, the DPS for the first time released to the public statistics on fire/arson events and traffic accidents. But crime statistics remain classified information. For additional information on this issue, see Gan, Lin, and Shen, 1987, p. 717.

33. Laws and Regulations of the People's Republic of China, 1982; C. A. Johnson, 1990; and Pinard, 1985, pp. 46–143.

34. Hardly any scholars in comparative legal study would agree that Confucianism is past history and is chronologically and politically irrelevant in the study of current socialist law and the legal system in China. Confucianism has found its way into Mao's revolutionary ideology. Without an understanding of the fundamentals of the Confucian law of morality, the convergence and divergence between the Maoist and Marxist orthodoxies and the legal culture in China cannot be fully appreciated.

35. Like their counterparts in the socialist camps, the Chinese communists openly denied any influence of the Confucian tradition on their ideology. As a matter of fact, numerous political movements launched by the Communist Party earned them the reputation for being iconoclasts. See Scalapino and Yu, 1985, and Spence, 1990.

36. In 536 B.C., Zi Chan, in the state of Zheng, cast penal law on a bronze vessel for the first time. See Bodde, 1973, and Pu and Zhou, 1986, for references.

37. Spence, 1990, suggests that Mao's attitude toward the humanitarian components in Confucianism serves as the best example of his iconoclastic tendencies.

38. Except in the case of plea bargaining, where the personal admission of guilt is the initiative for penalty reduction.

PART I

TRADITION OF THE LAW

CHAPTER ONE

The Chinese Legal Tradition: Law and Morality

CONFUCIANISM AND LEGALISM

THE CHINESE legal tradition developed from both Confucianism and Legalism, two influential, though adversarial, schools of thought. Unfortunately, the significant influence of the Legalist tradition in Chinese law and the legal system has often been overlooked historically because of the despotism and cruelty associated with the Legalist school during the Qin Dynasty,[1] the first unifier of the Chinese empire in 221 B.C. Although the Confucianist ideology provided the fundamentals for the substance of traditional law, the Legalist school constructed the important framework of the traditional legal system. For example, the Legalists first introduced to ancient Chinese society the idea of ruling by law and built up the judicial bureaucracy during the early Chinese empire.

Although the Legalist school and Confucianism were adversarial philosophies in terms of their political ideologies on how Chinese society should be ruled, they certainly shared some important ideas in common. For instance, both the Confucian and Legalist scholars insisted that the emperor had paramount power over all facets of life, including law. However, while the Legalists believed that the emperor had to rely on the rule of law to govern Chinese society, the Confucianists demanded that the ruler must appeal to the moralistic order backed up by a well-behaved bureaucracy of the gentry class. To compare the similarities and divergences of these two schools in the philosophical principles of social control and law, two fundamental issues must be addressed at length.

The first issue is their differing beliefs about the relationship between social order and law. The soul of Confucius's philosophy was the "superior man" and a well-ordered society. Departing from the concept of the "superior man" in a slave society, Confucius (551–479 B.C.) portrayed the superior man as a wise, humane, courageous, and benevolent being who is motivated by righteousness rather than profits and who studies the way of life and loves others. A well-ordered society is a result of behavioral exemplification of the superior man's moralistic virtue. To Legalism, on the other hand, the ruler's power and bureaucratic fabric are the keys to ruling a country. With law, the society will have peace; without law, the society will be in turmoil. Legalism was thus called the school of realism. Many Legalists were actively involved in the bureaucracies of states, while the Confucianists were primarily scholars or teachers prior to the Han Dynasty. The Legalists insisted that the moral order is inadequate to maintain social order because original human malignity would constantly drive people into trouble. A well-ordered society can be maintained only through a set of formally and publicly announced rules. Rulers of the states had the duty to establish and enforce law with uniformity, certainty, celerity, and severity. Shang Yang (commonly known as Lord Shang), a prominent Legalist, once elucidated that

> the ancient rulers fixed the standard of measures and weights as a continuous rule till today; without these standards, people would have to arbitrarily determine the light from the heavy, and subjectively guess the short from the long; therefore, law is the standardized rule. . . . Law is the authoritative force of the people, and the key of governing. . . . A wise ruler must signify the rule by law, so to speak, and act according to law so that the country would expand, the army would be strong, and the ruler would be venerated. Rule by law is fundamental to governing.[2]

Contrary to the Legalists, in Confucian phrases, *Li* replaces law. *Li* refers to the propriety that regulates "human desire that has been devised for the protection of the people."[3] In other words, *Li* is an important factor in the cultivation of the human personality. According to Confucius himself, *Li* governs social relationships, including those between the emperor and his ministers, between father and son, between husband and wife, between brothers, and between friends.[4] *Li* governs relationships between the ruling and the ruled, the senior and the junior, man and woman, and the blood-related and the acquainted. Achieving the state of *Li* requires *zheng ming*, "rectification of names," meaning that a person's position in relationship to others—such as a father with his son, or the emperor with his ministers—must be clarified by a ranking system that hinders social expectations and designates behavioral norms and moral responsibilities to others. When people are located in specific social positions with proper titles designating their role behavior, the society will be orderly and organized because everyone will know what he is or is not expected to do. *Li* sounds somewhat like the notion of natural law or laws of nature in the West.[5] Because of all their similarities, each was referred to as a set of natural rules that "judges human conduct by means of man's rational faculties."[6]

The second issue is the divergence between the two schools on crime and human nature. Confucian scholars[7] asserted that human beings were born with the good will to enable them to pursue four fundamental qualities as human virtues: humanity (*Ren*), righteousness (*Yi*), propriety (*Li*), and wisdom (*Zhi*). A man could achieve virtue through education. The evil in man was cultivated by bad environmental or external influences. Because the nature of human beings is good, wrongdoers could be taught shame and decency and, hence, reformed through education and moral persuasion. The individual's moral self-internalization was, for Confucius, the first step toward social harmony. A sound social order was the outer manifestation of the spiritual and moral capacities innate in the individual human being. Humanity (*Ren*) was a moral character, embodying a particular virtue—such as kindness, benevolence, and compassion—that enabled a man to attain his true manhood.[8] This moral character was developed in oneself and in one's relationships with others. The will of an individual is not free but is, rather, confined by his obligations to his family, clan, guild, emperor, and society as a whole. Criminal wrongdoing is a result of the faulty self-internalization of morality or an insufficient moral education and persuasion by family, clan, or governmental authority. Thus, the individual and the social institution to which he belongs are equally culpable of the wrongdoing.

Contrary to this humanitarian view of human nature and crime, Legalism believed in man's original malignity. Because all people are born with the desire for physical, material, and psychological gratifications, everyone has the potential to commit wrongful behavior. Original greed and selfishness distract men from obeying the moral order and lead them to mischief. Stiff penalties and the fear of punishment are the only forces powerful enough to stop people from drifting into crime. Although Confucianism and Legalism both agreed that people were born unequal in terms of their intelligence and wealth, the latter argued that original inequity is irrelevant in implementing law and punishing wrongdoers because all men have original malignity. To rule a state, the law ought to treat equally those who obey it because of their sound virtue and good nature and those who do not violate it for fear of being punished, since there is no difference between the former and the latter. Shang Yang insisted that "nothing is more basic for putting an end to crimes than the imposition of heavy penalties."[9] Law can, first, punish the evil of guilty persons and, second, reward the innocent. To strengthen the power of law, the punishment must fit the crime rather than the criminal. The uniformity of the imposition of law was the key to preserving the power of law.

As far as social order is concerned, Confucianism asserted that a society governed by a ruler who possessed all four fundamental qualities (*Ren*, *Yi*, *Li*, and *Zhi*) would be prosperous and harmonious. The Legalists, on the other hand, believed that social order could be attained only through the enforcement of law. A ruler must be able to enforce law swiftly and punish severely those who disobey the law in order to keep people's original greed and selfishness under control. In addition, both schools held different views on the real ends of a well-ordered society: for Legalism, a prosperous and powerful state; for Confucianism, a peaceful, harmonious, simple, and contented society.[10] Philosophically, the Confucianists sought spiritual self-perfection while the Legalists favored material gratification. Confucius believed that law can convict and execute people, but that it cannot teach them humanity, kindness, benevolence, and compassion. Only *Li* is able to do that. Law tells people what they cannot do, without teaching them why they should not do it. Therefore, law can keep people away from trouble for a moment but can never reform them.

The great harmony can be achieved only through moral persuasion and implementing *Li.*

It must be pointed out here that, although Legalism and Confucianism were recognized as two opposite schools of ancient Chinese philosophy, an important assimilation of these two schools appeared in the work of Xunzi (313–238 B.C.), a prominent Confucian scholar who, in diverging from the Confucian principle of moral persuasion, also expressed his strong interest in a state with centralized power and utilization of penal punishment. For instance, he stated in his book *Xunzi.zhenglun* that "the death penalty for murderers and punishment for assailants are common rules for all rulers . . . a nation will have peace if crime is punished, [but] otherwise it will be in turmoil."[11] Xunzi's advocacy of the state's power and heavy punishment for maintaining social order had significant meaning for the later development of the Confucianist philosophy on law and the state's role in social control, which absorbed some of the essences of Legalism.

The irony was that, although Confucianism had become the dominant official orthodoxy endorsed by generations of imperial rulers, it was the Legalists who helped Qin Shihuang, who eventually unified China by establishing the first imperial society, the Qin Dynasty, in 221 B.C. To implement rules of law, the government bureaucracy, a military force, and a vast taxation system were established. Because of their intensive suppression of undesirable social behavior and heterodox thoughts, the Qin emperor and his Legalist bureaucrats quickly earned a reputation for being the most vicious and cruelest regime in China's history; that reputation eventually brought about the downfall of the Legalist school in both the political and legal realms.[12]

CONFUCIANIZATION OF CHINESE LAW

By the time of the Han Dynasty (206 B.C.–A.D. 220), Confucianism had become the most favorable political ideology and eventually the official orthodoxy of law for successive generations of emperors.[13] During the Eastern Han Dynasty (A.D. 25–220) imperial law had undergone a process of Confucianization as it incorporated the idealistic vision of the Confucian "superior man" who is motivated by piety and good example, not by fear of the law, with the realistic view of Legalism that a system of reasonable criminal sanctions is necessary for those who cannot meet the minimum standards of social conduct.[14] Jia Yi (201–168 B.C.), one of the Confucianist scholars who pioneered the efforts to link Confucianism and Legalism during the Western Han Dynasty, shed new light on the different functions of *Li* (moral code) and *Fa* (law) in social control by assimilating the ideas of Confucianism and Legalism:

> With human sagacity and wisdom, we can learn things that already occurred, but we cannot be aware of things that will happen in the future. By the same token, Li can prevent sinfulness before it occurs, but law can reprimand wickedness after the wrong has occurred. Therefore, law is to be utilized for curbing evil, while Li has a difficult task that requires a lifetime to accomplish.

> . . . Li cultivates people, virtue and benevolence whereas punishment penalizes abominations.[15]

Jia Yi further declared that while *Li* (moral code) is more profound, law is also a necessary means for the ruler to maintain his prerogatives while he pursues social harmony. Like yin and yang, "you cannot dispense with either punishment or moral persuasion and put sole reliance on the other."[16] This comment indicates the assimilation of Confucianism with Legalism and other philosophical schools of thought such as Taoism and yin yang.

Dong Zhongshu (179–104 B.C.), another eminent Confucian scholar of the Western Han Dynasty, revised Confucius's classics by (1) combining the function of *Li* and law by emphasizing the supremacy of *Li* and the subservience of law; (2) emphasizing the emperor's sacrosanct power in governing the country and enacting the law; (3) establishing the "three authorities"—the emperor's authority over his ministers, a father's authority over his children, and a husband's authority over his wife—as the fundamental principles of law and punishment; and (4) officially solidifying Confucian ideology and prohibiting heretical beliefs.[17] Confucian scholars also incorporated the "three-duty" principle into the bureaucratic authority, simplifying it as the ministers' loyalty to their emperor, a son's filial piety to his father, and a wife's faithfulness to her husband. The three authority figures—the emperor, the father, and the husband—had legitimate authority to impose punishment upon their subordinates. Furthermore, law was regarded as a suppressive instrument that was controlled by the emperor, the ministers, and the gentry class.

Perhaps the most significant impact of Confucianization on law and the legal system was the so-called *chunqiu jueyu*—that is, determining the penalty according to the principles of *Spring and Autumn* (*Chunqiu*), a book of Confucian classics.[18] Introducing *chunqiu jueyu* into the judicial system symbolized the establishment of the superior status of the Confucian moral code over the law and the legitimacy of the emperor's superior power over the judiciary. In other words, the authority was legally recognized as having the power to determine guilt and innocence according to the Confucian classics, even when it sometimes had to sidestep the law. This moralistic characteristic of Chinese law and the judiciary was well documented in the chapter on "Penalty and Morality" in the *Discussion on Salt and Iron* (*Yan tie lun*):

> determining guilt according to *Chunqiu jueyu* actually means according to the will of authority, by which the law violator who follows moral rules is remittable, whereas the law-abiding person who violates moral code is punishable; in making this determination, sidestepping the law is, of course, a frequent occurrence.[19]

In addition, the Han Dynasty formally recognized four sources of law: *lü* (codified laws), *ling* (the emperor's order), *ke* (statutes inherited from previous dynasties), and *bi* (precedents),[20] among which *ling* has the highest binding power over the other three. Apparently the imperial legal system in China was in every sense a subordinate tool of authority for the purpose of social ordering.

LAW AND THE FAMILIST-ORIENTED MORAL CODE

The coexistence of Confucianism and Legalism in Chinese traditional law is often explained historically as the result of the Confucianization of Chinese imperial law. Legalist strands of formally structured penal controls and an emphasis on universally fixed penalties were modified during the Han Dynasty by the Confucian ideas of familism and the principle of differential status. The Confucian ideas created a humanitarian concern that resulted in greater clemency when penal punishments were determined. The official consolidation of the Confucian codes of morality—including paternalism, familism, loyalty, and filial piety—helped to shape the etiquette, customs, ethics, norms, and social structure that otherwise might be the manifestation of the legal formality of Legalism.

Law versus Family and Clan Rules

It has been said that two Chinese make a family; three Chinese make a bureaucracy.[21] Family unity and governmental bureaucracy are, indeed, two important features of the history of the Chinese imperial civilization. There is little doubt that the family system has been of utmost importance in the lengthy maintenance of social stability in imperial China. Central to the family values exemplified in the legal tradition are paternalism, filial piety, and the supremacy of blood relations. As an extended form of familism, the clan was a unilateral kin group, based only on patrilineal descent, whose members believed they shared a common biological ancestor, usually practiced exogamy, and often resided unilocally. Traditional law relied, to a certain extent, on the clan rules by incorporating excerpts from these rules or by upholding them. For instance, under both Tang (618–907) and Song law (920–1279), endogamy—marriage between those of the same surname—was an offense punishable by two years in prison; the law was an outgrowth of the clan rule of exogamy.[22] Because of the rules of blood purity and kin, primogeniture was also protected by law, under which it was a crime punishable by one year in prison or a flogging of fifty blows if a sonless couple adopted a boy from an outside clan.[23] The law also recognized the existence and practices of kangaroo courts within clans.

Although China has been the most populous nation in the world, the size of the Chinese family throughout history has averaged five to six persons, which is only slightly more than its Western counterpart.[24] The image of the large, joint Chinese family derives mostly from the significance of family unity and hierarchy in Chinese cultural antiquity. Feng Yu-lan, a prominent Chinese philosopher, noted that in China "the family became elaborate to such an extent that we may fairly speak of it as 'the Chinese family system.'"[25] The major characteristics of the Chinese family system are (1) the supremacy of seniority and patriarchy; (2) the emphasis on progeny, not romantic love, as the primary reason for marriage; (3) the intense family solidarity that gives individuals psychological and economic security through membership in a tightly knit group and that, at the same time, represses individualism;[26] and (4) the negligibility of maternal relations in the family system.[27] As a result of this familism, nepotism and favoritism were frequently practiced in Chinese society.

Furthermore, the family concept was even extended to state affairs, where the emperor was regarded as a father of the state and the ministers were called parental officers. In Confucius's own words to Duke Jing of the Qi State (*Qi Jing Gong*), "the Emperor must be an emperor; the minister must be a minister; the father must be a father; and the son must be a son."[28] The emperor's authority and relationship with his ministers and his people in general were the same as those found in the family. As Shu-ching Li put it: "insofar as the government was nothing but a projection of the patriarchal family, and the virtue which justified the sovereign's holding of the throne was a projected family ethics, there could never be a government of laws as practiced in the West, but a government of men."[29] The head of the government was the head of the extended family of the whole nation. Conventionally, government officials were called "parental archons." The government was not a public servant body, but a sacrosanct paternity. Though China was not without law and legal institutions, law was traditionally deemed as being inferior to the will of the ruler and Confucius's moral code. Interestingly, although the emperor's power to rule the country and his people was ultimate and sacrosanct, it sometimes gave way to the patriarch's supremacy. As a practical rule, when family/clan rules conflicted with law, the latter often yielded to the importance of the former. For example, during the Han Dynasty, the law recognized that if a son revealed his father's crime to the authorities, he should receive the same punishment as his father.[30] The son would be punished for impiety to his father while the father would be penalized for his contempt of government authority. Traditional law also gave the father judicial immunity for killing his son or for ordering his son's suicide for reasons of impiety. A son was also allowed to serve his father's sentence, an action regarded as a great filial piety, which often resulted in the mitigation of the father's original sentence for the purpose of rewarding his son's devotion.

The obligation to support aged or ill parents was also a consideration in decisions to grant immunity or suspend a sentence in both capital and noncapital cases.[31] An offender's execution could be reprieved until after his parents' deaths if he was their only son. However, if the murder victim was also an only son of his family, the murderer was not entitled to this clemency. This law not only demonstrated great consideration for family values in the traditional administration of criminal penalties but also tells us how a sentence was measured in traditional Chinese society. Although the victim himself might have no significant meaning for the magistrate in determining the sentence, his relationship with his parents and family obviously weighed heavily in the judicial disposition.

In addition to the integration of paternalism and law, family moral order, such as the husband's authority and the propagation of posterity, also permeated the law. Spousal assaults were treated differentially according to gender. A wife who assaulted her husband was punished more severely than was a stranger who assaulted another stranger; however, a husband's abuse of his wife was generally treated as nonoffensive unless serious injury or death occurred.

The continuation of the male lineage was a primary obligation for married couples. Historical evidence abounds that traditionally infertility was not only regarded as the worst characteristic of impiety to the ancestor and the family but was always blamed on women. During the Wei Dynasty, the law provided that if a married man had no male heir and refused to take a concubine, he could be punished for impiety against the ancestor.[32] This partially explained the common practice of polygamy and concubinage in traditional society.

The family feud or blood revenge had a special status in Chinese traditional law. According to the Confucian hierarchy of family relationships, the right to revenge was restricted to first- and second-blood relationships, that is, between parents and sons or between siblings. Otherwise, the law allowed family revenge only under certain conditions. For instance, Zhou law (770–256 B.C.) stated that if a person registered with officials in advance, his retaliatory killing was legitimate; but the vengeance was limited to one chance.[33] Although historical documents indicate that vengeance has been prohibited since the Western Han Dynasty,[34] blood revenge has always been considered as a mitigating factor in sentencing due to the moralistic character of vengeance for family members. Perhaps there is nothing better than revenge to account for moral heroism in Chinese culture. In traditional China, a family's pursuit of vengeance was not only something that had to be done to rectify harm inflicted against a family member but was also a moral responsibility one had to the victimized family members. Thus, revenge became a self-fulfilling goal to honor one's own egotism in Chinese tradition. As Madson put it, unlike retaliation, which is a means of achieving justice, revenge is an end in itself.[35]

Even the imperial government officials had to recognize the filial obligations of the individual to his family under many circumstances. According to the Tang and Song codes, for example, if a person who was an only son of his family was appointed by the emperor to serve an official post in a region other than where his parents resided, he had to take his parents with him so he could continue to take care of them; otherwise, he would be sentenced to either one year in prison and dismissal from his post or a flogging of eighty blows without dismissal from his post.[36] By the same token, if a son's parent died, he was prohibited from getting married, conceiving a child, or leaving home for official duty during the entire mourning period—which varied from three years during the Northern Wei Dynasty (386–543) to twenty-seven months during the Tang Dynasty (618–907).[37] In the Yuan Dynasty, if a son who was a government officer did not attend his parent's funeral, he would be flogged sixty-seven times and demoted two ranks.[38]

The vast historical evidence suggests that the importance of patriarchal relationships and familial obligations in traditional Chinese society has been a hallmark of Chinese traditional law and the penalty system. The Confucianist moral principle of familism served as the guiding light to define what might or might not become a matter of law and to govern the administration of criminal penalties in imperial China. What was even more significant about familism in Chinese history is the close resemblance of the patriarchal family structure to the structure of power in the imperial bureaucratic states. Therefore, familism profoundly shaped Chinese society and people's attitudes toward the role of law, the state, and societal harmony.

Individual versus Group

The rigorous consolidation of social harmony, family unity, and clan or guild obligations irreversibly overshadowed the possible growth of individualism in traditional China. Nevertheless, this does not imply that Confucianism totally denied individualism because of its overwhelming emphasis on family values and unity. As a matter of fact, Confucius and his loyal followers discussed in great detail the importance of the individual, the individual's personality, the individual's role, and self-cultivation and moral perfection as means to social harmony. But there is a fundamental distinction between the Confucian concerns of individualism and the Western concept of individualism. The latter concentrates on selfishness toward one's own interests, happiness, fulfillment, and personal tangible and intangible gratification, while the former embodied selfless altruism toward one's self-containment and moral fulfillment through unconditional commitment to family, clan, guild, and societal obligations.[39] As Lin Yu-tang, a modern Chinese thinker, put it: "The Chinese are a nation of individualists. They are family-minded, not social-minded, and the family mind is only a form of magnified selfishness."[40]

Furthermore, Chinese patriarchalism included the common gender prejudice of placing women in a subordinate position far beyond the common economic and political causes. A woman had no status in the continuation of her paternal family; once she married, neither she nor her children bore the name of her paternal family. Based on this fact, family inheritance was recognized not by blood relationship but by patriarchalism. The low status of women in the family and society was evident in the high incidence of female infanticide. Individuals became nothing without the family or clan affiliation. Unlike the West, the Chinese felt that the right to life was not something inborn but was rather a gift given by the parents. A person's life belonged first to his parents and the family and then to the ruler. Traditional law unequivocally affirmed this belief by giving the parents extended rights ranging from physical punishment to commanding their child's suicide to killing their children for moral causes.

More importantly, the family tie had also been introduced into the penal system by a collective punishment in the form of the death penalty or the "corruption of blood"[41] that could be extended to an offender's entire family. This type of collective punishment clearly reflected the family-value-oriented criminal penalty system that extended individual accountability in criminal liability to entire family members. The family provided psychological support for and social protection to the individual; at the same time its own fate was also determined by the behavior of each individual family member. The individual's obligations to his family and the family's obligations to the individual were dependent on each other. To conform with law was not a totally self-motivated decision for one's personal benefit but was often an altruistic decision for the family's well-being. The constraining power of the mutual obligations between the individual and the family certainly served as a social control agent to prevent individual deviance.

Furthermore, community condemnation or public humiliation was also frequently used by the authorities as a punitive measure that damaged a person's reputation and egotism because he relied on the community's acceptance for his psychological gratification and social and economic security. If it is true that an individual-centered culture could lead people to psychological independence and isolation, it is also true that a group-centered culture could lead people to psychological dependence and containment. Apparently, "dropping out, becoming invisible, or carving out an area of one's life and declaring it out of bounds to anyone but oneself or one's family seem to be impossible" in Chinese society.[42]

DIVINE PUNISHMENT OF MALIGNANT BEHAVIOR

Chinese imperial society was a flower with a wide variety of ritual observances and religious practices, although there were no unitary churches or centralized religious dogmas as there were in the West. The ritual practices were drawn mainly from Taoism, Confucianism, yin and yang, Buddhism, and ancestor worship. By Western standards, the Chinese practiced not religion but rather superstitious rituals such as family or kin ancestor worship and festivals of door and kitchen gods. These ritual practices reflected no more than a wish for a blessing for good health, prosperity, harmony, and peace. There was no belief in original sin and in the need for expiation in Chinese traditional culture because of the Confucian influence of original human virtue and the principle of secularity that underplayed the significance of the next life. People were inculcated to pursue happiness and fulfillment for themselves and their offspring in this life.

Nevertheless, similar to the Western religions, Chinese did believe that their behavior was constantly watched and recorded by a supernatural being; that is, if they violated the Way (*Tao*)—the cosmic order of Heaven—their errors and misdeeds would be registered in Heaven. When the time came, according to the cosmic cycle, they would be punished in some way—such as a shortened life due to a natural disaster or illness. In other words,

> calamities and blessing do not come through fixed gates; it is man himself that invites them. . . . But if he acts contrary to righteousness or behaves improperly, . . . [after a long list of crimes] if he commits these or similar crimes, the Arbiter of Human Destiny will . . . take away from the culprit's term of life periods of three hundred and three days. When these units are exhausted, he will die. If at death there remains guilt unpunished, the evil luck will be transferred to his posterity.[43]

Personal willingness to conform to moral orthodoxy led behavioral control in two ways. On the one hand, fear of punishment inflicted by the supernatural forces from Heaven kept people acting within the morally defined lines; on the other, personal conformity to the law of morality was essential in valuing a human life. An offender was viewed as possessing evil spirits that were against the Tao, the cosmic order, and detrimental to social harmony. To protect the cosmic harmony of the universe, people must commit themselves to conforming to the moral order.

Ritualistically, such obedience to the cosmic order was also preserved in judicial matters such as the execution of prisoners only during the autumn and winter seasons because these seasons represented decay or death according to the cosmic natural cycle.

Derived from a belief in supernatural forces, the infliction of punishment upon a wrongdoer was inevitably viewed according to the Way regardless of whether or not the offender was caught by the authorities. But what was the Way? Confucianism exerted secular *Li* ("righteousness") to explain that crime was a violation of moral codes that were substantiated by cosmic order and, therefore, were reprobative in behalf of Heaven's will. It appears that punishment was primarily retributive—not between the individual victim and the offender, but rather between the offender and supernatural forces. It was suggested that this superstitious belief in crime and punishment served as a psychological vehicle that effectively kept people within the letter of the law and deterred them from crime.

MORAL INTERNALISM AND THE ROLE OF LAW

Moral self-cultivation and self-containment, reinforced through socialization within the family, clan, guild, and other social institutions, were other important social control agents in Chinese society. The individual's internal ability to control his behavior was regarded as one of the greatest qualities of human virtue. Confucian scholars and the authorities zealously advocated moral perfectionism and internalism throughout imperial history. The legal proceedings, for example, attached a great deal of importance to self-motivated and self-initiated submission to the authorities, such as voluntary surrender and confession, and self-repentance that might be later regarded as important mitigating factors in penalty remission or reduction. The archaeological discovery of a Qin tomb in the Shuihudi area of the central Hubei Province provided the earliest evidence of imperial law regarding voluntary confession and the resulting penalty remission.[44] In the chapter of *Legal Dialogue* on the bamboo scripts, the question is asked: How should a penalty be imposed if a person fled with official property? The answer was: If he voluntarily surrendered to the authorities and confessed to the crimes of being a fugitive and committing theft (it was called *zichu*—"self-letting out"), he was guilty only of the crime of being a fugitive; otherwise he was also liable for the crime of theft. Nevertheless, if the penalty for theft is lighter than that for being a fugitive, the offender should be punished for being a thief.[45]

The chapter on penal law in *Han shu* termed voluntary confession as *zigao* ("self-report") and mandated that the offender who turned himself in and confessed to a murder before official discovery was entitled to a remission of penalty, except when the defendant was a principal offender in a conspiracy or had committed multiple offenses among which he had confessed to only one or two.[46] For example, according to a biography of Hengshan Wang (114–88 B.C.) in *Han Shu*, Liu Xiao, a son of Hengshan Wang, confessed to attempting to overthrow his father's power and was exempted from the penalty for plotting a rebellion. But he was still executed for the crime of adultery and incest with one of his father's wives, to which he had not confessed.[47] The succeeding dynasties, including the Republic of China, adopted this statute provision without exception.[48] Noticeably, timing was important in any possible penalty remission or reduction when the offender voluntarily confessed to the authorities. The offender was entitled to the full remission of his penalty if he confessed before the crime was known to the authorities; confession after the authorities pursued and arrested him was considered to be "under contemplation" and was eligible for a reduction in penalty by one or two degrees.[49] The penal law of the Southern Dynasty (420–589) specified that if a fugitive surrendered and confessed his guilt within a fixed time limit of one hundred days, he could receive a lenient sentence or amnesty.[50]

The timing of the confession was not just a matter of procedural technicality. From a moral point of view, confession, in the first place, represented a person's willingness to admit to both the factual guilt of the crime and the recognition of his moral faults; it indicated that he was returning voluntarily to the path of virtue. Although we do not know whether an offender's confession actually contained sincere repentance for a crime in imperial times, traditional law strongly upheld that a person's willingness to return to good virtue should nevertheless be rewarded. It is useful, perhaps, to note that the concept of free will—that a man has the choice of whether to commit a crime or to conform to social mores—has never had as much importance in the Chinese legal tradition as it has had in the West. The commission of a crime was viewed not as a rational choice by an individual but, rather, as the result of insufficient moral education or a lack of internal restraint to resist the bad temptations of the environment.

In addition, it has been noticed by many Western scholars that historically Chinese culture did not recognize an impaired or diseased mental capacity on the part of a criminal offender. To admit or accept the notion of mental illness and a person's diminished mental capacity was deemed a direct counterattack on the Confucian principles of moral persuasion and the ability of the human mind to be cultivated. Perhaps these principles explain the ignorance of mental illness and the poorly developed mental health services that existed in Chinese society.

Second, self-surrender and confession also implied an offender's submission to the authorities. In accordance with Confucius's three principal relationships,[51] crime was not just a simple violation of law but was often deemed a rebellion against authority. The offender's initiative in admitting to the facts of the crime was regarded as a personal willingness to submit to the authorities' control. Self-confession was not only personally beneficial for the offender himself, who might be rewarded with a penalty remission or reduction, but was also socially significant because it enabled the authorities to restore the power that had been challenged when the crime was committed. To ensure the restoration of the individual's respect for authority, the use of physical torture to obtain a confession was legally permitted if the offender refused to surrender. Thereafter, the voluntary confession was not totally voluntary at all, although theoretically it was the individual offender's choice under imperial law. In other words, on the one hand, the law recognized the necessity for a reasonable time interval between the commission of a crime and the offender's surrender; on the other hand, if the individual chose not to comply with the authorities, a coerced confession could be sought nevertheless. Thus, voluntary confession was a personal choice in theory but had little basis in reality.

Third, from the traditional point of view, Chinese society has highly valued self-sufficiency and self-reliance through internal restraint and discipline. Societal reliance on external control through the formal legal procedure, codified law, and official social control agencies was regarded as morally inferior to internalized self-constraint and virtually a dehumanization. In response to Alexis de Tocqueville's argument on the nature of external control forces in human society, Lee-Jan Jan states that "the increasing use and reliance on external control by law is a dehumanizing process, and eventually reduces human beings to the level of animals, who lack self control and a sense of morality and who have to be externally controlled by law."[52] Perhaps, it is indeed an ongoing dilemma for any society to develop external control mechanisms through law and the legal system without, at the same time, reducing the human capacity for internal discipline and self-control through the internalization of moral perfection.

Moreover, for a society that relies heavily on external mechanisms of social control, the procedural complexity and sufficiency of the legal system are essential for ensuring that justice can be rendered uniformly and precisely. Without due process there would be no justice. This is what is commonly referred to as "justice under the law." It has been established that "the rationality of law is formal rather than substantive."[53] Often this procedural justice is pushed so far that it reaches the point "where the question of substantive justice may not be an issue, and injustice may have no legal remedy so long as correct formal procedure has been observed."[54]

Compared with this kind of legal proceeding, Chinese law was, perhaps, skewed more toward substantive justice that focused on the factual guilt of crime and its impact on the social order. The responsibility of the legal system was to assure the community that the offender had been apprehended and punished so that order could be restored. Setting offenders free because of procedural errors was regarded as a greater evil than wrongfully punishing a few innocent people for the sake of restoring social order. The concept of justice was defined on the basis of public perceptions about social order and personal obligations to social harmony. Safeguarding justice in traditional China was left totally to the judicial officers and government authorities who, presumably, possessed good moral characteristics such as benevolence, impartiality, and incorruptibility. From a political point of view, China, of course, was a "totalitarian type of society, which is in a great hurry to settle some fundamental general social conflict or policy; [and in which, therefore,] law tends to go by the board."[55] After all, for the Chinese, it is not so much "justice under the law" but "justice above the law."

FINAL REMARKS

The most remarkable aspect of Chinese imperial law has been the competitive struggles between the Confucian and Legalist traditions, which are still relevant in today's China. After the dark age of political and ideological suppression advocated by the Legalist school during the Qin Dynasty, China gradually experienced the

Confucianization of law through the Han Dynasty. No matter how the imperial rulers intended to deny the influence of Legalism in constructing Chinese law and the judicial bureaucracy, Chinese law became a hybrid of Confucianism, which favors achieving social harmony through moral persuasion and thought reform, and Legalism, which endorses the state's absolute power in maintaining order. Although the differences between Legalism and Confucianism seem to be far more interesting to legal scholars than their similarities, we must keep in mind that their agreement on the ruler's absolute authority over every bureaucratic entity, including law making and the judiciary, provided the basic foundation for assimilating the two adversarial ideologies in traditional China. "Neither Confucianism nor Legalism can be associated with principles evocative of civil liberty and political freedom."[56]

Indisputably, Chinese imperial law bears a strong Confucian moral character. However, Confucian morality and imperial law were also two parallel behavioral codes joined hand-in-hand in ordering social conduct in Chinese society. Besides these overlapping areas, penal law was designed to preserve the inviolable status of the moral code, even though some conducts were not defined by law as offensive but were reprimanded by Confucian morality. The state served as an agent with a strong will and iron hands to preserve the sanctity of officially endorsed mores through both coercive moral cultivation and legal sanction. If we see the purpose of law and the legal system in other civilizations as controlling undesirable social behavior, Chinese traditional law and the legal system were aimed unequivocally at controlling both undesirable behaviors and unorthodox minds. Essentially, Chinese imperial law was enacted not to "secure natural equality . . . as to secure natural rights"[57] but to preserve the legitimacy of imperial hierarchical power and the order of the monarchical system.

On the eve of the Nationalist revolution, reform of law and the legal system was already under way due to the influence of the West. Nevertheless, the struggle between Confucianism and Legalism continues. Although the democratization of law[58] and society is an intellectually conscious and historically irrevocable process, its realization might be slower and might inflict more pain on China than on other nations because civil liberty and democracy had never been an important part of China's longstanding legal and cultural traditions. It is a given that China's three-millennia old legal tradition will continue to be in charge in the contemporary society. Robert Redfield intelligently asserted:

> In folk society the moral rules bend, but men cannot make them afresh. In civilization the old moral orders suffer, but new states of mind are developed by which the moral order is, to some significant degree, taken in charge. The story of the moral order is attainment of some autonomy through much adversity.[59]

NOTES

1. For chronological information on China's imperial dynasties, see the Appendix.

2. The quotation is translated from three chapters of *Shang Jun Shu*: Chapter III, 14, "Xiu Quan" ("The Cultivation of Request Standards"); Chapter V, 26, "Ding Fen" ("Fixing of Responsibilities"); and Chapter V, 23, "Jun Chen" ("Ruler and Minister"). See Hegao Yang, 1987, pp. 36 and 32, for the original text.

3. Chin-tsen Chang, 1960, p. 4.

4. Ibid., p. 1.

5. Comparison between *Li* in Chinese ancient law and natural law in the West was discussed in Bodde, 1957, p. 709; Chin-tsen Chang, 1960, p. 5; Chi-yun Chang, 1981; Dawson, 1948, p. 163; Needham, 1956b, p. 521; and John Wu, 1958 and 1979, p. 17. In debating the comparability of natural law in the West and *Li* in Chinese culture, Needham, 1956b, pointed out that, unlike the West, Chinese thinking on the interrelationship between the natural world and human society took a different path, that is, a self-contained, self-operated, and self-commanded cosmic harmony of wholes. For information on this debate, see the works of Bodde, 1957, pp. 722–23; Bodde, 1973, pp. 299–315; and Needham, 1956b, p. 582.

6. Chin-tsen Chang, 1960, p. 5.

7. Except for the Xunzi school.

8. Lo, 1983, p. 5; Lung, 1976, pp. 35–38.

9. Gao and Jiang, 1989, p. 28, for the original text (Zhong-xing lian qi zui, ze-min bu-gan shi) from *Lord Shang* (*Shang jun shu)*, Chapter XVII, "Reward and Penalty (*Shang xing)*."

10. B. Schwartz, 1959, p. 56.

11. This quotation is translated from the chapter titled *Zhenglun*. For the original text, see the reprint of *Zhuzi jicheng* by the China Book Bureau, 1958.

12. The best-known example of the Qin emperor's cruelty was "burning books and vivisepulting Confucian followers" (*fenshu kengru*) under what was known as the Statute of Burning Books (Fenshu Ling, 213 B.C.). See Ye et al., 1989, pp. 71–72.

13. Regarding the relationship between Qin law and Han law, a number of scholars, such as Ogawa Taksuki and A.F.P. Hulsewé, have suggested that the Han lawmakers made no mention of the antilegalism intent in the Han code although the Han emperor intended to abandon the Qin code completely. See Hulsewé, 1955, p. 29.

14. Borowitz suggested that the Confucianization of Chinese imperial law began when the Qin court (Ch'in court) adopted a penal code that "applied to all China after the establishment of a national government by the Ch'in Dynasty in the late third century B.C." (Borowitz, 1977, p. 522). Nevertheless, the Confucianization of law did not actually occur until the late Han Dynasty, from A.D. 25 to 220, when Confucianism was endorsed by the rulers of the Han Dynasty as the official orthodoxy (Ch'u, 1948).

15. Yang and Duan, 1988, p. 245.

16. Chin-tsen Chang, 1960, pp. 14–15.

17. Ibid., pp. 253–72.

18. *Spring and Autumn* is one of the important Confucian classics that provide the basic doctrine on Confucianist philosophy. For the most current edition of this work, see Zhong-shu Dong, 1975.

19. Ye et al., 1989, pp. 116–17.

20. Pu and Zhou, 1987, pp. 52–54.

21. Bhatia and Chung, 1974, p. 3.

22. Pu and Zhou, 1987, p. 168.

23. Ni et al., 1987, pp. 401–4 and 408; Shen, 1985, p. 1837.

24. Bodde, 1962, p. 44; Ch'u, 1948, p. 3; *China: Facts & Figures*, 1982, p. 5.

25. Feng Yu-lan, 1948, p. 21.

26. Bodde, 1962, p. 44.

27. Ch'u, 1965, p. 15.
28. Confucius, 1979, Book XII, p. 114.
29. S. Li, 1954, p. 4.
30. Ni et al., 1987, p. 70.
31. Qu, 1981, pp. 60–62.
32. Ibid., p. 384.
33. Ch'u, 1965, p. 268.
34. Qu, 1981, p. 70.
35. Madson, 1990.
36. Qu, 1981, p. 86.
37. See Bodde, 1981b, p. 187; Qu, 1981, p. 87; Ni et al., 1987, p. 384; and Shen, 1985, p. 1849, for detailed discussions on administrative and criminal penalties for officers who violated the moral piety code.
38. Qu, 1981, p. 89.
39. Family identity supersedes personal identity. For instance, according to Chinese custom, one's family name precedes the personal name. Westerners do just the opposite, asserting the personal ego in personal identity. See Bodde, 1962, p. 54.
40. Lin Yutang, 1935, p. 172.
41. "Corruption of blood," a term used in early English law, referred to the consequence of attainder, in that an attainted person could neither inherit lands or other hereditaments from his ancestor nor retain those he already had nor transmit them by descent to any heir because his blood was considered by law to be corrupted (*Black's Law Dictionary*, 1979, p. 311). This statutory provision was abolished in 1870. A similar type of statute also existed in the United States; see *John M. Avery, Appellant, v. George Everett, Impleaded, etc.*, Respondent, Court of Appeals of New York, 110 N.Y. 317; 18 N.E. 148, November 28, 1887, submitted October 2, 1888, decided.
42. Simon, 1985, p. 100.
43. This quotation is from *The Treatise of the Most Exalted One on Moral Retribution*, which has been considered to be the work of Lao Tzu, though its actual date and authorship are unknown. Some documents suggest that this work dates at least from the thirteenth century and is probably much earlier (de Bary, Chan, and Watson, 1964, pp. 632 and 634–35).
44. In 1979, Chinese archaeologists discovered 1,155 bamboo scripts that contained legal journals and court records of a local magistrate named Xi (Hsi, 262–217 B.C.). See Hulsewé, Brill, 1985, pp. 21–215, for a textual translation of the bamboo scripts.
45. Pu and Zhou, 1987, pp. 58–59.
46. See *Han shu*, 1962, which was a biographical book of history covering 206 B.C. to A.D. 20. The most recent reprint is the 1962 edition by the China Book Bureau.
47. Pu and Zhou, 1987, p. 59.
48. Bodde and Morris, 1967; Rickett, 1971, pp. 797–802. Rickett pointed out some obvious differences between the imperial statutes of voluntary surrender and confession and the statute of the Republic of China. One of the major differences is that the early remission of a penalty because of a confession in imperial law was invalidated in the Republic. The offender's confession could lead to mitigation and reduction of penalty only at the judge's discretion. Meanwhile, the Republican law expanded the range of crimes under which a reduction of penalty could be imposed resulting from a confession. However, the remission of a penalty due to self-surrender was evidently resurrected by the legal authorities of the Republic of China in a recent official campaign against amphetamine abuse. See "Voluntary Surrender—Remission of Penalty: Amphetamine Users Are Facing the Deadline," 1992, for the most recent revision of this statute in the Republic of China.

49. Kracke, 1968, and J. T. C. Liu, 1968.

50. McKnight, 1981, p. 43.

51. The heart of the three principal relationships—the emperor and his ministers, a father and his son, and a husband and his wife—is respect for and obedience to authority figures.

52. See de Tocqueville, 1956, pp. 303–4; Jan, 1983, p. 197.

53. Weber, 1969, p. 76.

54. Parsons, 1962, p. 71.

55. Ibid., p. 72.

56. Bozeman, 1982, p. 67.

57. Pound, 1922, p. 83.

58. In comparative legal studies, the concept of democratization of law is often used interchangeably with the notion of Westernization of law. See R. R. Edwards, 1978.

59. Cited in Nivison and Wright, 1959, p. vii.

CHAPTER TWO

The Rules of Punishment in Traditional Law

INTRODUCTION

CONFUCIANIST NOTIONS of law and order were well reflected in the punishments prescribed by imperial law against those behaviors deemed to be immoral and malicious. According to *Shang shu* (*The Book of Documents*), in the chapter "Shundian," by about 2200 B.C. the words *crime* and *penalty* were known in ancient China.[1] Although there was no archaeological evidence of the existence of formally written law at the time of the Xia Dynasty, *Shang shu* recorded the earliest forms of the "five penalties"—tattooing, disfigurement, castration, mutilation, and death—that were believed to be the components of *Yü xing* in the Xia Dynasty (2100–1600 B.C.).[2] *Tang xing* and *Lü xing* were said to be successive codified laws created by the mythical emperors during the Shang and Western Zhou Dynasties (1600–771 B.C.). The five punishments were modified into five forms of instruments used to carry out penalties in order of their severity: army, axe and hatchet, sword and saw, knife and chisel, and whip and rod.[3] As advocated by Legalist jurists, the early law was concerned primarily with making the penalty commensurate with the crime. The early codified law seemed to be more interested in defining instruments of penalty rather than crime per se. The task of deciding which conducts ought to be punished was left largely to social morality and norms. Systematically identifying crime categories did not occur until the year 550, when the Northern Qi State (550–577) of the Northern Dynasty for the first time classified crimes into ten categories in order of their severity. These ten categories, with modifications and revisions, survived and remained as primary categories of heinous crimes punishable by severe penalties throughout the entire imperial era (550–1911). Although the explanation of each category was modified slightly in each dynasty, the main scope and substance remained the same. Later they became known as the "ten abominations," somewhat equivalent to the category of common law crime in English law.

THE MORAL JUSTIFICATION FOR PUNISHMENT

In the Chinese traditional notion, punishment serves two ends: a compliment to moral conformity and the physical and spiritual elimination of malignity. The human body of the offender was believed to possess evil spirits and to be instrumental in substantiating the malicious spirit. Corporal punishment, such as cutting off the hands of a thief or castrating a rapist, was aimed at incapacitating the evil spirits by removing the instruments through which they worked.[4] Although the punishment was violent, its end justified its means because it was seen as less evil than the violence and disruption of social order brought about by the crime. Punishment was morally justifiable and a fairly reciprocal penalty for the commission of a crime.[5] Thus, punishment was retributive according to the principle of justice.

In the classic sense of Confucianism, rehabilitation through thought reform and moral persuasion should never be overlooked by any ruler of the state. In Confucius's own words, "Guide them by edicts, keep them in line with punishment, and the common people will stay out of trouble but will have no sense of shame. Guide them by virtue, keep them in line with the rites, and they will, besides having a sense of shame, reform themselves."[6] Obtaining an offender's admission of guilt before conviction was not a requirement under the law but rather a normative effort by justice personnel to fulfill their moral obligation to the state and the community. This practice emphasized the implantation of a sense of shame rather than a procedural finding of guilt. Whether offenders were found guilty of a crime according to law was not important for the purpose of restoring social order. What was important, however, was to shun offenders and make them feel ashamed of their crimes.

MIND CONTROL AND PUNISHMENT OF POLITICAL HETERODOXY

Throughout history, any attempts or behaviors directed against the current political order were considered to be the most heinous crimes and were punishable by the death penalty. This tradition can be traced back as far as 220 B.C., when the Qin emperor ordered the burning of all social, political, and humanitarian books and literature and buried alive more than 460 Confucian followers, thus marking the first use of legal sanctions against political and intellectual dissidents in Chinese history. For generations, rulers always treated political dissidents and rebellion as the number-one offense among the ten abominating crimes.[7] Noticeably, crimes under this category were not limited to the actual conduct of a rebellion or the overthrow of the government regime but also included any attempts, motives, or even critical expressions in scholarly writing, literature, poetry, the arts, and speech that were deemed to be inconsistent with official orthodoxy and offensive to the authorities. The dissenting expression was not only heretical to social conformity but also especially dangerous in plotting mass rebellion because of the dissident's power to tempt the masses perversely and because of their strong will to resist moral persuasion and reform; thus dissidents were suppressed severely and without mercy. China was not only an authoritarian state but also a totalitarian state. Although both models emphasized the maintenance of despotic political order, the totalitarian model was concerned with the control of both people's conduct and minds, whereas the authoritarian model was interested in controlling people's behaviors only. Such a brutal tradition was evidently perpetuated by China's harsh treatment toward political or intellectual dissidents who courageously pursued intellectual freedom and individualism in some modern eras.

DIFFERENTIAL TREATMENT OF OFFENDERS

Remarkably, both Legalism and Confucianism adhered to the inherent inequality of individuals before law and morality. The equal rights of individual persons before law were never honored by China's traditional ethics. Instead, inequality and differential treatment of individual offenders were the ethically prescribed norms in traditional China. For example, an important penetration of Confucian morality into the penalty system was the "five cardinal incumbencies,"[8] which introduced the idea of differential punishment in accordance with the offender's social status and relationship to the offender. Throughout Confucius's *Analects* (*Lun Yu*), the difference between gentlemen and the common people was discussed more frequently than any other subject. According to Confucius, people were born unequally—for example, some were more intellectual or wealthier and had the potential to become masters and rulers. A person's social status was predetermined before birth. This was said to lead to the diversity of occupations and the stratification of social classes into four groups in order of prestige: intellectuals, farmers, workers, and merchants.[9] The intellectual elite, selected through the civil examination system, constituted, along with the rural landlords, the patrician class within a complex network of official positions that were specialized, ranked, and salaried according to the knowledge they acquired about Confucius's classics.[10] Crimes committed by members of the gentry class were handled differently by the imperial judiciary according to the nature of the crimes, the member's rank and past achievements, and his loyalty to the emperor. During the Qing Dynasty, for example, *changwei* ("internal security"), an independent branch that had investigative and adjudicatory power over the three components of the formal judicial system—Xing Bu (trial court), Dali Si (appeal court), and Ducha Yuan (inspection branch)—handled cases involving governmental officials. It administered severe penalties to those who dared to rebel against their superiors and lenient administrative penalties for those who committed common crimes.[11]

The second example of the differential treatment of offenders derives from the Confucian code of filial piety. The severity of criminal behavior and its commensurate penalty would be ranked according to the interpersonal relationship between the victim and the offender, especially the victim's social status. The criminal conduct, per se, was of only secondary importance in determining the penalty. In the course of upholding the law, the moral code must also be preserved. For example, during the Qing Dynasty when a wife reported her husband's crime or a son reported his father's or grandfather's crime and the crime was verified, the accuser would receive the same penalty, ranging from a flogging of one hundred blows to a year in prison, as the accused; if the report was determined to be false, the reporting person would be sentenced to death.[12] In the case of murder, parricide was considered a more serious crime than filicide. Parents who killed their children were punished less severely than children who killed their parents, and parents were often not punished at all for intentionally injuring their children. In the case of assault between a married couple, if the wife was the assailant, she was subjected to a more severe penalty than was a husband who assaulted his wife. Specifically, a wife who assaulted her husband was punished by a flogging of one hundred blows regardless of whether there was an injury involved; an injury earned a punishment three times greater than the normal penalty for stranger-to-stranger assaults, in addition to the flogging; and the death of the husband resulted in the death penalty, which was administered by one thousand slices with a knife.[13] Women who did not attend their husbands' funerals or who remarried during the mourning period were also subject to severe penal sanctions. This indicates that, in addition to the penalty for common types of crimes, there existed "status offenses" under which a person could be punished for a conduct or an omission of a moral duty because of his or her relationship to the victim.

When crimes occurred between strangers, the rule of seniority and superiority also applied in determining criminal liability and punishment. For violent crimes, killing or assaulting senior family members, relatives,[14] or officials was deemed more severe than assaulting a stranger. For property crimes, stealing the state's or clan's properties was punished more severely than stealing from a private household, reflecting the emphasis of the collective over individual interests. On the other hand, however, the penal law decreed that stealing a stranger's property was a greater evil than stealing from family members, due in part to the primacy of clan law in governing property ownership and transactions.

THE PENAL EMPHASIS OF THE LAW

Historically, Chinese law was known for its emphasis on the penal aspects.[15] Due to the lack of recognition of individual rights and privacy, all social frictions were legally considered to be public matters, which thus must be dealt with by the state authorities. For instance, consanguineous marriage,[16] property inheritance, and failing to support aged parents were treated as public matters that carried a criminal penalty for the party found guilty as charged. Positive law was interested only secondarily in providing a legal forum for defending rights, especially property rights. Therefore, any type of social conflict with another individual, group, state entity, and so on, was surely subject to the scrutiny and judgment of the government authorities.[17] The civil justice system literally did not exist in the imperial society. It is easy to understand why the Chinese were so reluctant to pursue formal procedures in resolving their personal conflicts with others; they were hesitant not so much because the justice system was corrupt, but mainly because formal procedures always resulted in one type of criminal penalty or another. Surely, the legal system was the last resort for settling social conflicts because of the limited availability of civil justice.

COLLECTIVE PUNISHMENT—CORRUPTION OF BLOOD

Collective punishment against person and property was a popular form of penalty administered by the imperial legal system. Unlike penalties in the contemporary law of the West, which are aimed at individual culprits, China has traditionally extended a penalty to the entire family or clan of convicts who were guilty of the "ten abominations." Historically, this type of punishment, referred to as *yi sanzu*, executed three lines of the offender's family, including both parents' families, the offender's brothers' families, and the offender's wife's family.[18] Later, execution of the entire family was replaced by exile or penal servitude for the entire family and the "corruption of blood." If a person was convicted of committing one of the "ten abominations," his family members would either be exiled or become the property of the state. Surprisingly, collective punishment was not limited to ordinary offenders but was also extended to those who had held governmental posts. For instance, if a government officer was convicted of a crime against the emperor, his offspring would be banned permanently from serving in the officialdom.[19]

The administration of collective punishment reminds us once again about the socially and legally emphasized importance of family unity and continuity. It seems that Chinese society perceived that disrupting family unity and discontinuing the family lineage symbolically meant a stronger condemnation than simply depriving the individual offender of life, liberty or property ownership.[20] This notion of collective culpability has been revived in recent Chinese history under Mao's political regime.

JUDICIAL LENIENCY UNDER THE TRADITIONAL LAW

Although imperial law was generally regarded as cruel and harsh, there existed some humanitarian dispositions in imposing sentences. Age, physical condition, and social status were sometimes considered mitigating factors in rendering mercy or a remission of penalty. During the Han Dynasty, for example, Emperor Hui's (194–186 B.C.) statute mandated that "when a person above 70 or under 10 committed a crime, he shall not be immured under the law."[21] According to the statute of Emperor Jing (156–149 B.C.) of the Han, "a prisoner who was above age 80 or under 8, or pregnant or a midget should not wear a cangue or shackles while in custody."[22] The same humanitarian treatments can also be found in the Tang Code—for instance, pregnant women shall not be sentenced to death; a person over eighty or under ten, a blind person, or a midget shall be given a lenient sentence."[23] Nevertheless, the offender's mental condition was traditionally ignored by the law, as it still is today.

In addition, the emperors were also empowered to grant amnesty and periodically pardon certain groups of prisoners. As an important part of the judicial review process, the emperor reserved the power to review all cases involving the death penalty. Mercy was also granted based on the Confucian tradition of moral self-internalization—that is, if an offender had surrendered voluntarily, admitted his guilt, and showed repentance. For example, the Tang Code asserted that if an offender did not come forward to confess and was captured by the authorities before the end of the time limit, he would be tried only for the crime of being a fugitive, not for his original crime. However, if he still refused to confess before the deadline, he would be guilty of both fleeing and the original crime. Presumably, a certain period of time for repentance or confession was regarded as reasonable for people to reflect on the nature and consequences of their acts. This can be seen as another example of the law's intent to control undesirable social behavior as well as change people's hearts.

FINAL REMARKS

Clearly, Confucian morality was manifested in every principle of criminal sanction designated by the imperial authorities to penalize undesirable social behavior and heterodox thought. The state, as the enforcer of law, demonstrated its strong will and iron fists to preserve the sanctity of officially endorsed mores through both coercive moral cultivation and penal sanction. Confucianism and legalism might have been substantially different in terms of how Chinese society should be ruled, but they were incredibly similar on how the criminal punishment should be administered in order to preserve the imperial order and social harmony in Chinese society. Zero tolerance for political heterodoxy, differential treatment of offenders according to their social status and relationship to the victims, the imposition of collective responsibility in the administration of criminal penalties, and the use of judicial leniency all represented the penetration of Confucian moral teaching into the legal system of China.

NOTES

1. The usage of the words *evil* and *litigation* in ancient China first occurred in the earliest Chinese classic, *Shang shu*, in the chapter "Yaodian," which contains the mythological legends of 2300–2100 B.C. Litigation meant only public opinion without a complaining party in ancient China; in modern China it constitutes both verbal complaints and public opinion.

2. *Shang shu*, in the chapter "Lü xing," presents a traditional account of law. The legendary Emperor Yu (2100–2000 B.C.) conquered the southern region of China, which was occupied by a barbarian tribe, the Miao, who had invented the five punishments. Emperor Yu is said to have adopted these five corporal punishments from Miao tribal society and enacted them as a law that contained 3,000 descriptions: 200 descriptions of the death penalty, 300 provisions on cutting off feet, 500 items on castration, 1,000 items on cutting off noses and ears, and 1,000 items on tattooing (Ni et al., 1987, p. 15). Later this law became known as "The Law of Three Thousand Penalties of the Xia Dynasty" (2100–1600 B.C.).

3. Shen, 1985, p. 7.

4. Although Confucian scholars claimed that they believed in teleological philosophy, their view on punishment certainly reflected the similar philosophical stand of legalism that the socially beneficial end of punishment morally justifies the cruel means.

5. Regarding the moral justification of punishment, Moberly once pointed out:

> The deep-seated sense of fairness which revolts against punishment of the innocent revolts also against any treatment of the guilty which appears to confound guilt and innocence. It is felt to be unfair that a man's grievous fault should make no difference to the treatment he receives and that he should be treated just as favorably as if he had done no wrong. . . . [I]t is fitting and proper that, what others are to do to us, should be affected for better or worse by the quality of what we have done to them. (1968, p. 80)

6. Confucius, 1979, pp. 33–34.

7. For the text of the ten abominating crimes in the Tang Code, see W. Johnson, 1979; for the ten abominations in the Qing Code, see Bodde, 1973, pp. 93 and 139; Shen, 1985. MacCormick (1995) also provided a general discussion on this crime classification system used in imperial law in Chapter 8 of his book, pp.178–209.

8. The five cardinal incumbencies refer to the minister's duty to the emperor, the son's duty to his father, duty between brothers, the wife's duty to her husband, and duty between friends.

9. The merchants were traditionally regarded as morally inferior to the other classes because of their close association with greed, materialism, and hedonism. For further discussion on this aspect of economic development in the Confucian tradition, see Needham, 1956a.

10. The civil examination system was begun during the Han Dynasty, revived in the Tang, and continued until the end of the Qing. For the civil examination system in imperial China, see Bodde, 1962, p. 51; Drapkin, 1989, p. 140; and Rodzinski, 1984, pp. 93–95.

11. Pu and Zhou, 1987, p. 251.

12. See *Li lü* in *Da Qing lü jijei fuli* (*Qing Law*), 1706.

13. Ibid.

14. There is no doubt that traditional China was a gerontophilic society.

15. According to Bodde, the penal emphasis of law means that the Chinese traditionally treated all social frictions, including those that were typically regarded as matters of civil nature by the West, as publicly wrong. The civil law literally did not exist in imperial society (1973, p. 4).

16. During the Tang and Song Dynasties, the laws stated that marriage within consanguinity was a crime punishable by two years in prison (*Tang lü.14, Song xing tong.14*). During the Ming and Qing Dynasties, these same acts were punishable by flogging of one hundred blows plus three years in prison. Marriage between first or second cousins was defined as the crime of rape and was punishable by death (*Ming lilü.4, Qing lilü.10*).

17. Under the imperial system, judicial officers were also the administrators of the local government. Judicial duty was one of the important functions of the administrative body of government. Therefore, there was no concept of judicial independence.

18. During the Qin Dynasty, Shang Yang, a prominent legalist, invented this form of collective penalty. The scope of an offender's extended family varied slightly in each dynasty. For instance, during the Three Kingdoms Dynasty, the law excluded married women, such as an offender's sisters, from the offender's family. The Northern Dynasty extended this penalty to five family lines of the offender by including his uncles' families and his sisters' families (see Ni et al., 1987, p. 270). This punishment remained a major form of penalty throughout the imperial era and was not abolished until the early part of the twentieth

century. See Hulsewé, 1955, p. 112; Lewis, 1990, pp. 92–94; and Shen, 1985, pp. 71–79, for the origins and implications of this penalty system in different dynasties.

19. Hulsewé, 1955, p. 135.

20. Although China was not the only country that imposed collective punishment in its history, each culture has emphasized different entities that the law intends to deprive. For example, English law focused on property rights—inheritance—whereas Chinese law emphasized family unity and continuity.

21. Mi Zhou, 1985, p. 205.

22. Ibid.

23. Ibid., p. 232.

PART II

LAW OF THE TRADITION

CHAPTER THREE

Political Power and Judicial Independence: Marxist Ideology, the Communist Party, and the Role of Law

INTRODUCTION

THE ESTABLISHMENT of the People's Republic of China (PRC) was often viewed as a complete break with China's past. After the Chinese Communist Party (CCP) siezed power in 1949, the construction of a new legal order began immediately. Institutionally, the People's Liberation Army (PLA) supplied massive numbers of officers to staff the nascent police force, procuratorate, and court system. Legislatively, the legal statutes and laws previously enacted during the Chinese Soviet Republic and the Yanan period[1] and the temporary orders, amendments, and laws stipulated by the People's Government constituted the early body of Communist law. The masses were encouraged to participate in political affairs and the judicial process. The old legal machinery was officially abolished and condemned as a political accessory of the Nationalist regime that had suppressed and exploited the working class. Legal professionals were prohibited from practicing their profession because of their past associations with the legal system of the Nationalist government. Ideologically, the Marxist doctrine replaced Confucianism as the state orthodoxy in guiding all facets of societal affairs.

In 1954, the first Constitution of the People's Republic of China formally recognized the Communist Party's leadership in controlling all spheres of Chinese life. The Party's leaders declared that the goal of the socialist state was to establish a "proletarian democratic dictatorship" aimed at repressing class enemies. The working people constituted the ruling class, which was entitled to various political, social, and economic privileges. The new society seemed to display a distinguishable attitude toward law and the legal system in China. Law was said, for the first time in Chinese history, to truly "punish the wicked and reward the innocent." The new political establishment seemed to suggest that China's tradition had finally reached its historical impasse. Western commentators were also convinced that, indeed, "the

Communist attitude toward law has no connection with either the Chinese traditional attitude or the system introduced from the West."[2]

Undoubtedly, Marxism, as either a revolutionary doctrine or a philosophical ideology, is purely a product of Western culture; it exhorts the workers and intellectuals of the advanced industrialized countries of the West toward revolutionary change, but offers no political message to nationalist intellectuals and the masses in a largely precapitalist and mostly agricultural nation such as China. On the surface, Marxism has little in common with Chinese tradition. Nevertheless, for a political ideology to be adopted as the state orthodoxy in a totally alien culture and to govern a people for more than four decades, there must exist the foundation both for planting new ideological seeds that would spread across vast segments of the society and for a possible cultural assimilation.

This chapter examines the possible convergence and divergence between Mao Zedong's pro-Marxist principle of law and the Chinese traditional attitude toward law and political power. To do so, the chapter analyzes Mao Zedong's thought on the role of law and the function of judicial power with an emphasis on the relationship between judicial independence and the political power of the CCP. Without a doubt, China has been a Communist giant, second only to the former Soviet Union, since the 1949 revolution. Since then, China has been a state with a legal order that is designated, based on the Marxist ideology, to uphold the dictatorship of the Communist Party and the centrally controlled economic system. Although the recent economic reform in China has irreversibly shattered the mirage of the Chinese Communists, the CCP's paramount power in controlling the state and military forces remains largely unshakable. The economic boom and privatization of business enterprise have not brought the anticipated fundamental changes in China's politics and law.

Although Marxism is a product of the West, ideologically it is "less alien than either Buddhism or Christianity" to the Chinese because of the longstanding cultivation of Confucian secular morality.[3] The Marxist atheist tradition that focuses on changing the present world is analogous to the Confucian secular thinking of world harmony. The ideological analogy between the two traditions may have been the common point that enabled Marxism and Chinese traditional thinking to blend with respect to the role of law. The long inculcation of Confucian morality made China's adoption and assimilation of Marxism-Leninism easier and less discomforting.

In addition, the Marxist ideology was originally introduced to the Chinese, not as intellectual scholarship, but as a realistic and programmatic policy for launching revolutionary change in Chinese society. Mao and his revolution did attempt to sever its innate connection with the political tradition of Confucianism, which emphasized (1) elitism and hierarchy in political authority, (2) an organic relationship with society through family and clan, and (3) an ideological force of morality to justify political and legal rules, to define the purpose of the state, and to provide the legitimacy of political authoritarianism. Nevertheless, the influence of Chinese traditional values, customs, mores, and ideology remains a strong driving force in Communist China even without official recognition. Like most Chinese rulers in the past, the Communist leaders view law primarily as a political instrument of the

Party for maintaining the socialist order and one-party rule in China's politics. The legal system, for Chinese Communists, is preserved solely for the purpose of class suppression rather than the pursuit of justice for all. Thus, antagonism and violence against undesirable groups of people become inevitable social events.

The second issue to be examined in this chapter is the relationship between the Communist Party and judicial independence. Like those found in most socialist states in the world, the Chinese judicial system has been criticized for lacking an independent status from the political power of the Party and the government executive agencies, partly because of China's political identification with Communist totalitarianism and partly because China had neither the idea of judicial independence in its legal theories nor any experience during the prerevolutionary era to support this principle. Certainly, for the Communists, founding the People's Republic of China did not mean a victory for all the Chinese people but, rather, a triumph for the Chinese Communists. The legitimacy of the Party's leadership was established through military force and has been maintained continuously through coercion and suppression.

Yet it is indisputable that judicial independence is always relative rather than absolute in both totalitarian and democratic societies. Judicial independence in this chapter refers only to the minimal preservation of judicial power in independently reviewing particular cases brought before the judiciary without institutionalized political and administrative interference. To examine this issue, we shall not overlook the influence of the Chinese legal tradition, which enhances the ruler's real and symbolic status as the ultimate locus of political authority—the ruler who stood alone at the top of the hierarchy and held absolute power over all his officials and subjects. Specifically, the relationship between the Communist Party and the judiciary draws this discussion to three dimensions of the Chinese judiciary: the constitutionality of the Party's leadership, Party membership and judicial personnel, and the relationship between the Party's policies and law in China.

FROM MARXISM-LENINISM TO MAO ZEDONG'S THOUGHT

Mao Zedong's Appeal to Lenin's Marxist Ideology

Long before the Chinese Communist Party was born, the course of revolutionary change and an antitraditionalist tendency had already advanced in a number of China's intellectual movements that were aimed at destroying what remained of the Confucian tradition. The abandonment of the imperial examination system in 1905, which ended the bureaucratic gentry society, signified the political, social, and cultural crises in the faith of Confucianism. With the downfall of China's two-millennia-old imperial system in the collapse of the Qing Dynasty in 1911, Confucianism not only lost its official status as the state orthodoxy but was also undermined as an ideology by the Republic revolution led by Sun Yat-sen. Any preservation of the Confucian tradition was related immediately to the restoration of the old monarchical system and, hence, met insurmountable resistance from the intellectual class. This iconoclastic attitude was also reflected in the Chinese Communists' hostility toward the

Confucian tradition when the Party, on the eve of its birth in 1921, blatantly declared its commitment to the violent overthrow of the old order. Although Marxist theory had been known to the Chinese intellectuals long before the CCP was born, the Chinese reformers were not particularly impressed with the theory on capitalism, the working class, and the communist revolution because, in part, at that time China had developed neither a capitalist economy nor a working class.

The victory of the Bolshevik revolution[4] in Russia signaled the arrival of Lenin's version of Marxist theory, which was embraced by a significant number of Chinese intellectuals and which imbued them with a far more realistic and feasible revolutionary message than Marx's original writings. By welding the Bolsheviks, the Russian Communist faction, Lenin was determined to attain his goal of socialist revolution with an authoritarian approach. The excitement of witnessing the victory of the Russian revolution and the prevailing frustration and disappointment over the Nationalists' failure to implement Sun Yat-sen's liberal and democratic ideas and to fulfill the expectations of a better life also aroused an intellectual and popular enthusiasm that called for a wholesale change in Chinese society under the leadership of a new political force armed with a new ideology. Under these social conditions, Lenin found an eager student, Mao Zedong, and a newly emerged Chinese Communist Party in China during the 1920s.

It is important to point out that, unlike the introduction of Marxism into the Soviet bloc in Eastern Europe, Marxism was not injected from the outside into China but was, instead, pursued eagerly by a group of Chinese intellectuals who desperately sought social changes. Over the next thirty years, Mao Zedong and his Communist Party were determined to carry out the socialist revolution as they survived the Long March[5] and the siege of the Nationalist government, valiantly fought Japanese aggression, and eventually won the civil war in 1949 by driving the Nationalist government out of the Chinese mainland.

Beginning with Lenin, Marx and Engels's critique of capitalism and the theory of the proletarian revolution were no longer merely philosophical and political creeds but rather a revolutionary agenda for social reform. In order to weld the working class—including the workers, the peasants, and the transformed soldiers—Mao rephrased Lenin's theory of *partiinost* or "party-mindedness," which foreshadowed the dictatorship of the Communist Party in the former Soviet Union. For Mao the law was, in fact, "the program of the Communist Party uttered in the language of power" and the will of the new ruling class. Long before the establishment of the PRC, the CCP had enacted various decrees in the territories they controlled and enforced them mercilessly to carry out their revolutionary justice. By upholding the Party's leadership and Marxist doctrine, the judiciary was regarded as the consolidating organ of political, administrative, and legislative powers to carry out the Party's revolutionary agenda by means of law enforcement, mass trial, and penal sanctions.

Violence, Class Antagonism, and the Role of Law

To understand the nature and limitation of law and the legal system in China, an examination of two fundamental elements of the Marxist-Leninist ideological stands that significantly influenced Mao's political thinking will, perhaps, provide meaningful clues to Mao's revolutionary agenda. First, using brutal violence or armed force to establish a socialist state has been the heart of Marxist-Leninist ideology and has generally been practiced by Communists elsewhere as it has been by the Chinese. Marx suggested that "one of the final results of the proletarian revolution will be the gradual dissolution and ultimate disappearance of that political organization called the state,"[6] because the main objective of the capitalist state is to secure, by armed force, the economic subjugation of the working majority by the wealthy minority. The state, in nature, is a suppressive machinery that has traditionally served the interests of the rich and the powerful.

The goal of the proletarian revolution is to liberate people from this exploitive system. The Marxists, nevertheless, also realized that before the proletarian revolution could eliminate all the social conditions that create class antagonism, abandoning the state machinery "would be to destroy the only organism by means of which the victorious working class can exert its newly conquered power, keep down its capitalist enemies and carry out that economic revolution of society without which the whole victory must end in a defeat and a massacre of the working class."[7] In a socialist society, "the state can be nothing but the revolutionary dictatorship of the proletariat."[8] It is clear that the proletarian state is not a governing body formed to ensure the equal protection of the people, but rather an executioner of the will of the new ruling class to suppress class enemies ruthlessly. Lenin believed that "those who recognize only the class struggle are not yet Marxists. . . . Only he is Marxist who extends the recognition of the class struggle to the recognition of the dictatorship of the Proletariat."[9] He further asserted that:

> The dictatorship of the proletariat will produce a series of restrictions of liberty in the case of the oppressors, exploiters and capitalists. We must crush them in order to free humanity from wage-slavery; their resistance must be broken by force. It is clear that where there is suppression there must be violence, and there cannot be liberty or democracy.[10]

The same support for violence was also embraced by Mao Zedong in one of his earliest works, *Report on an Investigation of the Hunan Peasant Movement*, first published in 1927:

> [A] revolution is not the same as inviting people to dinner, or writing an essay, or painting a picture, or doing fancy needlework; it cannot be anything so refined, so calm and gentle, or so mild, kind, courteous, restrained, and magnanimous. A revolution is an uprising, an act of violence whereby one class overthrows another.[11]

Mao openly expressed his favorable attitude about armed force and violence as a necessary path way to overcome the power of the old ruling class. As he stated so aptly, "political power comes from the barrel of a rifle." The socialist state could not survive without the consolidation of the military forces and the use of violence to overthrow the power of the antagonistic class.

Although Marx, Lenin, and Mao made the same assertions about the violent nature of the proletarian revolution and the function of the socialist state, Mao's obsession with violent rebellion against the old social order was not something new and inspired by the Russian Revolution. Instead, it was a continuity of Chinese tradition: In his later works, Mao himself proudly cited generations of dynastic emperors who seized power by launching wars and slaughter many times over. It has been an important part of Chinese politics that the political power of the government must change hands through violent rebellion and revolution. Chinese people were historically and culturally unfamiliar with the peaceful transition of political power through democratic and free elections.

Second, the suppressive function of the socialist state was seen to extend to all bodies of the government—a concept created by Lenin and later continued by Stalin as a derivative of the theory of class antagonism.[12] Apart from Marx and Lenin, Mao emphasized the life-and-death struggle between the bourgeoisie and the working class in the post-Revolutionary era. According to Mao, the elimination of private property ownership in the post-Revolutionary society does not simply eradicate class antagonism because the old propertied class will not easily give up the political power it had used to promote and protect its economic interests. Therefore, the immediate task of the socialist state is to "strengthen the apparatus of the people's state. . . . The army, police and courts of the state are instruments by which classes oppress classes. To the hostile classes the state apparatus is the instrument of oppression. It is violent, and not 'benevolent.'"[13] To carry out the programs of the socialist revolution successfully, the state must lavish enormous attention on strengthening the suppressive function of the legal system, by which the class enemies will be identified, purged, and punished. The law is, first, a set of rules that protects the interests of the working class and, second, an instrument for maintaining the social order of socialist China so that the CCP's revolutionary programs, such as transferring privately owned lands to the collective ownership of the people's communes in rural areas, can be carried out smoothly. The law, after all, "is not a guarantee of rights or the protection of a realm of freedom for all, but simply the will of the dominant class elevated into a 'status' and its tool for the suppression" of the class enemies.[14]

Because law has the political functions of advancing the socialist revolution toward communism and of protecting the interest of the newly established ruling class in China, "law is arbitrary in so far as it is treated not as a set of inviolable canons but as a site in constant need of rearticulation to aid the development of socialism."[15] As it was suggested by Michael Dutton (1992), the CCP needed to be free from any procedural or substantive restraints of law and to limit public scrutiny on the administration of law in order to effectively utilize law and the judiciary, as a weapon of class struggle, for the furtherance of the socialist revolution. Obviously, the political function of law and the legal system was said by Mao Zedong to be the operational guideline for the legal system. Equal justice, under this decree, was never meant to be "equal justice for all," but rather "equal with exception," subject to change along with the Party's policy on class division.

Reminded by the ancient dictum of Julius Caesar that "arms and laws do not flourish together,"[16] Mao admitted that to obtain power, arms must be used; whereas to maintain control, law must be used. The Chinese Communists have never ignored the important functions of written law, statutes, regulations, and the legal system, which have existed from the era of the Chinese Soviet Republic to the founding of the People's Republic of China, even though the first penal law of the PRC was not enacted until 1979.[17] With the enhancement of laws and the legal system, class suppression was launched by the CCP through a series of "violent storms" in the form of political campaigns accompanied by terror and violence: the Land Reform Movement (1945–1952); the Suppression of Counterrevolution Campaign (1951–1953); the Three-Antis-Campaign (1952–1954) against corruption, waste, and bureaucracy among the Party members; and the Five-Antis-Campaign (1950–1953) against bribery, tax evasion, theft of state property, fraud in government contracts, and the theft of economic information from the state by private industrial and commercial enterprises. It has been a longstanding Chinese tradition that "killing a chicken to scare off the monkeys" must be waged by the authorities with ruthless terror and violence to eliminate evil individuals and deter others from committing the same acts. But what distinguishes Mao from this tradition is his belief in the antagonistic nature of class struggle. For Mao, the conflict between the working class and the old exploiting class exists without any possibility of compromise. In addition to persuasion for those who willingly surrender to the revolution, violent suppression is a necessary means to overcome those who resist revolutionary ideas.

Moreover, what is unique about Mao Zedong's approach is his obsession with the political roles of law and the judicial system, which held for him the same fascination he had expressed about literature, the arts, intellectuals, and education—the so-called components of the superstructure that Marx elaborated from the Hegelian dialectics of history. But Marx was an economic determinist. For him, change in the superstructure was determined by change in the economic basis, that is, the productive forces, although the superstructure is of prime importance in promoting or otherwise hindering the development of productive forces. The proletarian revolution occurs when the superstructure no longer matches up to the advanced productive forces in a capitalist society.[18] The advancement of productive forces over the development of the superstructure was the central premise of Marxist political-economic theory. But for Mao Zedong, the impact of the superstructure on the economic basis was more than just important. It was crucial and vital for consolidating the political power of the Communist Party. In order to consolidate the victory of the revolution, Mao insisted that the CCP must hold the commanding power over all facets of societal life—including the economy, politics, culture, and the judiciary—backed by the "iron-fist dictatorship" and the violent suppression of class enemies. The role of law and the legal system is, after all, to be a suppressive instrument against class enemies.

THE COMMUNIST PARTY AND JUDICIAL INDEPENDENCE

Whenever a legal system is the subject of a comparative study, judicial independence is always the chief concern in examining the role of law and the function of the legal system in that society. Although judicial independence is regarded by scholars in comparative research as one of the symbolic high points of Western democracy, it is often equivocal in different cultures and societies. To fully examine judicial independence in a society, one must explore the balance between positive and natural law and the interrelationship among legislative, administrative, and judicial organs.

First, upon closer examination, one cannot separate judicial independence from the issue of the balance between positive law (representing the will of the ruling body, i.e., laws enacted through either elected organs or by military dictatorship) and natural law (reflecting the rights of the people by nature). This issue is a by-product of the democratization of the West, which is deeply rooted in the culture of Western civilization and is historically self-explanatory. Through the historical struggle for democracy in the West, the rights to life, liberty, and property have generally been recognized as the inherent nature of a person and, as such, they are to be protected by law without qualification. Considered the natural rights of individuals, they cannot be violated by anyone, including powerful government officials. Nevertheless, this issue of an individual's natural rights, in the Chinese tradition, referred primarily to one's duty and responsibility to the interests and well-being of one's parents, family members, clan, community, and the state. Individual rights to life, liberty, and property were traditionally deemed subordinate to collective interests and societal harmony. The Confucian law of morality reflected this traditional concept of the individual in relation to society.

Second, positive law in Western culture represents the will of the people carried out through an elected body such as a parliament, congress, or assembly. In the Chinese tradition, however, it is a synonym for the will of the emperor, who is believed to possess the greatest human virtues as well as the qualities of integrity, fairness, and selflessness. The controversy that results when the people's rights as a body to make law encounter the people's rights as individuals to be protected from abuse by the law will always arise when an individual exercises his or her rights while the government attempts to maintain a minimum social order for all. When this controversy arises in Western culture, the courts are empowered to resolve friction between individual rights and governmental concerns for social order. In Chinese culture the will of the government will always prevail over individual rights. Thus, for the West, judicial independence has been not only a manifestation of democracy but also a means for achieving social justice. The division of governmental power into three coequal branches (administration, legislation, and the judiciary) is not merely an organizational arrangement of government bureaucracy but is also an institutionalized guarantee for a balance between private liberty and collective self-government. These principles, apparently, have had little significance and relevance in Chinese legal tradition although China has had both positive law and natural law. The laws in China, from enactment to enforcement, traditionally have been monopolized by rulers—along with their gentry elite—who make law, interpret law, and enforce law. The judicial or court system was created to extend a ruler's political power to manifest autocracy rather than democracy. It is important to note that the lack of judicial independence in China resulted neither from a statutory deficiency nor from an ill-designed legal system. Rather, it is a reflection of China's tradition and culture in the domain of politics and law.

Moreover, independence of the judiciary is a rather ambiguous concept in discussing the role of law in a society and often requires further clarification with respect to the degree of separation of judicial power from other government authorities. Perhaps it is a reasonable argument that there has never been absolute judicial independence, even in the most democratic of nations such as the United States.[19] But, "at a minimum, judicial independence should have signified that political organs will not interfere with the application of law to the fact of particular cases," at least in the adjudicatory process.[20] Specifically, one must ask: Does the Chinese judicial system have this minimal independence in the application of law? Most observers—both Chinese and international—have responded in the negative because of the dominant status of the Communist Party, which has overwhelmed all phases of societal life.[21] However, simply giving a negative answer does not help us to fully appreciate the criticism of the political dependence of the Chinese judiciary.

Certainly, political interference with judicial decision making is not a problem unique to China; in fact, it exists in every system at the individual level on a day-to-day basis. When prosecutors or judges make decisions—such as on the severity of a sanction against an accused, the validity of an accusation, or a possible remedy—their personal viewpoints on law, social justice, and order always subconsciously affect their decision making. Their various relationships and connections—either ideological, political, economic, financial, social, or personal—also potentially restrain their freedom in making a decision independently.

Without a doubt, scholars studying judicial independence in China have shown grave concern over the political interference that has existed at the individual level. But the greatest concern here is the Communist Party's role in the judicial decision-making process. To elaborate the Communist Party's interference with the judiciary, three dimensions of the Party's intricate relationship with law and the legal machine deserve a careful examination: the constitutionality of the Party's leadership, Party membership and judicial organs, and the Party's policy and the law.

The Constitutional Dilemma on Judicial Independence

Before we can discuss the relationship between the Communist Party and judicial independence, we must look at the constitutionality of the latter. As early as 1954, the first Constitution of the PRC proclaimed that "people's courts administer justice independently and are subject only to the law."[22] But we must keep in mind that not only did judicial independence have no status in Chinese legal history, but also that their experience of law and justice prior to the 1949 revolution gave the Communists no sympathy for the concept. Furthermore, before this principle was actually implemented, the storm of the Cultural Revolution quickly swept away the government's early intention to empower the judiciary with independent authority. Under the radical revolutionary agenda of Mao during the Cultural Revolution, this constitutional mandate of judicial independence was removed by the People's Congress from two subsequent revisions of the Constitution in 1975 and 1978.[23]

In bitter memory of the lawlessness prevalent during the Cultural Revolution, the 1982 Constitution reinstated text stating that "in accordance with the law," courts and procuratorates shall "exercise judicial power independently and are not subject to interference by administrative organs, public organizations or individuals. . . . [All] state organs, the armed forces, all political parties and public organizations and all enterprises and undertakings must abide by the constitution and the law."[24] The textual contents indicated, at least in the book of law, that the Chinese government intended to empower the judiciary with the authority to conduct judicial decision making independently without being subject to political pressure and individual or organizational influence. Under the Constitution, neither "law [n]or administrative [n]or local rules and regulations shall contravene the Constitution . . . [nor can any] organization or individual . . . enjoy the privilege of being above the Constitution and the law."[25] The independence of the judiciary is technically guaranteed by the Constitution.

However, one quickly wonders why the Communist Party has chosen to provide the constitutional guarantee of judicial independence if it has no political sympathy toward this principle? Does the Party really mean to subject itself to this legal restriction? Does the Party truly intend to enforce this constitutional provision as binding upon all political parties, including itself? The answers, perhaps, can be found in three important aspects of political affairs in China. First, there is a distinguishable political difference between the Communist Party and other political parties. It is commonly known that the Communist Party does not consider itself the same as other political parties in terms of political status and power in determining China's domestic and foreign policies, even though it acknowledges the coexistence of eight so-called "democratic parties," recognized by government officials as legitimate political associations. For instance, one of the chief officials of China recently stated that "China is a one-party-ruling country in which the Chinese Communist Party is the core of the leadership with cooperation from other political parties who 'participate' in governing China but will never rule China."[26] The Communist Party clearly differentiates itself from other political parties, which are constitutionally prohibited from seeking ruling power in China.

Second, the exclusive leadership of the Communist Party is also mandated by the Constitution of 1982 in the "four adherences"—adherence to the leadership of the Communist Party, Marxist-Leninist-Maoist thought, the socialist road, and the people's democratic dictatorship.[27] Recently, Ren Jianxin, chief justice of the People's Supreme Court, instructed fellow judges and judicial personnel that "the courts must exercise the independent power of the judiciary under the leadership of the Party. Adherence to the party's leadership means that the people's courts' independence in decision making must be monitored and approved by the Party."[28]

It is obvious that judicial independence is a paradoxical term according to Chinese judicial personnel—in part because of the dilemma in constitutional law which professes judicial independence at the same time it guarantees the Party's ruling power over the judiciary and in part because of the personnel's political affiliation with the Party. Whatever the reasons for the paradox, it is clear that judicial independence does not imply that judicial decision making can be free from the restraint of the Party's political line and its scrutiny. Despite efforts to separate judicial power from political interference in recent years, the Party's paramount leadership above the law not only reflects Mao's dictatorial style of communist totalitarianism but also exemplifies the political centralism in the Chinese tradition.[29] Ironically, the judicial independence guaranteed by the Constitution is actually an "independence" with dependence under the political power of the Communist Party.

But one might argue that being in a leadership position to rule China does not necessarily remove the Communist Party's responsibility to obey the law. As a matter of fact, even the new Constitution of the Communist Party agrees that "the Party can engage in activities only within the domains permitted by the Constitution and the law."[30] It makes one wonder why, if the Communist Party adheres to its paramount ruling power in the sphere of the judiciary and legislation, it has chosen to restrict its own activities within the domain of the law. Perhaps what the Party intended to do was to make individual Party members subject to the rule of law. As for the Communist Party as a political entity, it was never meant to be placed under the rule of law. Perhaps the answer is more complicated than one might think simply because the principle of judicial independence in the Constitution is only a showcase to appeal to the West.

This brings us to the third aspect—the real intention for empowering judicial independence. For the first thirty years of the People's Republic of China, a country with a population of 1.2 billion was ruled by a man, Mao Zedong, who almost considered himself a god, and its judicial policy and the application of law were determined solely by his catechistic thought. Worst of all, the Cultural Revolution destroyed the entire legal system and replaced it with the "red terror" and "mass violence" against the so-called "class enemies" through wiedespread persecution, incarceration, torture, hard labor, and even execution, all without due process. In reawakening these historical tragedies, the reformers of the Party urged the immediate formalization of law and the legal system in the 1980s. Subsequently, the separation of the Party's power from judicial authority was also listed on the agenda for modernizing the legal system. Alarmed by the threat of the Cultural Revolution to the survival of the CCP's ruling status, the Party sees providing acceptable independence to the judiciary as an imperative strategic move to restore the public confidence in the Party's ability to lead the country to recovery and prosperity.

Yet some top officials have shown a strong desire to preserve the authority of the judiciary and to prevent political interference with the application of law for a different reason: they want to tranquilly execute the economic reform program that require strong backup from an independent judicial system. Local Party cadres often ignore repeated warnings from the central government against interfering with the judiciary because of their past experiences in administrative bureaucracy and the lack of basic institutional change to pursue the separation of judicial power from other governmental authorities. This is a rather harsh reality that the recent economic reform must confront because administrative and judicial personnel are often unprepared, either personally or professionally, for the challenges of reform.

First of all, traditionally the Party cadres have been inculcated to be loyal to the Party. For many of them, "following orders from the top" becomes their motto as they seek to follow the traditional pathway up the bureaucratic ladder. From a professional point of view, although the majority of judicial personnel do not like interference from political and administrative powers, they do not feel particularly uncomfortable with it either, not to mention that in their ambitious climb up the bureaucratic ladder, they will choose to accept or even to seek such interference in order to show their loyalty to the Party. As far as the subordinate role of the judiciary is concerned, both Chinese traditional values and bureaucratic norms continuously offer plenty of reasons for psychological comfort.

Furthermore, inadequacy also exists among judicial personnel in terms of their professional training. Since the modernization program began in 1979, more than 70,000 judges have been appointed by the People's Congress, less than 5 percent (3,000) of whom have had formal legal training (four years of law school).[31] Following the old system of the cadres' promotion in the Chinese Communist judiciary prior to 1949, the judicial personnel have been traditionally selected based on Party membership—they must be Party members and preferably veterans of the People's Liberation Army in order to be selected. Understandably, their training in legal knowledge and professional ethics is rudimentary, and their experience with the standard of discipline during their previous military service makes them prone to obey orders "from the top," setting legal niceties aside.[32] With 3,424 courts established in thirty provincial or regional districts and one military tribunal, adequate legal education and training continue to be imperative if there is any hope of providing a basic professional guarantee for judicial independence.[33]

In recent years, the general mood of the public has been heated up by newspaper commentaries that criticize the political obstruction of justice. Some brave judges have also openly complained about the persisting interference of local, regional, or provincial Party officials in judicial decision making. These judges have reported widespread and serious corruption, extortion, and abuse of power on the part of Party cadres to obstruct justice. For instance, when a relative of a director of a regional treasury bureau was sentenced to prison, the director ordered his accounting office to close the account of the court to protest the judge's decision. As a result of this closure, the court's routine business was interrupted and was eventually forced to shut down for forty days because of the sudden fiscal crisis.[34] For those judges with a professional conscience who are prepared to fight for independent decision making, the frustration and misery of their lives are sometimes beyond reasonable imagining. It is not surprising to hear stories in which administrators and Party cadres threatened judges with removal from the bench or simply revocation of the judge's decisions.[35] Judges have bitterly described their lives and working conditions as "dining without a bowl, sleeping without a bed, working without a desk, and conducting trials without a bench" because many of them have constantly been chased by pestering messengers who carry reminders, requests, bribes, and threats from the local cadres who are seeking favoritism.[36]

The daily operation of the judicial system has often shown remarkable discrepancies between the attitude toward judicial independence displayed by some lower-level Party cadres and the intentions of the central government to prevent such interference. From the reformers' point of view, economic reform cannot succeed without firmly upholding the authority of law and the independence of the judiciary. But wished-for change does not always manifest itself easily in reality because change to a new legal order also means overcoming the traditional forces that have dominated people's minds, attitudes, and conduct for generations. Although Marxist-Leninist and Maoist teachings have zealously urged Party members to devote themselves to the Party's idealistic goal—communism—without any reservation or desire for personal gain, individual Party members have often sought acceptance and psychological comfort from personal networks created through favoritism and nepotism. Favoritism and nepotism have their deep roots in Chinese familism, which highly values family ties and interpersonal relationships. Kinship-oriented officialdom was regarded by Confucius as the greatest human virtue that would, in return, bring great harmony and rewards. It seems to be an irony of fate for the CCP that while the leadership invariably pursues a depersonalized and antifamilist autocracy, its members eagerly revisit familist tradition. There is no question that favoritism and nepotism among those who hold power have inevitably flourished at the expense of judicial integrity and independence. It reminds us that an old Chinese metaphor, "When a person becomes a minister, even his chickens and dogs will go to Heaven,"[37] is still an acceptable practice for Communist officialdom in Chinese society.

On the surface, these traditional cultural values have little in common with Marxist-Leninist and Maoist thought, which separates people based on their ideological conformity to Marxist orthodoxy and their political status. Mao Zedong, as a revolutionary, once said that the Party shall adopt a policy that "promotes people not by their personal relation to the Party's cadres" but "by their performance and merits" in order to unite more people for revolutionary change.[38] Unfortunately, the revolutionaries often do not really acknowledge their debt to the past, and eventually they reach the same impasse as their predecessors. The longstanding tradition of favoritism in Chinese culture continues to be a vital force, essentially determining the Party members' behavior. The persistent interference of individual Party officers with the judiciary has been recognized by the government as a major obstacle in normalizing the judiciary under the economic reform policy. But we must also remember that the statutory restriction on political interference with judicial independence was aimed not at constraining the Party's commanding authority, but rather at curbing inappropriate or favoritist conducts manifested by individual Party members.

Party Membership and Judicial Officialdom

There has been little effort to actually institutionalize the constitutional guarantee of judicial independence and to effectively curb the epidemic of favoritism and political corruption that interferes with judicial decision making and obstructs justice. There are two reasons for the lack of effort, both of which result from the political institutional arrangements in China. First, the vast size of the Communist Party's membership has had a far greater impact on China's politics than an ordinary political organization would have. Since the founding of the PRC in 1949, aggressive recruitment has steadily increased the total membership of the CCP from 4 million in 1949 to 38 million in 1986[39] to 57 million in 1996.[40] Since no opportunity to advance politically and economically exists without Communist Party membership, the membership card has become something of a Holy Grail to which ambitious men and women have aspired. Every profession—from the military to industry, from academia to the judiciary—has a glass ceiling above which only those with Party membership can rise in the bureaucratic hierarchy. According to a recent official acknowledgment, among 147,283 judges and 140,246 procurators, an overwhelming majority (95%) are Party members who are carefully selected for being politically loyal to the Party line and ideologically adherent to Marxism-Maoism. Many judicial officers also hold important positions within the Party organization. For instance, Ren Jianxin, current chief justice of the People's Supreme Court, is also the deputy secretary of the Political and Legal Commission of the Communist Party and deputy commissioner of the Ad Hoc Commission on the Comprehensive Maintenance of the Social Order to the Central Committee of the CCP.[41] Naturally, the Party's political agenda must be brought into the process of judicial decision making by those Party-affiliated judicial personnel. It would be naive to expect those Party members who hold judicial posts to exercise their judicial powers independently and objectively, since judicial independence and objective of justice are often potentially inconsistent with or even contradictory to Party policy.

Second, along with the existence of the administrative, legislative, and judicial powers of the Chinese governmental bureaucracy, there is a parallel political organ coexisting as part of the Chinese political power. This is the Communist Party Committee, usually headed by a Party secretary, which monitors the loyalty of Party members to the CCP as well as the consistency of administrative, legislative, and judicial operations with Party policy at every level of government and and in nongovernmental institutions—in every office, institution, and work unit—even though the legality of this type of Party control was never actually specified by the Constitution.[42] Yet the Constitution of the PRC and the Organizational Law of the People's Courts and People's Procurators mandate that the People's Congress and its standing committees at both the national and local levels are the only governmental bodies empowered to appoint or remove judicial (both court and procuratorate) personnel under their jurisdictions[43] and that the standing committee members are prohibited from serving in any administrative, judicial, or procuratory position during the term of their service on the standing committee. But personnel changes such as appointments, promotions, or demotions often cannot be validated unless the Party has given its approval. Therefore, although the People's Congress may have been designated by the Constitution as the only agency empowered to appoint judicial officers, the Party's supervisory power preempts that of the Congress.

With some 3.45 million Party committees being set up at every level of governmental and nongovernmental institution, the Party's control is literally ubiquitous.[44] For judicial systems at the state, provincial, or municipal levels, a Political and Legal Working Commission of the CCP was set up to monitor and supervise the day-to-day operations of law enforcement, procurates, and the courts.

Furthermore, judicial independence, as set forth in the Constitution, is not only institutionally impossible due to the Party committee's superior power over personnel appointments in the judiciary, but also politically impossible due to the political loyalty of the overwhelming majority of Party-affiliated judicial officers. It is, as a matter of fact, an unwritten rule for judicial officers to request approval from the Party committee in their jurisdictions before any judicial remedy, decision, or disposition can be announced publicly from the bench. The Party interferes with the judiciary or, more precisely, claims the judicial decision-making function as its own through the Party-affiliated appointment and installation of Party committees within the judiciary. Culturally speaking, the self-initiated appeal of judicial officers to the Party authority is not only politically astute but also moralistically normative based on the traditional attitude toward authority.

Party Policy versus Law

Our analysis of the relationship between the Communist Party and the judiciary would not be complete without an examination of the relationship between Party policy and the law. To understand the relationship between the Party and China's legislative bodies, as proclaimed by Chinese officials, it is essential to keep in mind that

> the Party is a part of the people; the Party guides Chinese people to enact constitution and laws. . . . [O]ur laws are established under the Communist Party's leadership, on the basis of implementing the Party's policies, and through the legislative process of the government. It is a unification of the people's will and the Party's volition.[45]

In addition to the unshakable status of the Party's leadership at every level of the judiciary, the leadership has substantiated political control by the Party at the administrative and operational levels. Party policy is regarded as indispensable for initiating any legislation; laws are therefore a reflection of the Party's political agenda. As the head of the Party Propaganda Ministry explained, "The law must be stable and cannot be changed rapidly; thus, only the Party's policies, which are mature and correct through practice, can be formalized as law. The law is, after all, well-developed, codified, and formalized Party policy under the Party's guideline."[46]

Nevertheless, the law is also a reflection of social change. When social conditions require modification or abrogation of law, who should initiate the action? The Party must do so, of course, the minister continues, based on the guidelines of Party policy. Compared to law, "policy has more flexibility, suitability, and appropriateness. It can be altered according to changes in reality."[47] When social issues arise, Party policy takes effect even before the law becomes available. If the law and policy are in conflict, Party policy will always prevail "because, to the Party officials, political policy is the soul of law and law is but the formulation of policy into decrees."[48] The relationship between the law and Party policy is clearly defined by the above statement. Although the Constitution has given the ultimate power of legislation and interpretation of the law to the People's Congress, the consistency between Party policy and the law is, nevertheless, an important hidden agenda that must be preserved at all times and under all circumstances.

In addition, although China has a constitutional law whose guarantees of various rights and freedoms are rhetorically equivalent to the rights provided by the Bill of Rights, the practice of the judiciary indicates that Chinese constitutional law is not meant to be a substantive law but rather a symbolic statute that provides general guidelines for justice administration and social control policy. Since the inception of the 1982 Constitution, the courts have not heard a single case challenging constitutional law. In other words, the enforceability of constitutional law has never been allowed to be tested in the courts. It cannot be true that no legal controversies have ever arisen from the clashes between individual citizens' exercise of the constitutional rights and governmental measures to constrain these rights in China. As a matter of fact, such clashes have occurred repeatedly in recent decades. However, the court is not meant to be a forum for Chinese citizens to challenge the government authority on constitutional grounds. Instead, the court is operated as an extended arm of the Party's political will in executing its political, economic, and social policies. The following two cases best exemplify the Party policy in relation to the enforceability of law in China.

In 1982, for instance, there were numerous workers' strikes and demonstrations across the country to protest inflation, lower wages, and widespread corruption among Party cadres and managers of units. Theoretically, the workers were exercising their legal freedom to strike, which had been guaranteed by the 1978 Chinese Constitution.[49] The strikes and demonstrations were quickly suspended, however, when the leaders of the strike were detained, arrested, or given administrative or disciplinary penalties. The government officials also publicly declared the strikes as being illegal. When the public and some legal professionals criticized these official crackdowns and questioned the constitutionality of the government's accusation that strikers had violated the law, the Party Politburo quickly instructed the standing committee of the People's Congress to convene an ad hoc committee (the Constitution Revision Committee) to propose the removal of citizens' right to strike from constitutional law. The Party's wish quickly prevailed, of course, when the right to strike was stripped from the subsequent 1982 Constitution.[50]

In a recently reported case, Guo Luoji, a former professor of philosophy at Beijing University, filed a lawsuit in 1992 with the Nanjing People's District Court against Li Tieyin, commissioner of the National Education Commission and a member of the Party's Politburo, and the Party committee at Nanjing University for violating his constitutional rights of free expression and engaging in political persecution because of his unorthodox publications on socialism and Marxism. In the lawsuit, Mr. Guo's alleges that Commissioner Li (1) illegally ordered Beijing University to revoke his professorship without any academic reason and (2) physically removed him and his family from Beijing to Nanjing. In his lawsuit against the CCP committee at Nanjing University, Mr. Guo alleges that the committee illegally infringed his constitutional rights by (1) banning his publications, (2) depriving him of his faculty privilege of teaching, and (3) prohibiting him from attending an academic conference abroad. This was believed to be the first lawsuit filed with the court by a private citizen against a local CCP entity and a high-ranking official of the CCP on constitutional grounds in Communist China's history. On March 2, 1992, the Nanjing People's District Court responded that it would not hear Guo's allegations simply because (1) the alleged punishments against him were administrative or disciplinary sanctions in nature; and (2) the CCP committee, as a nonadministrative organ, has immunity under the administrative law, even though the CCP committee had obviously interfered with the university's administration to launch political persecution against Guo.[51] Mr. Guo has since appealed the Nanjing court's ruling to the Provincial Supreme People's Court. Although Guo's case may never be heard by the court, the significance of this lawsuit may not lie in the outcome for Mr. Guo, but in the wakening of Chinese citizens' desire to challenge the constitutionality of the enforcement of Party policy and the interference of the Party with the daily operations of administrative bodies.

FINAL REMARKS

Without a doubt, Mao Zedong and the Communist Party have directed a revolutionary change in China for the past forty years. Mao introduced Marxist ideology to the Chinese masses, which eventually enabled him to consolidate full control over economic, political, and social affairs in China. Although his ideology was generally within the framework of Marxism and Leninism, the Confucian traditional values regarding society, politics, the state, and the role of law persistently manifested themselves in Mao's philosophical and political writings on the role of the proletarian state and the functions of the legal system in socialist China. Like the Confucian tradition, Maoism insisted on the head of state's totalitarian control in ordering the society and maintaining the bureaucratic fabric; they differed, however, in that Confucianism centered on the emperor's individual power while Mao claimed the Party's leadership in controlling the state's throne. Mao also clearly displayed his favorable attitude toward the Legalist tradition of law, which zealously advocated control and order with certain and ruthless suppression. For Communists, the law is a political weapon for overcoming the power and resistance of their class enemies. The primary function of law and the judiciary is not to protect all people in Chinese society but rather to protect only the interests of the proletarian class and its vanguard, the Communist Party. In Mao's own words, law and the legal machine are instruments of class struggle.[52]

To further understand the role and limitation of law in China, we must consider the relationship between the Party and judicial independence. The Party at present is no longer just a small band of enthusiastic revolutionaries but rather an enormous bureaucratic organ with nearly 57 million members, who hold most of the important legislative, administrative, and judicial posts. Party membership has practically "been a principal road to power and the perquisites of power such as housing, food, education, job, health care, travel, and the like."[53] All the personnel in the top positions of the government and the judiciary are also important members of the Party. Obviously, Party membership and judicial positions go hand in hand. It is hard to imagine how the judiciary can maintain any independence in determining a judicial matter according to the law without getting interference from the Party secretary or being sidestepped by Party policy.

To be fair, under the modernization program there have been some signs of change from the liberal reformers within the Party and the government in an effort to limit the Party's power in the judicial process. However, the reform effort has been overshadowed by the constitutional guarantee of the Party's unchallengeable leadership status over all affairs in China. In addition, the institutional blend of the Party's political power and judicial power further undermines any attempt to sever the connection between Party affairs and judicial matters. The reluctance to dissolve the Party cells in every office and institution does not come from just the fear of the economic consequences of making 57 million Party cadres jobless or the political consequences of the social instability that would result. Dissolution requires a moral commitment among the public, including those cadres, to overcoming the psychological crisis that may result when they abandon what they have had faith in and devoted their entire lives to, since Party membership has been regarded by the society as a symbol of mankind's highest virtues. Moreover, the favoritism and nepotism that have derived from the familist tradition have continued to offer plenty of psychological and materialistic comforts to the Communist officials, allowing them to sidestep the rules of law or ignore legal niceties. Although Mao and his Communist Party attempted to sever any political and ideological connections with China's past by inculcating the masses with Marxism and Leninism, they could not escape the same historical impasse by ruling China in a Chinese traditional way.

NOTES

1. For the civil government and law of the Chinese Soviet Republic (1931–34) and early Communist legislation prior to 1949, see W. E. Butler, 1981 and 1983; Lotveit, 1973; Selden, 1971; and Vladimirov, 1974.

2. Michael, 1962, p. 135.

3. See Shaffer, 1990, p. 2., for more discussion on the secular characteristics of the Chinese cultural tradition.

4. Bolshevik comes from the Russian word for the "majority," who won control of the party in 1903. Their opponents among the Social Democrats would become known as the Mensheviks, from the Russian word for "minority."

5. The Long March began officially on October 15, 1934, with 85,000 soldiers from the Red Army, 15,000 men who were Communist Party and Chinese Soviet Republic government officials, and thirty-five women who were the wives of highly placed leaders. After a year of extreme difficulties in climbing snow-covered mountains, crossing rivers and swampland with insufficient food, clothing, and medical supplies, and constantly fighting off military attacks launched by the Nationalist government, Mao and 8,000 survivors of the Red Army ended this epic 25,000-li (12,500 kilometers or 6,000 miles across eleven provinces) march in Shanxi Province. The end signaled the turning point for Mao and the CCP. See Hsu, 1990, pp. 559–62.

6. Engels, 1979, p. 164.

7. Ibid., p. 165.

8. Marx, 1963, p. 261.

9. Lenin, 1973, p. 399.

10. Ibid., p. 63.

11. Mao, 1960e, p. 870.

12. See Marx and Engels, 1973, p. 30, for a further discussion on the theory of class antagonism in a capitalist or pre-revolutionary society. The theory of class antagonism in a socialist or postrevolutionary society was developed from Lenin's work.

13. Mao, 1960b, p. 892.

14. Michael, 1962, p. 135.

15. Dutton, 1992, p. 284.

16. Barber and Watson, 1988, p. 125.

17. In the early years of the Communist revolution, the CCP enacted various laws, statutes, regulations, and decrees to carry out the Party's revolutionary agenda through its civil and military governments in the regions it controlled. These laws, such as those promulgated during the Soviet Republic and Yanan periods, were immediately adopted by the PRC after 1949 and laid the groundwork for legislation and the operation of the people's justice for the next thirty years.

18. Ironically, the proletarian revolution portrayed by Karl Marx did not occur in advanced industrial nations such as England or Germany. Instead, it occurred in backward industrial countries and predominantly agricultural nations such as Russia, China, and Cuba.

19. In the United States, judges are often endorsed by a political party, nominated by the president, or appointed by a governor and, therefore, cannot be totally free of their association with those political entities. The practice of judicial independence has often diverged considerably from the professed ideals of justice. Realistically, no one can really

> expect any country to staff its judiciary with men whose views and acts contradict the premises of that country's governmental system. . . . Judges must implement many of the fundamental values and policies of their society as those values and policies are embodied in the Constitution, statutes, regulations, rules of decision, and other sources of law furnished by the state. (Cohen, 1964, pp. 125–28)

20. Ibid., p. 125.

21. For a commentary on and critique of judicial independence in China, see Asian Watch Committee, 1990, pp. 41–43; Cohen, 1968, pp. 107–43; Townsend, 1980, pp. 317–20; and Ingraham, 1987, pp. 4–6.

22. See Article 78 of the Constitution of the People's Republic of China, September 1954, in Chai, 1972, p. 269.

23. The two subsequent revisions of the Constitution were passed by the national People's Congress in 1975 and 1978, respectively. In addition, in 1970, Lin Biao, then defense minister and vice-chairman of the Party, allegedly distributed a discussion draft of the constitution nationwide. However, that draft was recalled after Lin Biao's failed coup against Mao in the fall of 1971. For the historical evolution of Chinese constitutional law under the Communist regime, see H. Chiu, 1989a, pp. 50–60; Hsia and Johnson, 1986, pp. 30–38; W. C. Jones, 1989, pp. 39–49.

24. Articles 126 and 131 of the 1982 Constitution, in Folsom and Minan, 1989, p. 967.

25. Article 5 of the 1982 Constitution, in ibid., pp. 947–48.

26. "Prime Minister Li Peng's Conversation with Malio Warsckis, President of Mexican Sun Times, May 30," 1991.

27. The Preamble of the 1982 Constitution, in Folsom and Minan, 1989, p. 946.

28. "People's Courts Must Consciously Accept the Party's Leadership and Strenghten Judicial Work to Serve the Reform," 1990.

29. China's centralism differs from European centralism, which unifies with diversity. China's centralism is uniformity without diversity, from politics to ideology, economic policy, social norms, and lifestyle.

30. Dong Liquin, 1987, pp. 665–70.

31. Li, 1988.

32. Kaminski, 1982, p. 12. Kaminski provides an overview of the promotion system in the Chinese judicial system, especially for military veterans among judicial personnel, who essentially followed a paramilitary norm to take orders from the top. This norm substantially undermined judicial independence.

33. *Law Year of China*, 1992 (Beijing: Press of Law Yearbook of China, 1992), p. 859.

34. Xiao Du, 1988.

35. Ibid.

36. Ibid.

37. This metaphor implies the nature and extent of the traditions of favoritism and nepotism in China, in which the privileges of one's official ranking were extended to all his family members and relatives and even his pets.

38. Mao, 1972c.

39. For more detailed data on the historical development of the CCP's membership, see Schurmann, 1968, p. 128; and Spence, 1990, pp. 533, 634, and 728.

40. Yan Chen, 1996.

41. "The CCP's Central Committee's Ad Hoc Commission on Comprehensive Maintenance of Social Order Held First Meeting in Beijing," 1991.

42. The Party cell's role as the real master and commander in every factory, village, work unit, academic institution, military unit, and government office is a continuation of the Party's tradition, which dates back to the civil war. Griffin, 1976, provides more discussions on this aspect.

43. Articles 62, 63, 67, and 101 of the 1982 Constitution, in Folsom and Minan, 1989.

44. Yan Chen, 1996.

45. Dong Liquin, 1987, p. 667. Dong's assertion in the 1980s is virtually a reiteration of the Party's early position on the issue of judicial independence in the 1950s. For example, in 1958 Wu Defeng, the vice-president of the Chinese Political Science and Law Association, stated in an article of counterattack against the so-called Rightists that "the courts are created by the country's organ of state power and ought to be responsible to it. Since the Party is the

heart of the leadership of the state and the people's courts are only one of its organizations, naturally the courts cannot be independent of the Party" (Rickett, 1982, p. 106).

46. Dong Liquin, 1987, p. 668.

47. Ibid.

48. This quotation is from Wu Defeng's speech in 1958, which is cited in Rickett, 1982, p. 106.

49. Under Article 45 of the 1978 Constitution, Chinese citizens "enjoy freedom of speech, correspondence, the press, assembly, association, procession, demonstration and the freedom to strike." See Laws and Regulations of the People's Republic of China, 1982, vol. 1, p. 14, for a textual translation of the 1978 Constitution.

50. See Peng, 1991.

51. "Guo Luoji, a Well Known Scholar, Charges Li Tieying with Political Persecution." 1992; "Guo Luoji Sues the National Educational Commission Again." 1992; and "Writ of Appeal to the Nanjing District Court and Supreme Court of Jiangsu Province by Guo Luoji, March 10, 1992," 1992.

52. The class division and its influence on law and judicial policy will be discussed in the next chapter.

53. Folsom and Minan, 1989, p. 47.

CHAPTER FOUR

The Class Division and Equal Rights before the Law

INTRODUCTION

THE THEORY of class struggle was the hallmark of Maoist thought with regard to the proletarian dictatorship during the postrevolutionary era. Despite Mao's early claim in the 1950s that the *antagonistic* class struggle between the "enemy and ourselves" had been brought to an end and that the barriers to soaring victories in the battle of production had all fallen away,[1] the class struggle was, nevertheless, carried on for another two decades with or without an antagonistic class enemy. Throughout the first three decades of socialist revolution, Mao's class struggle theory served as the sole guideline for the legal system to launch numerous campaigns of official suppression against so-called class enemies. From 1949 to the 1970s, tens of millions of Chinese were subjected to merciless persecutions, political purges, social disenfranchisement, economic discrimination, and legal sanctions as a result of the political "cleanup" in Chinese society. Although China did not promulgate its first penal law until 1979, such absence of codified penal law never hampered the government's ability to utilize legal machinery, such as public security forces, the people's procurate, and the court system, to carry out official sanctions against politically undesirable groups for the purpose of both political and social stability. To understand the operation of this "lawless" legal system, any discussion of the role of law and justice policy in China would be incomplete without a thorough examination of Mao's political obsession with the antagonism of class struggle during the postrevolutionary period.

Upon Mao's death and the subsequent political downfall of the Gang of Four in 1976, the CCP's devotion to the political struggle against class enemies quickly faded away. The post-Mao leadership of the CCP quickly shifted its attention to the economic development and basic needs of the people in the society under Deng Xiaoping's economic reform agenda. Nevertheless, the Party hard-liners continuously insisted that class struggle had not yet ended under the new economic reform, despite widespread political indifference among the public in the post–Cultural Revolution period. According to one Party official, "the chief targets of the current struggle are serious economic criminals . . . [w]ho embezzle, steal, speculate and profiteer."[2] What is even more important is that to accomplish this task, the current class struggle will be carried out not through "tempestuous mass movement," as in the past, but through the application of law and the formalization of the legal system. It is clear that this new line of Party policy redirected the class struggle, through intensified legal sanctions, against enemies of the newly established economic order.

The discussion in this chapter centers on the impact of Mao's class line on social control and on differential treatment under the law from the 1950s to the present. As stated earlier, the social control mechanism has existed since the PRC was founded or, perhaps even more precisely, since the legacy of the Soviet Republic in the 1930s, which formed the Communist tradition of formal control and the nascent form of the judicial system. For most of Chinese Communist history, the formal (legal) sanction has been carried out by means of mass tribunals, the so-called people's justice. For this judicial tradition, the formally written laws are more concerned with the range of penal sanctions against particular categories of crimes and relatively less interested in defining the scope of criminal acts, simply because the Party policy, responding to the priorities of its political agenda, has prempted the written law in identifying offensive acts.

To understand the essence of Mao's idea of the antagonistic class struggle and its influence on Communist law and the social control mechanism, one must examine three dimensions of Mao's class struggle theory. First, to understand Mao's obsession with class struggle, it is important to look at the philosophical origins of his ideas about the antagonistic nature of class struggle. It is well known that class struggle is one of the important premises of Marxist dialectics, which viewed the development, advancement, and eventual, death of capitalist society as resulting from the ongoing struggle between the proletariat and the capitalist class. From a political point of view, the antagonism of class struggle has little in common with Confucian theory, which primarily promoted humanitarian benevolence and moral persuasion in maintaining social harmony. But this does not mean that Mao's theory of class division had no historical root in Chinese tradition. Yin-yang philosophy, for example, might be just one of the traditional philosophies that inclined Mao toward the Marxist dichotomy of human society and class struggle theory. This philosophy claims that the world, including both nature and humans, comprises two opposite but reciprocal and interdependent forces—yin and yang—that coexist everywhere in an incessantly contradictory state. Yet yin-yang philosophy neither claimed a political division of human society nor ever used the term *antagonism* to explain the relationship between yin and yang. Yin-yang philosophers, however, believed that the world's cosmic order resulted from the competition between the two sides.

Politically, Mao's class struggle theory inherited a great deal from Marx and Lenin as well as Stalin. But what distinguishes Mao from Marx and the Soviet

Communists is that he developed his theory within the framework of traditional Chinese philosophy. That is, the antagonistic struggle was not just an ideological weapon to help the proletariat gain control of political power in a society but also a necessary pathway toward a communist utopia in the world.

Second, the central targets of class struggle were periodically altered according to the political priorities set up by the Party, which primarily determined the agenda and policy of both legal and extralegal control over undesirable groups of people. Like every other society, Chinese society is concerned with the issue of social equality. To be sure, China's Constitution does guarantee equality and democracy for the Chinese people.[3] But the democracy professed therein is not what is commonly understood as "democracy with freedom"; rather it is "democracy with dictatorship."[4] Similarly, the equality guaranteed by the Constitution does not mean "equal before the law for all." Instead, it is "equal but different." Remarkably, sanctions against the remaining reactionaries, intellectuals, and Party officials and members during the official campaigns—such as the Three- and Five-Antis Campaigns in the 1950s, the socialist educational movement in the 1960s, the Cultural Revolution in the 1970s, and attacks on antieconomic crime in the 1980s—reflect Chinese officials' adherence to Chinese traditional ways for dealing with politically and officially undesirable groups of people: that is, treating people according to their political status. Mao was deeply concerned with people's ideological conformity and their political stand (whether or not they sided with the Communist Party), while Confucianism divided people according to their relationship to authority within the family, clan, or governmental hierarchy.

Third, the traditional ethos about the family was very vivid in Mao's class struggle policy with respect to the suppression of antagonistic individuals. In accordance with China's traditional notion of collectivist punishment—which, in general, has ignored the importance of the individual—criminal responsibility has long been regarded as belonging to a family or a blood line.[5] Ironically, the law of corrupt blood in eighteenth-century England was also practiced in twentieth-century China. Discrimination, persecution, and penal sanctions imposed by the authorities against the entire family of the accused demonstrate that Mao's class struggle theory was somehow connected to the Chinese legal tradition. One person's misdeed might often bring misfortune or even tragedy to his entire family. Therefore, the older generations of a family had to remain extremely cautious about their own behavior in order to protect their offspring. Collective responsibility and extended punishment served to deter involvement in those conducts which were undesirable from the authorities' point of view.

THE ANTAGONISTIC NATURE OF THE CLASS STRUGGLE

The term *class struggle* was first used by Marx in his elaboration of Hegel's dialectic of history. According to Marx, the level of production and the power struggle between the materially dominant and the economically exploited classes determines the advancement of human society as it moves from primitive communism to slavery, to feudalism, to capitalism, then to socialism, and eventually to communism. After a systematic study of Marx's so-called "material dialectic," Mao provided a definitive interpretation of the Chinese revolution and class struggle in a simple "catechetical style, [with] vigorous and unadorned prose":

> The contradiction between imperialism and the Chinese nation, and the contradiction between feudalism and the great masses of the people, are the principal contradictions in modern Chinese society. . . . The struggles arising from these contradictions and their intensification inevitably result in the daily developing revolutionary movements.[6]

Although this social evolutionist idea, which centered on the dichotomous and antagonistic struggle, was affirmed by Mao in 1937,[7] it has continued to underscore the chief theoretical tenets of revolutionary orthodoxy for Chinese Communists for nearly half a century. The struggle, for Mao, was not just a temporary phenomenon; it contained sufficient power and dynamics to move the entire society forward. It has also followed certain patterns, of course, including a dialectic one. "Great world chaos leads to great world peace. This is the law of class struggle."

Obviously, class struggle performed an instrumental part in achieving Mao's goal of a communist utopia. Mao strongly believed that this utopia could be realized only through a continuous class struggle. Furthermore, similar to yin-yang philosophy, he insisted on the universal existence of struggle between two opposite forces. "Opposites in contradiction unite as well as struggle with each other, and thus impel all things to move and change."[8] Even "with the arrival of Communism there will still be struggle between the old and the new, between the correct and the wrong."[9] It is clear that Mao diverged from his Soviet counterparts by regarding this struggle as part of the natural forces that follow a natural rule of law. Whether it was willingly or unwillingly, Mao followed yin-yang philosophy to pursue his revolutionary goal by dividing Chinese society into two antagonistic classes. Where Mao parted from yin-yang tradition was that the latter emphasized the reciprocity of two opposite forces that coexist to achieve cosmic harmony, whereas the former proclaimed the unchangeable antagonistic nature of the two classes in postrevolutionary China. To Mao, the struggle by which one class eventually eliminates another was both the means and th end of the communist revolution.

Noticeably, the antagonistic nature of class struggle was a unique feature of Mao's dialectic. Although we do not know if he had overestimated the strength of the capitalist class or was phobic about being surrounded by external and internal anti-Communist enemies, Mao consistently expressed his fear and insecurity about the possible overthrow of the Communist ruling power by foreign imperialism and domestic reactionaries. He characterized class struggle as the folktale of Wu Sung on Chingyang Ridge: "either kill the tiger or be eaten by him—one or the other."[10] Therefore, "it is necessary to bring about a brief reign of terror."[11] Mao was convinced that the antagonistic class will never give up its intention to overthrow the ruling power of the working class.

Mao himself declared the end of the antagonistic class struggle in the 1950s, after the Communist government firmly consolidated its political power and successfully transformed the national economy to collective ownership and central control. But he also reminded the Party cadres that the nonantagonistic class struggle would continue on the ideological front and that there was every possibility of transforming this struggle into an antagonistic one because of the remaining reactionaries at home and the threat of foreign imperialism abroad.[12] Thus, suppression on this front became a necessary measure for handling contradictions between officially advocated political doctrines and politically undesirable social groups. For Mao, after the collectivization of property in China, the essential criterion for identifying potential elements of the antagonistic class was no longer their social status as determined by their personal wealth, but rather their political stand on the ideological correctness of communism. Therefore, personal loyalty to the Party and to the socialist revolution was zealously advocated by the Party as a means to redivide the class camps.

SOCIAL CLASS AND EQUAL RIGHTS BEFORE THE LAW

The Notion of Equal Rights

Equity—concern for equality, fairness, and justice—has been an important concept in the critical study of society and law. To provide equality for all, it is necessary to assume that all people or citizens are viewed equally regardless of the differences in their race, age, sex, socioeconomic status, personal merit, and ideological or religious beliefs, at least within the letter of the law.[13] That is what is meant by "all people are created equal." Nevertheless, theoretically speaking, equality often means one of two things. In one instance, it could mean that two men who are equal in relevant respects should be treated in exactly the same way.[14] For that to happen, a set of precisely defined rules—the law—must be established and announced publicly beforehand so that the law will "treat equals equally." This set of rules must have the qualities of certainty, uniformity, and rigidity. In another case, equality could also imply that all people are treated equally based on their circumstances. In other words, a remedy or burden will be rendered to people proportionate to the quantity of the relevant attribute or need they possess.[15] Contrary to the rule of law, the proportionality principle requires flexibility and greater discretion in order to guarantee equal opportunity to all for enjoying proportionate treatment. Potentially, this principle may be socially or politically equal but quantitatively unequal, whereas the principle of "treat equals equally" may be quantitatively equal but socially or politically unjust. Equity normally follows the principle of proportionality. Essentially, what is equal may not be just. In a sense, justice is a relative rather than an absolute concept. After all, each society not only prefers one principle over another but also culturally defines what is fair, just, and equal. Equally important, regardless of which principle is more prevalent and acceptable in a society, equity is often implemented to counterbalance an overly harsh rule of legal formalism.[16] If equity "begins where the law ends" and supplies justice in circumstances "not covered by law,"[17] its application, whether supported or restrained by cultural tradition, may also keep the law in abeyance.

With regard to the concepts of justice and equality, there are three dimensions in Chinese society of equal treatment before the law—the political notion of "people" in Chinese law, the criteria for dividing social classes, and the impact of class status on equal rights before the law—that deserve an examination in order for us to understand the political significance of "equal rights before the law" under the Maoist regime.

The Notion of "People"

Diverging from the orthodox Marxists in the former Soviet Union, who proclaimed the nation as the essential unity of all elements that made up the Soviet Union, the Chinese Communists assert that only the "people" make up the nation, thus excluding those elements that constitute political forces opposing the Communist government.[18] But who are the "people"? Mao declared that:

> They are the working class, the peasantry, the urban petty bourgeoisie and national bourgeoisie. These classes, led by the working class and the Communist Party, unite to form their own state and elect their own government [so as to] enforce their dictatorship over lackeys of imperialism—the landlord class, the bureaucrat capitalist class, as well as the representatives of these classes, the Guomindang reactionaries and their henchmen representing these classes—to suppress them, allow them to only behave properly and not to talk and act wildly.[19]

Clearly, the Chinese nation, according to Mao, is not a state comprising all Chinese citizens but is rather a state composed only of the people who accept and support the Communist leadership. This political division of people provided the fundamental guidelines for the political function of the legal system in the postrevolutionary period. Without an understanding of this essential distinction between the people and the "reactionaries" in the legal vocabulary of Mao's Communist regime, any critique of China's unequal rights before the law would inevitably be, inadequate at best or misleading at worst.

Further, although Mao divided Chinese society into two politically adversarial classes, it was commonly recognized that Chinese society was traditionally separated less by socioeconomic class than by the social distinction between the rulers and the ruled. Unlike Western democratic society, where the people elect their own government and voice their opinions about politics through their elected bodies, Chinese society was historically governed by a ruler advised and assisted by a handful of the gentry class who had been carefully selected through a civil examination system based solely on the Confucian classics. Despite the Communists' claim of a complete break from Chinese tradition, the antiquity of the Chinese imperial bureaucracy provided not only cultural continuity but also the political blueprint for the formation of the Communist bureaucracy under Mao's leadership. Although Confucian classics and Maoism seem to have little in common, Mao maintained the same line of ideological teaching as Confucian China, that is the unchallenged status of officially endorsed ideology. The selection of Mao's party elite was based purely on their political loyalty to the Communist leadership and their complete ideological acceptance of Maoist teaching.

Has this ruling elite ever represented the entire people or the working class in governing China? Even Mao himself did not really believe that China could be truly ruled by the people. He admitted that the Communist government does not always voice people's concerns because of the existing contradictions between the people and the government.[20] Mao himself was once troubled with the declaration that the government represents the interests of all the people.[21] In reality, Chinese society was divided not only between the people and their enemies but also between the political ruling elite and the people under them.

The Criteria for Dividing Classes

The criteria for determining an individual's class status has varied considerably in the course of different political campaigns. One's class status could be determined either by his occupation prior to the revolution—such as being a member of the intellectual class, a factory owner, a manual laborer, or a farm laborer—or by his family's status, as classified during the class division campaign in the early 1950s, or based on one's political loyalty to the Communist Party. For example, during the Land Reform Movement from 1941 to 1945, the social classes in rural areas controlled by the Communists were divided into five categories based primarily on the land ownership of each family, with middle-class peasants, poor peasants, and landless farm laborers comprising the people and with the landlords and rich peasants constituting the class enemy.[22] Under the supervision of the Peasants Association, land redistribution was carried out by means of coercion and violence against the landlord class. The local CCP leaders encouraged violent confrontation between the poor peasants and the rich landlords. This sanctioned violence was probably comparable to the intensity of the harsh fighting with the Guomindang troops during the civil war.

It has been estimated that one in every six rich landlord families, totaling one million class enemies, had a member executed during the violent confrontations led by the Peasants Association during the Land Reform Movement.[23] Those confrontations were a primitive form of the mass tribunals and a formal sanction of the "people's power." The same class division campaign was also launched nationwide to sweep out the bureaucratic capitalist class[24]—the Nationalist reactionaries and their henchmen who represented these classes.[25] Accordingly, some 800,000 people classified as class enemies were sentenced to death or to prison within the first few years of the PRC.[26] Noticeably, this early class division was based mainly on the property ownership of individual families.

The earmark of this campaign was the individual's inheritance of his or her parents' class status, though some people might have escaped this rule because of their pro-Communist choice prior to 1949. Still, many members of the CCP who left their well-to-do families and participated in the revolution long before the campaign of class division had to denounce the exploitative behavior of their parents or grandparents and sever their personal ties with their antirevolutionary families in public to prove their absolute commitment to the revolution and their loyalty to the Party.

By the early 1960s, Mao himself had recognized that the so-called class enemies—such as the rich landlords, the bureaucratic capitalists, and the Nationalist reactionaries—had vanished from Chinese society, either because they had been executed or had fled or because their property had been confiscated and they had been coerced into labor. Nevertheless, Mao insisted that "it would be naive to imagine that there are no more contradictions" even though the old exploiting classes had been eliminated.[27] Two fundamental contradictions will continue to exist in socialist China: one among the people and the other between the people who support the Communist leadership and the class enemies who reject it. The former is nonantagonistic whereas the latter is antagonistic in nature.[28]

To identify the new class enemy, Mao suggested that the contradiction between the national bourgeoisie and the working class would become antagonistic, even though the national bourgeoisie were considered to be part of the people during the Democratic Reform or potentially able to be reformed to become part of the people through the "benevolent administration" of political propaganda and education.[29] The shifting criteria in classifying class enemies were apparently driven by the priority of the Party's political agenda of property ownership reform. As the Party tried to consolidate the transformation from private to public property ownership, the national bourgeoisie were placed squarely on the front lines in the confrontation with the socialist revolution.

During the Cultural Revolution, Mao once again shifted the criteria for defining class enemies due to the intensified struggle within the Party for political control, which overrode other economic and social priorities. Anyone who did not totally agree with Mao's political line and who refused to conform to his radical factionalism was declared to be a counterrevolutionary or revisionist. It seems that Mao saw the adversarial factions within the CCP not only as the ultimate challenge to his personal paramount ruling power in China but also as forces threatening to make the country diverge from his revolutionary goal.

The escalation of the class struggle during this period reflected Mao's strong belief that the two different types of contradiction dynamically and mutually transform each other, especially from nonantagonistic to antagonistic. It is not totally clear why Mao chose to constantly create an antagonistic political enemy, considering the risk of the internecine consequences. Perhaps he did so because of the psychological insecurity he had experienced in the early years of his revolutionary career as he was consolidating his political power, or perhaps it was because of his obsession with dialectical materialism, which insists that communism must be realized through class struggle. What is clear, however, is that the scope and definition of the people and class enemies were changed constantly based on the political priorities of Mao's agenda. Being a membe of the Party elite qualified a person as the representative of the people during one campaign but did not necessarily exempt him from becoming a class enemy during others.

EQUAL BUT DIFFERENT BY CLASS STATUS

As early as 1954, the Constitution of the PRC guaranteed that Chinese citizens shall enjoy the right of equality before the law; the rights of freedom of speech, of the press, of assembly, of demonstration, and of religion; and the rights of work, leisure, education, and social assistance.[30] But as we discussed earlier, who would enjoy these rights was determined not by the nature of men nor by their Chinese citizenship; instead, it was defined along class lines. In a catechetical fashion, Mao declared that "only the people are allowed to have their right of voicing their opinions . . . [g]iving them freedom of speech, assembly and association. The right to vote is given only to the people and not to the reactionaries."[31] More precisely, those defined as the antagonistic classes do not have the same right to enjoy the freedoms provided by the Constitution.

Moreover, these unequal rights are manifested not only in the spheres of politics—the freedoms to vote, speak, assemble, or associate—but also in areas such as employment, education, housing, medical benefits, welfare, and even military service. Opportunities for public service and social competition are reserved only for those who qualify as people according to Mao's political standards of class division. Inequality before the law—often enforced through means of political purges, social humiliation, economic discrimination, and penal sanctions under the socialist system—was manifested as a continuity of Chinese familist tradition. Individuals were not classified into different political classes based on their personal political and ideological conformities; rather, class status was ascribed to each extended family as a social unit. In practice, the class status of the offspring of those grouped into the antagonistic classes was the same as their parents' class status. Therefore, any discriminatory and punitive policies toward the older generations of the antagonistic classes were also equally applicable to their offspring, for three generations down the paternal line. Thus, many youths were denied access to the equal rights guaranteed by the Constitution or to fair participation in social competition solely because of their parents' political debts to the revolution.

Although we found little of the humanitarian quality of the Confucian familist tradition in Mao's revolutionary ideology, the negative side of the familist tradition, which focuses collective responsibility on the family, had a strong influence on the Communist policy of unequal rights before the law. Despite the Communist Party's claim that personal performance rather than parental class status should count in social competition and political officialdom, China's longstanding tradition of collective punishment, by which children are held to be culpable for their parents' "crimes," was endorsed by the Communists in many of their political campaigns against politically undesirable classes throughout the first three decades of the PRC.

During the post-Mao era, the new leaders of the CCP finally seemed to give up their indoctrination of the class line, which had affected the lives of tens of millions of people. The Constitution of 1982 reaffirmed in Article 33 that "all citizens of the People's Republic of China are equal before the law."[32] The most important change was that the Communist Party finally abandoned Mao's doctrine of the inherited class status of individuals. The socialist pragmatists replaced Communist idealists.

But the Party insisted that class struggle continues because of the "threats from domestic bourgeois liberalists backed by the international antagonistic forces" who attempt to "peacefully alienate China from the socialist system."[33] Therefore, under the new guidelines, inconsistency with Marxist ideology and infidelity to the Communist Party are still regarded as intolerable or even offensive behaviors. Noticeably, the new Party leadership shifted from the collective responsibility of the familist tradition to individuals culpability. As a Chinese jurist asserted in a law school textbook, the new class enemies of the proletariat practically "have no rights whatsoever under the Constitution. . . . Nor did the Constitutional guarantee of equal rights before the law mean that law is created for all and treats individuals from different classes equally."[34]

It is not clear at this stage, under the new environment of economic openness, how the antagonistic class will be formed to alienate China peacefully from the Communist camp. But we do see a clear trend: the new Party leadership is placing greater emphasis on the antagonistic elements on the ideological front. Consequently, the Constitution and the law, which seem to promise equality, are not equivalent to "a securing of natural equality" or "a securing of natural rights"[35] but only intend to provide limited equality to certain groups of people who do not oppose the "four fundamental principles of adherence—adhering to Marxism, the Party's leadership, the socialist road and the people's democratic dictatorship." Chinese law students are taught constantly that "penal law has a class nature" which potentially serves only the interests of the working class.[36] Who shall enjoy equal rights and protection and what degree of freedom shall be enjoyed are determined not by the nature of man but rather by the Party's policy on class division.

Obviously, for the Chinese Communists, what is equal, just, or fair is not a legal concept but rather a political notion. Coincidentally, the concept of class in Chinese society has less to do with economic status than with one's political conformity to the Communist Party and the official ideological orthodoxy. For the Chinese authorities, constitutional law is a symbolic manifesto of legal formalism that merely provides general guidelines for justice policy, rather than a substantive law that should be applied uniformly and that can be challenged by individual cases in the courts. Naturally, this type of judicial authority must possess a great deal of discretion so that the Party, through its requirement of Party membership for holders of judicial posts, will be allowed to manipulate the rule of law according to political priorities.

Differential Treatment among Ordinary People

In accordance with Mao's theory of the two types of contradictions,[37] minor disputes among people or crimes committed by proletarian people could be handled informally by community and administrative organs, such as a popular program of mediation and conciliation, because such offenses were seen as nonantagonistic in nature. Serious crimes, especially those acts viewed politically as being detrimental to the "four fundamental principles of adherence," were certainly subject to rigid penal punishments. Arguably, the Chinese way of differential treatment of offenders might not be so unique if we consider how the seriousness of the crime is assessed in other judicial systems in other cultures or societies. Nevertheless, we cannot simply assume that the severity of the crime, in the minds of the Chinese legal authorities, is determined by the degree of tangible harm or damage inflicted, as it is commonly understood in other systems. Although both act (*actus reus*) and intention (*mens rea*) are relevant elements in determining criminal liability under Chinese penal law,[38] the Chinese have traditionally put greater emphasis than other societies on the detrimental nature of criminal motives, especially political motives directed toward the existing authority, in rendering criminal penalties. In measuring the severity of an offense, one's class roots were often taken into consideration to assess his potential political motives. The same act engaged in by people from different classes could be interpreted as having different legal degrees of severity. Thus, differential treatment could be imposed accordingly.

The severity of one's "offensive behavior" could be aggravated simply because of one's antagonistic class roots—his parents' class status. For example, in 1967, a twenty-four-year-old man, Yu Luoke, published his essay on class origin in an unofficial newspaper to criticize Mao's doctrine of the inheritance of class status. He argued that the popular motto, "A revolutionary father will raise a revolutionary son while a reactionary father will produce a reactionary heir," was both politically wrong and socially discriminatory.[39] Whether one would become a revolutionary or a reactionary, he argued in the essay, is not so much determined by one's father's class status but rather by one's own choice of conduct; as a matter of fact, a revolutionary father can produce a reactionary son and the heir of a reactionary can become a revolutionary.

His critique against the widely implemented policy of discrimination and inequality under the class line quickly resulted in furious attacks from the Party radicals who controlled the power during the Cultural Revolution. Jiang Qin (Mao's wife), Yao Wenyuan, and Qi Benyu,[40] the members of the standing committee of the Party during the Cultural Revolution, quickly labeled Yu's essay counterrevolutionary and launched a nationwide counterattack in the officially controlled press. In 1968, Yu was arrested for the crime of "maliciously attacking" Mao's class theory, tried by a mass tribunal, and sentenced to death. He was executed on March 5, 1970.[41]

But what was striking in this tragedy was that Yu was not the only person who openly doubted Mao's class inheritance theory. Even Mao himself said that individuals in an antagonistic class could be reformed through socialist education and persuasion. Yu's tragedy was due less to his mischief of independent thinking, his critique of inequality before the law, and his iconoclastic challenge to Mao's authority than to the fact that he was the son of a member of the antagonistic bourgeois class. Therefore, his critical expression, which was assumed to be rooted in his reactionary family, had become a serious crime of counterrevolution.

Why was Yu executed when others who had expressed the same opinions and presumably had committed the same offenses were not? The answer, perhaps, can be found in Mao's comments on good and bad behavior, in which he asked

> how can we tell the good from the bad here—by the motive (subjective intention) or by the effect (social impact)? Idealists stress motive and ignore effect, while mechanical materialists stress effect and ignore motive; in contradiction from either, we dialectical materialists insist on the unity of motive and effect. . . . [S]ocial practice and its effect are the criteria for examining the subjective intention or the motive.[42]

It is true that, unless clearly stated by an actor, a subjective intention can seldom be proven by direct evidence but must be proven by circumstances, from which it may be inferred or deduced and from which a harmful result has ensued. Based on one's class background, a counterrevolutionary motive suspected by authorities is critical for determining the seriousness of the crime under Mao's political doctrine of class division.

On the other hand, criminal acts—that is, conventional crimes—committed by people, especially by members of the "proletarian class," could be interpreted as mistakes or omissions without any malicious intent to threaten the Party's leadership and the socialist system and thus could be diverted from the formal channel of criminal justice. Koeltl has noticed that "in China for a long time to come some citizens will surely be more equal than others, [and] the new constitution does not try to hide this fact."[43]

Differential Treatment for the Party Elite

The Communist Party may have had an intention to diverge from the tradition which viewed codified law primarily as an instrument for controlling the undesirable behavior of people—the ruled, not the rulers. Legally, neither the Constitution of the PRC nor the constitution of the Communist Party has preserved any privileges for the Party elite outside the law. In fact, the constitution of the CCP specifically prohibits the Party from engaging in activities beyond the limits of the law.[44] Thus, the critical question is not whether Party members are legally allowed to act above the law but whether they would be punished in the same way as other law breakers when they crossed the boundary of law in Chinese society. Although Party members theoretically have equal rights—no more, no less—before the law, just like any other ordinary citizen, in practice they have enjoyed greater privileges than ordinary citizens in numerous ways. The Party's practice and institutional arrangements for handling corruption and other crimes committed by the Party elite exemplify their privileged status before the law.

In 1988, the Standing Committee of the National People's Congress adopted the Supplementary Provision Relating to the Punishment of Corruption and Bribery, which addressed three types of crime—corruption, bribery, and misappropriation of public funds—committed by state and other public service personnel.[45] This legislation obviously reflects grave official concern over the widespread official corruption and crime by the Party elite in China, which threaten not only the economic order during economic reform but also the political survival of the Party itself. In responding to the increased public outrage about official corruption, the

Disciplinary Inspection Committee (DIC) of the Central Committee of the CCP[46] issued On the Regulation of Disciplinary Actions against the Violation of Socialist Morality and Discipline of the Communist Party.[47] The penalties range from a warning to demotion in one's Party position to revocation of one's Party membership for crimes of abusing public funds and defalcation for personal weddings, funerals, and housing improvements; extortion; taking bribes; corruption; sexual assault and harassment against women, and so forth.[48] The Party's determination to alleviate these survival-threatening problems is absolutely critical, especially in the aftermath of the political turmoil of the 1989 student-led pro-democracy movement. But the remaining question is whether Chinese officials are capable of enforcing, and willing to enforce, the law based on the institutional arrangements for handling these problems.

The evidence shows that some impressive efforts were made by officials in the 1980s to crack down on crimes committed by Party members in the course of conducting their government responsibilities. By 1990, eleven provincial procuratorates and 155 local procuratorates had established anticorruption bureaus specializing in investigating and prosecuting corruption and abuse of power committed by public service personnel—mainly Party members.[49] According to the official report, in 1989 a total of 197,424 alleged corruption cases involving Party members were investigated; 89.5 percent of them were adjudicated, a 100 percent increase over the previous year. As a result of this crackdown, in 1989 alone, of 158,826 Party members who received disciplinary penalties, 33,487 were expelled from the Party; 37,734 received probation while retaining their Party membership; and 4,498 were removed from their Party posts.[50] But these impressive results were achieved primarily by administrative and Party disciplinary penalties rendered by the DIC rather than criminal sanctions decided by the courts. Of public concern is whether those Party members who had violated the law also received a criminal penalty under the law in addition to their internal Party disciplinary penalty. Both the administration and Party officials may have felt compelled to control the detrimental impact that crime by the elite had on economic reform and the stronghold of the Party's leadership. But what is the relationship between the judicial authority and the DIC's power in disposing crimes committed by the Party elite? Are Party members who committed crimes subject to double or more severe punishments than ordinary law violators or vice versa? Does the DIC assist the courts in investigating and prosecuting alleged crime committed by the Party elites, or does it actually help those elite criminals escape from criminal adjudication and penal sanction?

Establishment and Operation of the DIC. First, the establishment of the DIC has produced an unexpected gap between the Party's desire to control elite crime and its ability to do so. When the Party set up the DIC, its intention perhaps was to promote better behavior and uphold higher moral standards for Party members. Following the traditional doctrine that the better the behavior of the ruling elite, the greater the harmony a society will experience, the top officials believe that the exemplary behavior of Party members, especially the higher-ranking cadres, is critical for controlling widespread economic crime in the society. To the party officials, the establishment of the DIC was intended to uphold a higher behavioral norm for the Party elite through disciplinary sanction for the purpose of consolidating the Party leadership and restoring the public trust. For instance, under the Party constitution and other disciplinary regulations, Party members are subject to disciplinary penalty if they deliberately do not assist someone whose life is in danger or do not rescue public property that is being damaged;[51] these actions would not otherwise constitute a crime or violation if the actors were ordinary citizens. In addition, the Party disciplinary code also overlaps a great deal with penal law. However, the public concern for Party elite crime does not lie in the area in which the conducts are so defined as wrong solely because of the actors' Party status but lies primarily in the area in which the conducts are deemed wrong by both the Party's disciplinary codes and criminal law. Thus, what really matters here is not whether the perpetrator will be punished twice—first by the internal Party disciplinary code and then by penal law—but whether he or she will be punished at all under the penal law for the criminal violation.

Second, the DIC is not operating merely as an internal Party disciplinary inspection agency but is also functioning as an adjudicatory organ parallel to the judicial system. Procedurally, the DIC, with the investigative and disposing power over any alleged violation of the Party disciplinary code, does not appear to have a clear guideline to distinguish disciplinary wrong from criminal wrong in its disposition of cases. As a common practice, the determination of whether a case which involves Party elite, especially high-ranking officers, should be referred to the judicial system for prosecution does not lied in the seriousness of the crime itself but often lies in the area of actor's *guanxi* ("relationship") to the Party, such as his personal loyalty to the Party leadership, his past contribution, and his current political value to the Party. Further, the constitutionally guaranteed superior status of the Party over the judiciary provides the DIC with a legal status that allows it to operate above the judicial system. Not surprisingly, most of these cases investigated by the DIC were never referred to the judicial system for criminal investigation and prosecution; instead, the DIC meted out disciplinary penalties, such as stripping away one's Party membership, removing a perpetrator from a current administrative or Party position, or proclaiming a demotion, which are considerably more lenient than the punishments would have been if the cases had been adjudicated in the courts. The DIC functions as a legal shelter or safe haven that routinely replaces criminal penalties with lenient disciplinary actions against Party elites or exempts Party elites from equal treatment under the law.

Conventional Norms Regarding the Official Figures. It may be too farfetched to conclude that the Party intentionally provides such privileges or covers up for its elite's violations of law when they are legally subject to judicial inquiry. The Party may have intended to treat its members differently than ordinary perpetrators, but perhaps not more leniently. On the contrary, it seems to attempt to subject its members to tougher standards in order to display the higher morality of the Party. Unfortunately, the odds are that actual outcomes often go against the Party leaders' intent. For example, a newspaper article reported that a deputy director of a foreign trade bureau of a city accepted a bribe in the form of a television set and a camera from a Hong Kong businessman in exchange for a signed false contract that resulted in a five-million-dollar loss for his bureau. When the case was exposed, the city's DIC office immediately investigated it and eventually announced the penalty of removing the deputy director from his position while exempting him from criminal adjudication. Under the pressure of public criticism, the DIC explained that it decided on a disciplinary penalty rather than criminal punishment because the deputy director was an old high-ranking member of the Party who "had made a great contribution to the revolution" during his thirty-year-long political career and because it would be "too embarrassing" for the Party to see such a distinguished officer go on trial like common criminal offenders.[52] The notion of "face," highly valued in traditional ethics, once again comes to play an important role in dealing with law violators among the Party elite.

Although the law does not specifically state that the Party elite may be exempted from criminal sanction, the traditional values, customs, and norms regarding official figures and the interpersonal *guanxi* of Party members with the gentry class continue to provide individual Party members with greater protection and privileges above the law. Because of the notion of collective responsibility, punishing an elite member for his criminal violation would be viewed by the Party as a public admission of its own failure in not selecting a cadre with higher moral standards and in not monitoring its members' conducts. Such an admission would certainly be devastating for maintaining the Party's leadership image in public. One may specultate that though the DIC was established to hold the Party members to high behavioral standards, the traditional norms in officialdom often drive the individual officers of the DIC to act as parents dealing with mischievous children rather than as public officials in charge of a matter against public interest.

FINAL REMARKS

Do the people demonstrate their objection to the existence of the DIC, which undermines the authority of the judiciary, and do they challenge the practice of unequal treatment before the law? To answer the first question, the people certainly do. To answer the second question, few have voiced their concerns about the issue of equal rights before the law. We certainly have reason to speculate that lenient or privileged treatment for elite criminals occurs not because Party leaders intend to protect their fellow members but largely because many people, including DIC members, do not seem to be uncomfortable with the reality that the operation of the DIC is actually undermining the sanctity of the judiciary and the law.

NOTES

1. MacFarquhar et al., 1989, p. 25.
2. Yan Zhou, 1982, pp. 17–19.
3. See the *Constitution of the People's Republic of China, 1954.*

4. This is described as the "people's democratic dictatorship" in the Constitution of 1982. See the Preamble of this Constitution. The democratic dictatorship is an invention of the CCP. How democracy can be achieved under a dictatorship is discussed in Mao, 1972c.

5. See Yutang Lin, 1966, pp. 135–51 and Bodde's discussion of group responsibility in traditional Chinese culture, 1973, pp. 24 and 28–29.

6. Mao, 1960a, p. 880.

7. Mao's idea of the antagonistic contradiction between the proletariat and the reactionary class was systematically formed in his work "On Contradiction, August, 1937." See Mao, 1972a, pp. 75–94.

8. Mao, 1972b, p. 311.

9. Ibid., p. 309.

10. Mao, 1972c, p. 237.

11. Mao, 1960e, p. 871.

12. For Mao's idea of the continuous existence of the antagonistic class struggle in the postrevolutionary period, see Mao, 1989, p. 329.

13. Of course, law consistently favors some groups over others because the wealthy and the powerful always have greater influence over how the law should be written. For a philosophical argument about equality for all and the pursuit of social justice, see Ackerman, 1980.

14. This is what Miller once called the "principle of treat equals equally." See D. Miller, 1979, pp. 20–21 for more discussions on the philosophical reasoning behind this principle.

15. This is the "proportionate principle" or "distributive justice." See Ackerman, 1980; D. Miller, 1979, pp. 21–22; Rescher, 1966.

16. There are several distinguishable qualities between equity and formalism of law—for equity: standards, good faith, discretionary, and uncertainty; for formalism: rules, legal imperative, ministerial, and certainty. See Abadinsky, 1990, p. 13; Kelman, 1987, p. 48.

17. Abadinsky, 1980, p. xii.

18. Mao, 1960a, pp. 878–79. For Mao's departure from his Soviet counterparts, see Schurmann, 1968, pp. 115–18.

19. Mao, 1972c, pp. 238–39. The national bourgeoisie refers to those capitalists who were not members of the Nationalist bureaucracy or representatives of foreign imperialism, such as commercial entrepreneurs, petty shopkeepers, owners of small factories and workshops, and managers of industrial and commercial establishments. See Meisner, 1977, p. 87, for clarification.

20. Mao, 1960d, p. 935. According to Mao, there are two types of contradictions existing in socialist China. One is the contradiction among people, which is nonantagonistic in nature and should be resolved by nonviolent and nonpunitive methods, whereas contradictions between people and class enemies are antagonistic and must be resolved by violent suppression.

21. Meisner, 1977, p. 273.

22. For a discussion of the definition and classification of social class during the Land Reform Movement in the 1940s and the 1950s, see Spence, 1990, pp. 480 and 548; and Chen Yung-fa, 1986, p. 133.

23. The violence and mass tribunals utilized during the Land Reform Movement were highly celebrated at the time in literary writings by pro-Communist writers. For example, Ding, 1955, reported a great "red terror" and "violent confrontation" between peasants and the landlord class. See also L. Zhou, 1955.

24. *Bureaucratic capitalism* was a term created during the Democratic Revolution in the early 1950s. This concept refers to those who held prominent positions in the Nationalist

government, personally possessed the vast majority of China's national wealth, and controlled the major industrial, domestic and international trades, transportation, and financial institutions. They were also commonly referred to as the "four prominent families: Chiang Kai-Shek, Song Ziwen, Kong Xianxi, and Chen Lifu." See Meisner, 1977, p. 92, for a definition and description of the oppressive measures launched against the bureaucratic capitalist class.

25. Mao, 1960a, p. 892.

26. Leng and Chiu, 1985, p. 12.

27. Mao, 1972b, pp. 313–14.

28. Mao, 1960b, p. 893.

29. Mao, 1972c, p. 239.

30. *Constitution of the People's Republic of China, 1954,* Articles 85–103, pp. 4–31.

31. Mao, 1972c, pp. 238–39.

32. "Constitution of the People's Republic of China, 1982," 1989, p. 952.

33. Hu, 1991, pp. 4–5.

34. Leng and Chiu, 1985, p. 15.

35. Pound, 1922, p. 83.

36. Gao and Gao, 1981, p. 15.

37. Mao, 1960d, pp. 933–41.

38. See Articles 10 and 90 of *The Criminal Law and Criminal Procedure Law of the People's Republic of China* for a definition of criminal acts and criminal intent (1984, pp. 12 and 35).

39. This was a well-known antithetical couplet written on scrolls during the Cultural Revolution. It translates as "If a father is a hero, his son will be noble; if a father is a reactionary, his son will be corrupt."

40. The first two are best known as members of the Gang of Four.

41. Yu Luoke's tragedy also extended to other members of his family. His sister published several biographical novels after the Cultural Revolution to provide firsthand accounts about her brother, herself, their parents, and their suffering and tragic fate under Mao's class struggle doctrine. For more information on this case, see Yan and Gao, 1986, pp. 111–16.

42. Mao, 1960c, p. 932.

43. Koeltl, 1982, p. 748.

44. Da-ning Wang, 1987, p. 689.

45. For the original texts, see the *Legal System Daily*, January 25, 1988, p. 2; "The Disciplinary Inspection Committee Issued a Regulation on Handling the Problems in Complaints, Accusations, and Appeals," 1988, p. 4, and "The State Department Issued a Regulation on Punishing Embezzlement and Bribery," 1988, p. 3. Also see Conner, 1989, pp. 8–14.

46. For the history and function of the Disciplinary Inspection Committee of the CCP, see James Wang, 1981, pp. 248–58.

47. See "Central Disciplinary Committee's Regulation on Disciplinary Penalty against Party Members Who Violated the Party's Disciplines," 1990.

48. Ibid.

49. See "Prosecutary Prority in Next Year: Advancement of Anti-Embezzlement, Corruption, and Bribery," 1990.

50. See "The Disciplinary Organs Seriously Investigates Cases of Violating Party Discipline," 1990.

51. See "Central Disciplinary Committee's Regulation on Disciplinary Penalty against Party Members Who Violated the Party's Disciplines," 1990.

52. "The Director of a Foreign Trade Bureau Was Dismissed Because of Bribery," 1983.

CHAPTER FIVE

Punishing for Thought: Counterrevolutionary Crime in Chinese Law

INTRODUCTION

IN THE WESTERN legal tradition, the concurrence of criminal acts (*actus reus*) and criminal intent (*mens rea*) is essentially the foremost material element in determining the offender's culpability and in rendering his punishment.

> Indeed, to make a complete crime cognizable by human laws, there must be both a will and an act . . . [in] all temporal jurisdictions. [A]n overt act . . . is necessary in order to demonstrate the depravity of the will, before the man is liable for punishment. . . . [A] vicious will without a vicious act is no civil crime.[1]

Under this principle, the law "does not punish mere criminal thoughts" nor does it punish one for "status."[2] In determining criminal liability, which Chinese law seems to honor the same principle, which prohibits penal coercion upon people for what they think. As stated by a Chinese jurist, "thought, even counterrevolutionary thought, does not constitute a crime."[3] In 1991 a government "white paper" once again reaffirmed that "in China, ideas alone, in the absence of action which violates the criminal law, do not constitute a crime; nobody will be punished merely because he holds dissenting political views. So-called political prisoners do not exist in China."[4] Rhetorically, the text of Chinese law may not differ substantially from that of the West. Western and Chinese law do not differ on the basis of a simple contrast—Chinese law punishes for thoughts while Western law punishes for acts—but rather on the basis of what constitutes an act and who has the ultimate power to determine whether a speech or an expression constitutes a criminal act before the court of law. Specifically, for legal scholars the most troubling category of Chinese penal law is the section on counterrevolutionary crime, which has drawn intense criticism from the international and domestic legal communities. It should be pointed out that unlike the Western legal tradition, under which the goal of punishment is to control undesirable social behavior, for the Chinese there is a long and deeply rooted tradition that punishment aims to control not only undesirable social conducts but also deviant and heterodox minds. The socially harmonious state, as the goal of social control, is not limited to the conformity of social conducts to social norms but also extends to the harmonious spirit of the people. The creation of counterrevolutionary crime in the penal law echoes the traditional role of the state in promoting social control in China.

With regard to the wide range of counterrevolutionary crimes in Chinese penal law,[5] this chapter emphasizes the issue of penal sanctions against those political dissidents who never advocate the violent overthrow of the Communist government but who merely express their dissenting opinions about the policy or political system in China. For the past four decades many jurists, human rights advocates, and political scientists have been deeply troubled by China's arbitrary and brutal persecutions against political dissidents under the counterrevolutionary statute. Due to ideological resentment toward Communism, using the legal machinery to persecute and suppress political opposition as well as individuals who do not agree with Marxist ideology has been regarded as one of the hallmarks of legal practice in all the Marxist states. The scholarly criticism against China's implementation of the counterrevolutionary crimes law—from the early treatment of counterrevolutionary crimes during China's Soviet Republic era[6] to the New Democratic Revolution in the 1950s[7] to the mass internecine conflict of the Cultural Revolution in the 1970s[8] to the current criminal trials of pro-democracy students and intellectuals[9]—has also emphasized ideological and political attributes of the counterrevolutionary crimes law.

It may be true that legal sanctions against counterrevolutionary crime in China are largely attributable to Marxist ideology and the Communist totalitarianism founded by the Soviet Communists. Nevertheless, the use of formal sanctions against political dissidents and ideological heteroclites has a long history and longstanding cultural roots which are deeply ingrained in the Chinese traditional model of control. Unfortunately, these historical and cultural aspects of political persecution have long been overlooked by legal scholars, except for a handful of Sinologists and Sino-historians who have studied the role of law and the function of the traditional Chinese legal system on inspirational and aesthetic grounds.[10] The impressive volumes of legal literature produced during the past decades have regarded counterrevolutionary crime as primarily the political and ideological substantiation of Marxist-Leninist and Maoist thought in the legal sphere and have ignored the historical and cultural reinforcements, such as the traditional Chinese belief in authority and social order, that are deeply rooted in the minds of the Chinese people.

Thus, this chapter elaborates on the historical and cultural dimensions of the official campaigns against counterrevolutionary crimes by analyzing the ideological origins of counterrevolutionary crimes, the conceptual evolution of counterrevolution, and the legal sanctions utilized against such crimes during different stages of revolution. The Chinese traditional model of social control in suppressing political dissidents is another theme that will be addressed in this chapter. To elaborate the legal relevance and significance of the counterrevolutionary statute in the current social control policy in post-Mao China, this chapter hopes to convey historical and social understanding of the treatment of counterrevolutionaries and to show the convergence between the Confucianist and Marxist social control models.

THE LEGAL AMBIGUITY IN DEFINING COUNTERREVOLUTIONARY CRIME

Counterrevolutionary crime, as a categorization of criminal acts, has not drawn as much attention as have single types of political crime in the critical study of comparative law. As a matter of fact, counterrevolutionary crime in Chinese law has been traditionally a category that covers a wide range of illicit conducts, rather than just one type of political crime. Crimes against national unity, security, and sovereignty are universally acknowledged to be punishable by the laws of every society.[11]

Most of the critical literature on counterrevolutionary crime has showed a particular concern with counterrevolution as a single type of political crime—namely, nonviolent and anti-Communist expression—rather than as a category of criminal offenses. The major criticism was derived from Articles 98 and 102, which address the crimes of counterrevolutionary association and propaganda, which involve nonviolence and are primarily an expression of political opposition.[12] Thus, in this chapter we will call this type of counterrevolutionary crime "political crime" in order to distinguish it from other types of counterrevolutionary crimes which involve the use of force or violence—such as assassination, hijacking, or sabotage against the government.[13]

To provide a general definition for counterrevolutionary crime, especially criminal intent, Article 90 of *The Criminal Law and the Criminal Procedure Law of the People's Republic of China* mandates that "all acts endangering the People's Republic of China committed with the goal of overthrowing the political power of the dictatorship of the proletariat and the socialist system are crimes of counterrevolution."[14] To be more specific Articles 91–104 enumerate twelve types of counterrevolutionary crimes ranging from treason, espionage, hijacking, sabotage, terrorism, and coup d'état to counterrevolutionary association and propaganda.[15]

This general definition of counterrevolutionary crime can be interpreted in numerous ways. First of all, we must not forget the monopolistic relationship between the Communist Party and the government. Because the Party declares itself to be the vanguard and representative of the proletariat and the working class,[16] the dictatorship of the proletariat described in the statute is synonymous with the dictatorship of the Communist Party. Therefore, issues of national unity and government sovereignty may become issues of the legality of the Party's ruling status in China's political affairs. The criminal conducts enumerated in the counterrevolutionary statute become socially significant and legally relevant only if the legality of the Communist Party's ruling status and the socialist system are accepted by every citizen in Chinese society. Theoretically speaking, an act endangering the People's Republic of China may not constitute a counterrevolutionary crime unless it is solely aimed at overthrowing the Communist leadership and socialist system. By the same token, an act aimed at overthrowing the state government of China may not necessarily constitute a counterrevolutionary crime unless that act is aimed specifically at overthrowing only the *Communist* government.

Although terms such as "Communist Party" and "Party leadership" were never mentioned in the counterrevolutionary crime statute, the absolute monopoly of the Communists in China's politics and the unity of the Communist Party and the government often make opposition to and even disagreement with Communist Party policy into acts against national security and sovereignty. It is equally possible that any act against the unity and security of the PRC and the sovereignty of the government can be interpreted as a crime against the ruling authority of the Communist Party and vice versa. Political partisanship in China is not regarded merely as an issue of ideological endorsement and membership in a political association. Thus, the significance of a counterrevolutionary crime in Chinese law lies not in the dangerousness of a criminal act to China's national interests but in its detriment to the interests of *Communist* China. The political nature of counterrevolutionary crime underscores the ideological emphasis in the legal practice of imposing criminal sanctions against political opponents—that is, criminal law potentially could punish one either for one's heterodox thoughts or for one's political status.

Second, the categorization of counterrevolutionary crimes creates another dilemma because people might commit a listed crime, such as sabotage or hijacking, without the specific intent to overthrow the Communist government. Therefore, the legal definition of counterrevolutionary intent and act implies a differential treatment of counterrevolutionary offenders. The often-pronounced intention of the Communist government hints at more severe punishments for those who, in speech or in writing, express dissident opinions toward the Party's political ideologies and policies. The seriousness of acts such as espionage, sabotage, and hijacking may be determined not according to the nature of the acts and their consequences for national security but rather according to the nature of the criminal motivations—that is, if the acts were directed at the Communists or were intended merely for monetary or personal gain.

To substantiate this political function of criminal law, two special categories of counterrevolutionary crime—"organizing or leading or participating in a counterrevolutionary group"[17] and propagandizing for or inciting the overthrow of the proletarian dictatorship and the socialist system by means of "slogans, leaflets or other means"[18]—were created to curb political opposition. Practically speaking, any individual who chooses to exercise the constitutional rights of free speech, press, association, and assembly will inevitably run a high risk of being labeled counterrevolutionary even though these rights are guaranteed by the Constitution.

Third, the ambiguity of Chinese law, which has long confused legal scholars, can also be found in the statutory definition of counterrevolutionary crime. Many legal scholars have noticed that Chinese law traditionally has been obscure in defining what constitutes a criminal act so that the criminal penalty can be rendered accordingly.[19] This ambiguity also exists in the counterrevolutionary statute, which, for example, provides little clarification of what actually constitutes a counterrevolutionary group or counterrevolutionary slogans, leaflets, and so on. Where should people draw the line between "prorevolutionary" criticism of the Party's policy or of the misconduct of Party leaders and a counterrevolutionary expression against the leadership of the Communist Party in general? Who will make the ultimate determination when disputes arise as the result of the exercise by individual citizens of the constitutional rights of free speech, press, association, and assembly for the purpose of expressing their criticism of, dissatisfaction with, and even objections to Marxist ideology and the Party's policy? And how much freedom are they actually entitled to enjoy under the counterrevolutionary statute?[20]

Furthermore, Chinese traditional law was always oriented toward penal sanctions rather than toward civil remedies.[21] From the imperial era to the Communist regime, the primary purpose of codified law has been not a clear definition of criminal acts but rather a meticulous categorization of criminal penalties. The ambiguity in the legal definition of criminal acts will inevitably give the authorities a great deal of flexibility in judging a conduct according to officially endorsed ideological orthodoxy and social mores.

In addition, unlike the West, the ultimate goal of penal sanctions for the Chinese authorities was never limited to controlling undesirable social behavior but also includes reinforcing moral or ideological conformity. It was a central notion of Confucianism that merely punishing a misdeed cannot prevent recidivism of similar conduct. Controlling the mind of a person or changing the heart of that person is the only effective way to stop misdeeds. To Chinese authorities, social control is not and cannot be limited to controlling human behavior. It must be extended to controlling heterodox or free thinking. Confucianist moral persuasion historically was an officially planned and coercive process of inculcation without any freedom of choice. Although the educational function may have been a characteristic of socialist law, the codification of counterrevolutionary crime in Chinese law may not be so much socialist as purely Chinese.

In an effort to clarify the above dilemma, a Chinese expert on criminal law suggested that counterrevolutionary crime comprises two essential elements: (1) objectively there is "an act that is detrimental to the People's Republic of China" and (2) subjectively the purpose of the act is to

> overthrow the power of proletarian dictatorship and socialist system. . . . [T]he law neither allows suppression, purge, persecution and retaliation against political oppositionists nor punishes those who criticize the Party's guidelines, directions, and policies for counterrevolutionary crimes. . . . [H]owever, the law also absolutely forbids those so-called "democratic," "political dissidents" from opposing Marxist-Leninist and Maoist thought and opposing the leadership of the Communist Party, the socialist road, or the proletarian dictatorship under the slogan of democracy.[22]

Unfortunately, this statement created perhaps even more confusion than the statutory definition itself. Despite the confusion, at least one thing becomes clearer according to this legal expert—that is, being politically opposed to Marxist-Leninist and Maoist thought or the Communist Party is certainly subject to punishment. In other words, Chinese penal law does punish for anti-Marxist and anti-Communist thought. The questions that remain unanswered are (1) does criticism against an individual Party leader or a group of the Party elite constitute a crime against the Party leadership? (2) can an individual opinion that opposes the Party's policy be considered an act against the socialist road? and (3) when the statutory definition is challenged by individual cases, who has the ultimate authority to decide? Despite the constitutional guarantee of Chinese citizens' rights to free speech, press, and association, the counterrevolutionary statute in Chinese law limits these rights to speaking with only one voice and supporting only the one Party's ruling power and policy.

THE HISTORY OF LEGAL SANCTIONS AGAINST COUNTERREVOLUTIONARIES

Historically, the CCP's efforts to combat counterrevolutionary elements can be divided into five time periods, in each of which a certain political priority was dominant. The earliest campaign began during the Chinese Soviet Republic era (1927–1934) for the purpose of consolidating the Chinese Soviet Republic territory by means of land reform and massive army recruitment. This campaign served two purposes: political agitation and military enhancement.

The second period, the Yanan period, spanned the end of the Long March of the Red Army to the Communist triumph over the Guomindang in 1949. Following the military retreat from the Soviet Republic region, consolidation of the Party's leadership became a critical issue for the survival of the CCP and the Red Army. Mao Zedong and his close associates—including Zhou Enlai and Zhu De—launched several campaigns to cast out the alien factions in an effort to enhance the Party's strength and to reunify the severely enervated Red Army forces. The law of the anti-counterrevolutionaries—which had been promulgated on April 8, 1934, by the Soviet Republic government but had not been implemented because of the military retreat and the Long March—was finally carried out in order to establish new political order in the Yanan region, the headquarters of the Communist government at that time.[23]

The third wave against counterrevolutionaries came during the early stages of the socialist revolution from 1949 to 1965. Immediately after the Communist conquest of mainland China in 1949, restoring social and economic order and increasing national productivity were at the top of the CCP's agenda. To achieve its goals, the Party instituted a nationwide sweep of land reform and the confiscation of property and assets that had belonged to the Nationalist government, foreign imperialists, bureaucratic capitalists, and feudalist lords. The Statute of Suppression of Counterrevolutionaries was enacted on May 21, 1951, to purge the adherents and reactionaries of the Nationalist government and foreign imperialism.[24] The propertied classes were once again identified as counterrevolutionary elements and were subject to punishment. One of the important developments in treating counterrevolutionaries was the educational function of law, which was addressed for the first time in the statute.

The following period constituted the so-called lawlessness of the Cultural Revolution from 1966 to 1976. The term *counterrevolution* was used arbitrarily to punish people for the status they inherited from their families, for their ideological stands, or for their occupations, such as being a government administrator or an owner of a small private shop. Although one's acts, speeches, expressions, and writings were important criteria for determining whether he or she was revolutionary or counterrevolutionary, status alone—such as being the offspring of a member of the propertied class—was sufficient for rendering punishment.[25] The judicial authority was completely ousted and replaced with a mob law enforced by groups of self-proclaimed radical revolutionaries. The label of counterrevolution was used as a weapon to shake down the revisionists among the Party officials and their adherents. Purging, persecution, incarceration, torture, execution, labor-camp confinement, banishment, and forfeiture of property were carried out on a massive scale for reasons of political cleansing, personal revenge, or mob madness. The turmoil finally ended after more than a million people had died and hundreds of thousands were traumatized, injured, or scared as a result of the enforcement of mob law.

In stepping away from the bitter past of the lawless Cultural Revolution, in 1979 China eventually promulgated its first criminal law, under which counterrevolutionary crime formally became a category of criminal offenses. The judicial process was also formalized under the criminal procedural law. Although the legal system was restored institutionally in the early 1980s, it continues to operate under the shadow of the Party's interference and total control. As the new Party leaders shifted their political priorities from the ideological persuasion of the masses to economic reform, the targets of the counterrevolutionary statute have also shifted—from class enemies and alien factions within the Party to the activists of the pro-democracy movement—as the Communist Party hopes to restore public faith in itself and the socialist system. In order to do so, the authorities have resorted to the legal system to carry out the new anti-counterrevolutionary campaign against the opposition, as we witnessed in the 1980s and 1990s during the trials of the activists of the pro-democracy movement.

The Campaign against Counterrevolution in the Soviet Republic (1927–1934)

Ironically, the term *counterrevolution* was not invented by the Chinese Communists. Rather, it was introduced to Chinese law by the Nationalist government—the Guomindang (GMD)—during the era of the Republic revolution (1911–1927)—led by Dr. Sun Yat-sen (Sun Yi-xiang)—to label those who attempted to revive the Manchu imperial system; the term was later used against Communist propaganda.[26] "Counterrevolution" became a special term in the vocabulary of the Communists, initially referring to members, collaborators, and adherents of the

Nationalist government soon after the CCP and the GMD officially split in 1927.[27] Later it was extended to include all elements aimed against the Communist Party and its revolution.

The earliest wave of anti-counterrevolutionary activity occurred from 1924 to 1934, before and during the regime of the Chinese Soviet Republic.[28] At this time, on the one hand, the CCP desperately needed the support and participation of the masses of peasants, workers, and soldiers in order to form the military muscle necessary to oust the Nationalist army and to consolidate the territory of the Soviet Republic. On the other hand, the CCP was also occupied with an internal struggle for a strong and unified leadership because the Party members were still puzzling over the best ideological uniformity and revolutionary tactics to overcome the Guomindang's political and military purges. Thus, the campaign against counterrevolution took place simultaneously on two fronts: the class front of the revolution against the Nationalist government and the Party front against the moderate factions within the Party.

As part of the effort to consolidate the Communist influence among the peasants, workers, and military deputies, the Constitution of the Chinese Soviet Republic, enacted in 1931, identified seven classes of people as the imminent counterrevolutionary elements of the proletarian revolution: "capitalists, landlords, the gentry, militarists, reactionary officials, *tuhao,*[29] monks and all exploiting and counterrevolutionary elements."[30] The antagonistic struggle against the counterrevolutionary classes was substantiated further under the Land Reform Law, which provided for the expropriation and distribution of the estates of all the landowners—including the feudal lords, big private landlords, the gentry, the monasteries, and other private landowners[31]—as well as capital punishment against those classes. The law was carried out immediately in the peasant and land reform movements in Hunan, Jianxi, Fujian, and Anhui Provinces.[32] With the slogans of "down with the *tuhao*" and "redistribution of the land," the peasants were encouraged and led by the Party members to confront the landowner classes by means of violence and "red terror." For instance, in the Hailufeng district of the Chinese Soviet Republic, the peasants' associations captured, publicly paraded, tried, and executed nearly 2,000 landowners within a matter of months.[33] A statistic released by the People's Commissariat Justice of the Chinese Soviet Republic reported that between July and August 1932, 70 percent of the cases adjudicated by the Soviet judicial organs were counterrevolutionary, while only 30 percent were common criminal cases.[34]

Apparently, ferreting out anti-counterrevolutionaries was a major task of the people's judiciary during this era. The violence and destruction against the propertied classes swept through on an enormous scale and with revolutionary vehemence. To many Western commentators, the peasants' movement demonstrated the sheer madness and brutality of the Communist revolution. However, the violence engaged in by the poor peasants was not completely "arbitrary," as has been suggested by some scholars,[35] but rather very specific retaliation against a class of enemies who exploited, brutalized, and slaughtered hundreds of thousands of the poor. The massive acts of violence and destruction witnessed during the Land

Reform Movement represented the peasants' final break from their long silence during the propertied classes' brutality, devastation, and exploitation of the poor. In order to survive the Nationalist military campaign against the Communists, the government of the Chinese Soviet Republic had chosen an aggressive tactic: to crush the classes that were protected by, and that supported, the Nationalist government. Generally speaking, on the class front of the anti-counterrevolutionary campaign, those who were rich and members of the exploiting class were subject to the people's justice.

On the Party front, the struggle between the radicals and moderates regarding the Party's tactics for overcoming the Nationalist government and its troops also intensified. The campaign of the anti-Trotskyites, in opposing the Stalinist line of socialist revolution in the USSR, took an active role—alongside the Guomindang's military purges—in influencing the CCP's policy on punishing counterrevolutionary elements within the Party. During the Chinese Soviet Republic, hundreds of CCP members were purged, exiled from the Party, or even executed.[36] The early practice of persecution and using penal sanctions against the political opposition undoubtedly left an indelible mark on the CCP's later policy on the treatment of counterrevolutionary activity. Opponents of the dominant faction within the Party were often subjected to both political purges and penal sanctions.

In the absence of a centralized government structure during the Soviet Republic, the judicial organs were rather rudimentary. As an extended part of the apparatus of the Central Executive Committee of the National Soviet Congress, the People's Commissariat of Justice, the State Political Security Bureau, and the Supreme Court were established to oversee the arrests, interrogation, trials, and executions of criminal offenders.[37] Mass tribunals were commonplace at that time for crushing the class enemies of the peasant class and the Soviet Republic. During the Land Reform Movement, the bloody uprising between the landlord class and the peasants expanded the territory of the Soviet Republic. The peasants' and workers' associations also formed an ad hoc committee for the suppression of counterrevolutionaries at various levels of the rudimentary governmental body.[38] This committee served a paralegal function for supervising the arrest, prosecution, and sentencing of those identified as counterrevolutionary. In aiding the Red Army forces in eliminating the elements hindering the revolution, it intensively cracked down on the anti-Communist elements within the region. Although the accused counterrevolutionaries had the right to appeal a guilty verdict to a higher level of the governing authority, they were presumed guilty with little chance for a reversal of the verdict. For class criminals, the mass tribunals generally functioned as the judicial forum for public trial and execution. Public opinions were taken into account in rendering punishment for those class enemies who were accused of counterrevolutionary crimes such as exploiting the poor, aiding or supporting the Nationalist government, brutalizing family members and relatives of the Red Army forces and Communists, and so on.

One striking feature of the Statute for Punishing Counterrevolution in the Soviet Republic was the recognition of analogy—a formal rejection of the rule of *nullum crimen sine lege,* or "no crime without a law." For example, the statute mandated that "all other counterrevolutionary acts which are not professed by this statute shall be punished according to the *most suitable* provisions in this statute."[39] In other words, besides the legal definition of counterrevolutionary crime provided by the statute, there was an extralegal criterion, perhaps a political one, for validating any conduct as a counterrevolutionary crime. It should be mentioned here that the legal allowance of analogy in adjudicatory proceedings is not an invention of the Communist government but, rather, a longstanding practice that can be traced back to the imperial system and that was honored by Nationalist law as well.[40] The legal recognition of analogy in law and adjudication is a prime example of the Chinese legal tradition, which allows judicial judgments to be subject to political interpretation and administrative interference.

The practice of analogy was also exemplified in punishing the Party's offenders, which was the sole jurisdiction of the Party's Central Committee.[41] This committee identified counterrevolutionaries within the Party and the Red Army and determined their punishments according to the "most suitable" provisions provided by the statute. Since the Soviet Republic was encircled by Nationalist troops, which made sovereignty of the Communist government and the Soviet Republic region unstable, imprisonment was rarely carried out even though such a penalty was prescribed by the statute.[42] Thus, the Central Committee often imposed disciplinary penalties—such as exile from the territory of the Soviet Republic, expulsion from the Party, discharge from the Red Army, or demotion in Party or military ranks—against Party members who were accused of counterrevolutionary crime. Of course, severe penal sanctions, such as the death penalty, were also commonly used against more serious and incorrigible counterrevolutionaries, such as political opponents of Mao's revolutionary faction.

The most important impact of the early anti-counterrevolutionary campaign is that this dual mechanism of justice provided the basic model of counterattack against counterrevolution for the next half century. The justice structure of the Chinese Soviet Republic also implied the overwhelming political function of the judiciary in fighting the battles both on the class front against domestic capitalism and international imperialism and on the Party front in striving for ideological purity and political unification. The Party's objective was "to combine the struggle against counterrevolution with political agitation."[43] The Statute for Punishing Counterrevolution[44] formalized the CCP's policy on counterattack against antagonistic political forces as a means of preserving the social, political, and economic order of the Soviet Republic. It affirmed the Party's position of prohibiting any act[45] that could be deemed detrimental to the CCP's "goals of establishing national power of the proletarian and working class dictatorship."

The Campaign against Counterrevolution during the Yanan Period (1935–1949)

When the survivors of the CCP and the Red Army finally settled down in the Yanan district of Shanxi Province, following the end of the Long March in 1935, the two-front campaign against counterrevolution underwent some dramatic changes. Externally, although land reform continued throughout the Shan/Gan/Ning and Jin/Cha/Ji regions, which were controlled by the Communists,[46] its scale was considerably restrained under the CCP's new priority: dealing with the urgent threat of a Japanese invasion. Compared with the Soviet Republic era, much more moderate tactics were applied to alleviate encounters between the propertied classes and the peasantry in order to ally all the social and political forces in resisting the Japanese invasion. The expropriation of the land of the propertied class was suspended temporarily.[47] In an effort to prepare for fighting against the Japanese invasion under a strong leadership, unified military forces, and mass support, the CCP took a moderate position in the campaign against counterrevolution on the class front; instead, the CCP was committed to allying with the Guomindang in order to facilitate the unification of all the Chinese people. Members of the landlord class were even invited to join the Yanan representative assemblies of the people's government.[48]

Nevertheless, the mass campaign against class enemies resumed in 1943. Departing from the early moderate policy toward the landlord class during the Anti-Japanese War, Mao's faction escalated its purge against the political opposition within the Party—especially Wang Ming, the most influential expert on the Soviet Union during the Yanan period, who had returned to China in the late 1930s—in an intensive rectification campaign in 1942. Those who breathed the air of free speech, which offended Mao's political adherents at that time, were quickly reprimanded, demoted, purged, incarcerated, and even executed for counterrevolutionary crimes. Mao aggressively reinstated the role of the CCP in determining the limits of intellectual expression and inquiry regarding Party policies and ideological beliefs. He launched mandatory distribution and study sessions of his and Stalin's essays in preparation for a new wave of ideological purification.

To restore social and economic order in the regions, several important laws were enacted to govern property, marital relationships, and legal procedural issues, such as the administration of prisons, self-surrender, and confession procedures.[49] The laws promulgated during the Soviet Republic were reinstated during the Yanan period; and the formal legal system—including a public security force, a procurate, and courts—was established.[50] In addition, the educational function of law was formally introduced into the judiciary at this time. In other words, leniency was allowed in the adjudication of counterrevolution in part because of the relatively stable governmental power and the politically moderate environment. Whether a person received a lenient or harsh penalty depended primarily on his personal willingness to confess and his display of remorse for his wrongdoing. Following the introduction of the educational function of law during the Yanan era, voluntary surrender, self-confession, and self-criticism became hallmarks of Yanan-style justice and features of the Communist model of justice in China.[51]

Furthermore, criminal trials during this period also formed the foundation for the development of adjudicatory procedures after 1949. The Party's Central Committee served primarily as a judicial organ, along with mass tribunals, in addition to the formally established public security, procuratorial, and court systems. Unlike their early counterparts in the Soviet Republic, mass organizations—such as the committees for weeding out traitors, peasants' association, or workers' union—in Yanan held limited judicial authority for apprehension and brief detention.[52] Whether counterrevolutionaries who were Party members should be arrested or tried by the court was decided not by the formal judicial organs but by the Central Committee of the Party. Although the central government of Yanan actively facilitated the formalization of the legal system, the judicial system in Yanan was not only inferior to the political power of the central government and the Party but was also constantly disrupted by the mood of the mass organizations. It seems that mass sentiment toward certain types of individuals played an important role in judicial determinations of the severity or leniency of punishments.

Because the CCP initially occupied primarily rural areas, most of its officers were from poor rural or mountainous regions. They joined the Red Army, then the Eighth Route Army, and later the People's Liberation Army and the Party as a means of surviving the devastation, the rebellion against brutal exploitation, and the oppression of the rich and powerful. Naturally, most of them were educated and trained within the revolutionary camp. They were taught through both the reality of the Nationalist government's practices and China's long history that the justice system had always been a powerful instrument for political suppression regardless of who was in control of the government. Surely, the CCP leaders never dared give judicial power recklessly to those who were well educated but who might be less loyal and possibly prone to be independent of the Party line.

Instead, the initial judicial personnel were selected carefully from the most reliable and loyal military officers to assure the Party's control over the judiciary. Most of those judicial officers, of course, had neither opportunities to obtain a formal education nor any judicial training or experience. Undoubtedly, the recruitment of judicial personnel in Yanan bred the basic model of judicial appointment for the PRC, which remains one of the major obstacles to judicial independence in the 1990s.[53] However, the lack of higher education and formal legal training among the appointees was not something the CCP intended, nor did the Party understand its importance, for these certainly could have been easily improved in the forty years following the establishment of the PRC. Political loyalty to the Party—rather than to the people, their country, or their profession—as the foremost criterion in selecting judicial officers reflects the influence of China's longstanding legal tradition, which essentially treats the judiciary as an extension of political power and a subordinate branch of the administrative organs and political parties.

Anti-Counterrevolution in the Socialist Revolution (1950–1965)

In 1949, the CCP finally triumphed over the Nationalist government and its army. In order to restore the urgently needed social, political, and economic order, the campaign against counterrevolution was implemented immediately, especially on the class front. The primary task of this campaign was to remove physically and institutionally from Chinese society the Nationalist bureaucrats, the adherents of the Guomindang, representatives of the foreign imperialists, and the feudal landlords. Initially, the goals of the Campaign of Suppression of Counterrevolution on the class front were twofold. First, eliminating elements antagonistic to the Communist government was crucial for consolidating the political power of the newborn government. Second, the government desperately needed to seize the assets and property possessed by the economic and financial elite of the Nationalists in order to reassume social production and to revitalize the nation's economy.

To crack down on the sabotage, assassinations, and espionage launched by the Guomindang and the foreign anti-Communist countries, the CCP once again resorted to mass tribunals to intensify the campaign. For instance, in Shanghai alone some 2,000 mass committees were formed to apprehend counterrevolutionary elements. Within a year, hundreds of thousands of people had been arrested, interrogated, detained, tried, and sentenced to prison or death,[54] and some 500,000 firearms that had passed through the hands of the bewildered masses during the long years of warlord and guerrilla fighting were confiscated.[55] During the early stages of the campaign, political affiliation with the GMD, either publicly acknowledged or privately concealed, was the criterion used to identify counterrevolutionary elements. Because the PRC was established as a victory of the working class, those who displayed antagonism toward the people's government—by being a member of the exploiting class, engaging in espionage for the Nationalist government or a foreign country, or being the leader of a religious group or secret society which disliked Communists—would be identified as elements of counterrevolution.

Two movements, the Three-Antis and the Five-Antis Campaigns,[56] were launched simultaneously to crack down on corruption, abuse of power, and defalcation involving Party cadres and elements deemed detrimental to the socialist economic order and production. Although the campaigns on the Party front were not as widespread and violent as those on the class front, they did lead to the thorough investigation of some offices and enterprises which might have benefited illegally.

In a further effort to purify political ideology among Party members and intellectuals, Mao Zedong also launched an Anti-Rightist Movement to purge those whose politics or ideologies were inconsistent with his idea of a Marxist orthodoxy. The intellectual class, including card-holding Party members, became the primary target of the campaign.[57] By the end of 1957, over 300,000 intellectuals had been branded "rightists," a political label effective enough to ruin their careers as they were sent to labor camps, to prison, or to punitive exile in the countryside for the rest of their lives.[58]

During the campaign, the CCP also invited the public to join a new type of committee to scrutinize the performance and behavior of the Party's cadres.[59] Getting the masses involved in the Three-Antis and the Five-Antis Campaigns was a precisely calculated tactic to expand the Party's popularity among the people and to help Mao consolidate his control of political power in the Party and the government. Although the number of executions of Party members accused of crime under the campaign was far less than that for offenders on the class front, voluntary surrenders, mandatory confessions for financial malfeasance, mutual denouncements of the Party cadres, and self-criticism were used widely to secure further investigations, detention, and prosecutions.

Following these campaigns, the socialist educational movement was established in the early 1960s to tend to the unfinished business of the CCP in the countryside—that is, to organize the peasants and farmers into the people's communes-agricultural production teams-and to complete the transformation of private property to collective ownership. This was also the beginning of the mass movement that systematically inculcated the public with Marxist orthodoxy and Maoist thought in both the rural and urban areas.

Counterrevolution in the Cultural Revolution (1966–1976)

The campaign against counterrevolution during the Cultural Revolution showed a dramatic increase in intractability. Counterrevolution virtually became a label for any element that did not agree with Mao's ideology and the radical line of the Party's revolutionary policy. Being a member of the propertied class or even the son or daughter of the past exploiting class made one a political opponent of Party policy and subject to criminal penalties and various punitive treatments. The legal system not only was smashed by the mass movement led by the young Red Guards but also became the target of mass campaigns for helping political revisionists and members of anti-Maoist factions such as Liu Shoqi and Deng Xiaoping. Whoever actually was or claimed to come from a revolutionary or working-class family could form a revolutionary committee to arrest, detain, interrogate, torture, try, and punish in kangaroo courts those who were accused of counterrevolution. Coerced confessions and fabricated evidence, often obtained through torture or speculation, sent tens of thousands of innocent people to labor camps and prisons. Over a ten-year period, it was estimated that 40 million people died from mass riots, torture, execution, and self-inflicted or forced suicide.[60] Millions of people fell victim to the class struggle.

As in the past, the anti-counterrevolution campaign was also launched on two fronts. On the class front, the old elements of the antagonistic class were sought much more thoroughly than ever before under the slogan of the "cleansing class brigade." A history of association with the Nationalist government, foreign imperialism, or the imperial gentry class, or even a well-to-do family background traced as far back as three generations, became sufficient evidence to warrant a verdict of guilty of hidden counterrevolutionary activity.[61] The intensity of the purge was unprecedented in its madness and revolutionary obsession. Even those who had worked as undercover agents or spies for the Communist Party in the Nationalist government or army prior to the 1949 revolution and were prominent Party members could not escape this thorough purge. Furthermore, this intensity was also reflected in another innovative effort to purify the Party of any political disloyalty: "using mass movement to attack inner Party cadres who hold power and travel the capitalist road." Thus, unlike other campaigns in which the Party encouraged the masses to encounter the antagonistic class in society, Mao used his cult to convince the masses that today's dream of the communist millennium would become a reality tomorrow if they tossed out those so-called revisionists who were, though Mao did not tell the masses, also political opponents of his faction.

Ironically, the revolution somehow diverged from Mao's aim—by destroying his myth of the communist millennium and public faith in the Communist Party. The ten-year-long turmoil was not only an internecine melee for the sake of personal revenge among people, but it also brought about the destruction of China's economic and social stability. Paradoxically, if China ever achieved anything from this nightmare, it must have been the awakening of the people from their deification of Mao's dogmatism and their consequent loss of faith in the socialist system and in the Communist Party.

Counterrevolution in Post-Mao China (1977–Present)

It took two years for China to recover from this state of madness and normlessness. In awakening from the nightmare of the Cultural Revolution, the new leadership felt the urgency to restore the public's confidence in the Party's leadership and their ability to lead China to modernization. In a departure from previous methods of treating political defeatists, the Party applied moderate and formal measures to get rid of the Gang of Four in order to consolidate the new leadership.[62] The open-door policy and relaxed political climate quickly brought about new opportunities for public criticism and demands for more political and intellectual freedom.[63] The new leadership also acknowledged the importance of the formalization of law and the legal system in restoring economic order and carrying out economic reform regardless of whether they felt comfortable with it or not.

It is important to note that while the Party realized that the formalization of law and the legal system was not only necessary for the new economic order but also crucial for the survival of the Party leadership, the Party also insisted that the fundamental principles—such as Party leadership, Marxist ideology and Maoist thought, the socialist system, and the proletarian dictatorship—are also indispensable. In upholding these four principles, the objectives of the anti-counterrevolution campaign shifted to new groups of people—pro-democracy dissidents. In 1979, when a group of people demanded the fifth modernization—political democracy—their leaders, such as the well-known figure Wei Jingsheng, were quickly arrested, tried, convicted, and sentenced to prison for counterrevolutionary crime under Articles 98 and 102 of the criminal law. The so-called Democratic Wall Movement, whose participants were geographically limited to young people in Beijing, ended after less than a year when the participants were sent to prison. The fate of the Democratic Wall Movement was inevitable, in part because of the independent thinking and forceful pursuit of basic rights and freedom of expression and in part because of the disrespectful and challenging attitude toward the authorities displayed by the participants. Although Wei Jingsheng, along with other advocates of political reform, had applauded Deng Xiaoping's willingness to engineer four modernizations in the post-Mao era—modernization of industry, agriculture, science and technology, and education—his open criticism against Deng's refusal to modernize China's political system nevertheless brought an inevitable defeat to the movement.[64]

After the student-led pro-democracy movement in Beijing in the spring of 1989 was brutally crushed by military forces, the counterrevolutionary statute once again became a powerful weapon for the authorities to use to purge the student and intellectual activists.[65] Unlike past campaigns against counterrevolutionaries, while the authorities utilized their law machine in a crackdown on participants that resulted in thousands being detained, tried, convicted, and sentenced to penal institutions or execution,[66] they also launched a countrywide purge against supporters and sympathizers. It was reported that hundreds of thousands of people were purged with administrative or disciplinary penalties ranging from warning, demotion, suspension or firing from their jobs, or forced resignation to loss of housing and medical or other benefits.

The new campaign against counterrevolution was specifically aimed at freedom of speech and press. For example, to further elaborate Articles 98 and 102 of the penal code, on November 26, 1989, government officials in Shanghai enacted the Temporary Provisions of the Shanghai Municipality on the Banning of Harmful Publications. According to Article 4 of these provisions, "reactionary publications" oppose the people's democratic dictatorship and the socialist system and include publications containing one of the following elements:

1. opposition to the Chinese Communist Party and its leadership,
2. attacks against the People's Republic of China and the socialist road,
3. attacks against and vilification of the people's democratic dictatorship,
4. denial of the guiding position of Marxist-Leninist and Maoist thought, and
5. serious distortion of historical facts, advocating the disintegration of the nation and people, and vilifying the Chinese people.[67]

The penalties for infringing on these rules range from a fine of 30,000 Chinese yuan[68] to unspecified terms of imprisonment.[69] It should be noted that using analogy has been a legally acceptable practice in Chinese society for more than two thousand years. By Western standards, many acts of the accused counterrevolutionaries may fall in the category of *casus omissus*; that is, the statute did not specify such act as a crime. However, the ambiguous definition of counterrevolutionary crime conveniently provides a legal basis for the judicial authority to prosecute those activists under analogy.[70] Further, though formally established criminal procedure has forced the authority to meet minimal standards of trial under due process, criminal procedural rules were repeatedly tossed aside under political pressure. For instance, many detainees, without ever being charged for any crime, were held in police custody for several months or even years, periods of time that far exceeded the legally allowed period—twenty-four hours or three days—under the Criminal Procedural Law.[71] In a change from the past practice against counterrevolutionaries, the judicial authority allowed the accused pro-democracy activists to be represented by legal counsel at trials. Nevertheless, the courts commonly do not allow the defense counsel to have access to the evidence mounted by the state against their clients until seven days before the trials begin and generally do not grant defense's requests to postpone the trial. Many defense lawyers were rushed to trial without completing a review of the investigation files or personally conducting an investigation by interviewing their clients and witnesses.

Clearly, though the formalization of law may have provided some forms of guarantee for due process in the present campaign against counterrevolutionaries, the fundamental practice against political dissidents and ideological heteroclites has not been changed substantially. Mind control continues to be a main method by which Chinese authorities seek social control. Deeply shaken by the rapid collapse of the Soviet Communist camp in Eastern Europe, the Party leaders faced a psychological crisis, as well as a political one that convinced them of the urgent need to crackdown on those who dare to challenge the last gasp of the Party's leadership. In a departure from the early campaigns against political rebellions, this time the Party members have showed less political enthusiasm and loyalty toward the Party hard-liners and more sympathy and support for the causes of pro-democracy activists. With this newly formed public mood, hundreds of dissidents were able to escape to the West with silent help from local or high-ranking Party cadres, police officers, and army personnel. Such widespread disloyalty toward the Party's campaign against political dissidents is unprecedented in Communist history.

MECHANISM TO ENFORCE THE COUNTERREVOLUTIONARY STATUTE

Unlike Western culture, China traditionally pursues unity without diversity and promotes homogeneity with centralism. This unifying tradition can also be seen in the legal domain. For example, although the Constitution guarantees Chinese citizens the rights to "enjoy freedom of speech, the press, assembly, association, procession, and demonstration," it also mandates that all Chinese citizens must obey "the leadership of the Communist Party of China and the guidance of Marxist-Leninist and Maoist thought" and must "adhere to the people's democratic dictatorship and follow the socialist road."[72] Therefore, the right to enjoy freedom of speech and the press actually means the right to speak in only one voice, which must be consistent with the official orthodoxy. This rule has been honored by China's rulers throughout the country's history.

Coincidently, with regard to settling disputes involving freedom of speech and the press between the state and individuals who aim to overthrow the current government and incite violence, Western society may not differ substantially from Chinese Communists.[73] The laws in both societies prohibit this type of political voice and expression and punish those who attempt to engage in such violent conduct. But what is unique is that Chinese law is also designed to penalize those whose dissenting speeches and writings primarily promote nonviolence and who have no intention of overthrowing the current government but who only criticize government policies and call for wholesale social reform.

Furthermore, China has also created a unique social control mechanism to suppress those who dare to speak in opposing and critical voices. The smooth and effective administration of this mechanism against political crime relies on three prerequisite conditions. First, political interference with the judiciary potentially undermines the authority of law and eventually opens the door to widespread abuse of judicial discretion. On the one hand, the political priority of the Party serves, in fact, as a measuring rod to forecast the political climate of the justice system; the Party's agenda determines, for example, whether more people should be apprehended and punished more severely under particular political campaigns. On the other hand, the Party also actually participates in the process of adjudicating political crime through the work of the tens of thousands of Party secretaries, judges, and prosecutors at every level of the judicial agencies. Frequently apprehension and penalty are determined not by judges or judicial officers according to the facts of crime and law, but rather by the Party secretaries based on the political impact which Party leaders think the dissenting expression will have. Any expression that potentially challenges the leadership status of the Party and threatens the stability of the socialist order is certainly subject to the most severe form of punishment. After all, the Chinese Constitution does not guarantee the right of free expression. It merely allows people to exercise the rights of free speech and press in a voice consistent with officially endorsed ideological orthodoxy.

Ironically, the Chinese people, including legal professionals and jurists, do not seem particularly uncomfortable with this political interference even though it has been widely criticized by Western legal scholars. It has been addressed by only a few Chinese legal professionals. Possibly, on the one hand, the cultural propensity of Chinese society traditionally regards the legal machinery as a property or vehicle which belongs to the rulers and which can be manipulated at a given ruler's wish; on the other hand, critics of the political manipulation of the law run a high risk of being accused of the crime of counterrevolution. Therefore, the public—including the legal professionals—have become culturally accustomed to judicial dependence, even though some may object to such political and administrative interference.

The second necessary condition is a law which contains many gray areas in defining conducts that constitute counterrevolutionary crime. Such ambiguity gives the authorities sufficient latitude to impose sanctions against those whose undesirable behaviors are not explicitly defined by the law as criminal. As a Communist invention, "policy" is often used as a law or guideline for criminal adjudication in imposing criminal penalties against political offenders.[74] Many legal scholars, from both the West and China, recognize that the ambiguity in defining counterrevolutionary crimes in Articles 98 and 102 potentially opens the door for political interference and abuse of judicial discretion.[75] Nevertheless, from the imperial era to Communist China, penal law has always meticulously categorized and elaborately specified penal sanctions, at the same time leaving the ultimate determination of offensive acts to the political and administrative authorities. Bodde pointed out that Chinese law was traditionally penal in emphasis, meaning that matters of a civil nature were either ignored entirely or given limited treatment within the penal format.[76] Perhaps we can also add that Chinese Communist law is also sanction-oriented, meaning that the law is primarily interested only in grading penalties and that it leaves the definition of crime to the Party's policy. As proclaimed by a Party official,

> Chinese law is promulgated based on the Party's policy and is legalization and formalization of the Party's policy. . . . [O]f course, implementation, application, [and] revision as well as abrogation of law must also accept the guidance of the Party's policy. . . . [G]enerally speaking, the Party's policy is more flexible and suitable than the law.[77]

In practice, although the Chinese authorities no longer claim that the words of the ruler are law, they still believe that the policy or will of the political authorities must be vindicated, even at the expense of the law. For this reason, the law, of course, must be enforced in a vertical direction, from the state down to the individuals, and certainly not vice versa. The Chinese judicial system is not and was never meant to be a legal forum for individual citizens to challenge the law and its application on constitutional grounds.

Third, unlike the United States Constitution, the Chinese Constitution is considerably less stable and permanent regarding the rights of citizens and is subject to frequent revisions along with political changes at the top. For example, in 1979–80, the famous Democratic Wall Movement in Beijing, which accompanied a number of workers' strikes across the country,[78] drew considerable attention from both domestic and international communities. When the activists of the Democratic Wall Movement—such as Wei Jingsheng[79]—were imprisoned for writing articles and editing unofficially published magazines which urged Deng Xiaoping's commitment to democracy,[80] the Central Committee of the Party immediately instructed the Legal Reform Committee of the National People's Congress—headed by Peng Zhen, the most important Party official in charge of judicial and legal matters since 1949—to remove the right to strike from constitutional law. This was subsequently accomplished during the fifth session of the Fifth National People's Congress on December 4, 1982.[81] Similar legislative actions were taken to repeal the Chinese citizens' right to freedom of demonstration and assembly following the bloody crackdown on the student-led pro-democracy movement in the spring of 1989.[82]

Under the new amendment, the constitutional rights to demonstration, assembly, and rally are restricted by provisions which prohibit inconsistency with the fundamental principles of the Constitution; are seen as being detrimental to national unification, sovereignty, and territorial unity; incite national separatism; and are believed to be detrimental to public security and destructive to the social order.[83] Citizens are also prohibited from demonstrating in places other than the districts in which they reside, and they must register with the authorities and obtain official permission before they can enjoy the freedom of demonstration and assembly guaranteed by the Constitution.[84] The new amendment further specifies more duties of citizens and, at the same time, restricts individual rights originally guaranteed by the Constitution.[85] The constant alteration and further restrictions of constitutional rights provide a tool for the authorities to prevent any further political uprising which might potentially threaten the legality of the Party's leadership.

FINAL REMARKS

To sum up the official control of counterrevolutionary crimes, the chief feature is the political motives in defining these crimes, regardless of whether the suppression was aimed at class enemies on the class front or was launched against political dissidents on the Party front. Although the law does not provide specific punishments for certain social statuses—such as being a rich landowner, a wealthy entrepreneur, or even the child of a family classified as the propertied class under Mao's class division—some members were often subjected to widely prescribed legal punishments and extralegal persecution. Before 1979 the constitutional right of equality before the law was subordinated to the class line. There is no doubt that this kind of political suppression was urgently needed for the CCP to seize power from the Nationalist government, using military conquest and sweeping revolution in the rural areas, which were occupied by 90 percent of China's population before 1949. In effect, anti-counterrevolution campaigns against the propertied classes also helped the CCP form the initial framework of a socialist economic system so that the Party's power could be enhanced without being challenged by marginal factions of the Party and by society as a whole. These suppressive measures—reinforced by familist traditions, such as the criminal implication of "corrupt blood"—had sufficient power to enable the CCP to maintain political control for more than four decades.

A second important feature of the official suppression of counterrevolutionary crimes is the political manipulation of the judicial process. Although constitutional law requires that the judiciary must discharge its duties independently, this requirement is crippled by the system of promoting and recruiting only Party cadres to judicial positions. We cannot deny that the Party may have intended to move gradually toward independence of the judiciary—at least at a minimal level—to decide legal cases brought before it. However, the desire to formalize the legal system was handicapped by a fear that consistently haunts the oldest Party members, a fear of losing control over other areas such as economics, the mass media, the army, and eventually political power itself. The superiority of loyalty to the Party over honesty to the people and integrity to the legal profession often further undermines the ability of the judiciary to conduct legal matters independently without bending to political pressure. In addition, the CCP's supreme power in legislation provides an additional political vehicle to mobilize the legal system against political opposition at the authorities' wishes.

In a move to respond to international and domestic criticism of legal sanctions against political dissidents, the fourth session of the Eighth National People's Congress, held in March 1996, further restricted the discretion of police, prosecutors, and courts in conducting investigations, arrests, searches and seizures, pretrial detentions, and indictments in criminal matters. For example, the pretrial detention was shortened from the original twenty-four hours to twelve hours. Seized property, assets, or accounts must be returned to the owner if the person is not charged for any crime within the legally required period of time. Legal representation of the accused has been extended from seven days before the trial to the day of indictment. If the accused desires, defense counsel shall be allowed to provide legal advice during the first police interrogation for investigation purposes.[86] To improve the protection of individual rights guaranteed by the Constitution, the People's Congress also further revised and limited the administrative authorities' discretion in imposing administrative and disciplinary penalties against private citizens or organizations.

NOTES

1. Blackstone, 1765–69, vol. 4, p. 20.

2. Klotter, 1988, pp. 22–23.

3. Liang, 1987, p. 16.

4. *China: Daily Report,* Foreign Broadcast Information Service (F.B.I.S.), November 21, 1991, at 11.

5. The definition of counterrevolutionary crimes includes various criminal offenses ranging from treason, espionage, sabotage, and hijacking to organizing counterrevolutionary groups and engaging in propaganda to overthrow the Communist government.

6. Griffin's study (1976) provides a comprehensive review on the early legal sanctions against counterrevolutionaries from 1924 to 1949. See Kun, 1934, for the texts of the original statutes on counterrevolutionary crime. See also Y. Chen, 1986, for a description of the early Communist movement in China, and Leng, 1967, pp. 1–26, for the early development of the Chinese Communist system of justice from the Soviet Republic to the Yanan era.

7. For a discussion of the Chinese legal system and mass dictatorship during this period, see Cohen, 1968, pp. 312–14; Leng, 1967, pp. 27–76; V. H. Li, 1970, pp. 66–111; 1973, pp. 144–219; and 1978; Teiwes, 1979; and Moody, 1977, pp. 71–74.

8. For a comprehensive chronology of the anti-counterrevolution during the Cultural Revolution, see Yan and Gao, 1986. See also the works on the mass tribunals against class enemies by Butterfield, 1982, pp. 342–69; Hsia, 1972, pp. 48–60; Goldman, 1981, pp. 117 55; Madson, 1990, pp. 175–202; and Meisner, 1977, pp. 167–203.

9. For the Chinese Communist Party's general policy toward the Chinese intellectual class, see Goldman, 1981, pp. 214–46, and Schell, 1988, pp. 35–52. See also Asian Watch Committee, 1990, for the maltreatment of political dissidents following the 1989 pro-democracy movement. See Chow, 1989, pp. 23–31; Croghan, Chen, and Zhang, 1989, pp. 13–21; and K. A. Johnson, 1989, pp. 7–12, for an analysis of the revolutionary tradition in Chinese society.

10. Bodde, 1962 and 1973; Hulsewé, 1955 and 1985; Michael, 1962; and Rickett, 1971, pp. 797–814, and 1982, among others, have written extensively on the role of law in the Chinese legal tradition.

11. The provision on counterrevolutionary crimes specifies seventeen types of crime against the government of the People's Republic of China—including treason, espionage, inciting riots, terrorism, counterrevolutionary association, and propaganda—and penalties ranging from three years' imprisonment to the death penalty. See *The Criminal Law and Criminal Procedure Law of the People's Republic China,* 1984, pp. 35–39, for the text of the statute. See also Gao et al., 1983, p. 329, for a list of the seventeen categories.

12. Counterrevolutionary crimes described in Articles 98, 99 (using superstition or a secret society to carry on counterrevolutionary acts), and 102 are nonviolent in nature. Article 103 of the Criminal Law specifies that the death penalty is inapplicable to these three categories.

13. The violent crimes of counterrevolution are specified in Articles 91 (collusion with foreign states in plotting to harm the sovereignty, territorial integrity, and security of China), 92 (plotting to subvert the government or cause the disintegration of the nation), 93 (instigating, luring, or bribing state, military, or police personnel to defect to the enemy, to turn traitor, or to rise in rebellion), 94 (defecting to the enemy and turning traitor), 95 (ringleaders in armed mass rebellion), 96 (ringleaders in a prison raid or in organizing a jailbreak), 97 (espionage or aiding an enemy), 100 (sabotage such as using explosives, setting fires, breaching dikes, hijacking, etc.), and 101 (spreading poisons and disseminating germs or viruses that kill and injure people). Offenders who are convicted of these crimes and who caused severe harm to the state or death and injury to people may be sentenced to death (Article 103).

14. *The Criminal Law and Criminal Procedure Law of the People's Republic of China,* 1984, p. 35.

15. See note 12 of this chapter and Gao et al., 1983, p. 329.

16. See the Preamble of the 1982 Constitution of the PRC, 1989, pp. 945–46, for the legal status of the Communist Party's leadership in relation to the National People's Congress, the government institutions, and the People's Liberation Army.

17. Article 98 of *The Criminal Law and Criminal Procedure Law of the People's Republic of China* states:

> whoever organizes or leads a counterrevolutionary group is to be sentenced to not less than five years of fixed-term imprisonment; others who actively participate in a counterrevolutionary group are to be sentenced to not more than five years of fixed-term imprisonment, criminal detention, control, or deprivation of political rights. (1984, p. 37)

18. Article 102, Section 2, of *The Criminal Law and Criminal Procedure Law of the People's Republic of China* states:

> whoever for the purpose of counterrevolution commits any of the following acts is to be sentenced to not more than five years of fixed-term imprisonment, criminal detention, control, or deprivation of political rights: . . . 2. through counterrevolutionary slogans, leaflets or other means, propagandizing for and inciting the overthrow of the political power of the dictatorship, of the proletariat, and of the socialist system. (1984, p. 38)

19. For a discussion of the ambiguity in Chinese law, see P. M. Chen, 1973, pp. 10, 57, 145–46. He argues that while traditional Chinese law has been primarily a codification of punishment, it is weak, obscure, and equivocal in providing a definition of crime. Therefore, it has been a general practice that the law punishes not only those conducts specified by the law as crimes but also those not covered by the law but part of the social norms, customs, or ritualist rules. Literally speaking, the legal principle of *nullum crimen sine lege*—"no crime without law"—has never been honored by the Chinese legal tradition. Because of this ambiguity in defining criminal conducts, the practice of analogy was allowed by the judiciary in rendering penalties.

20. See Articles 35 and 41 of the 1982 Constitution.

21. For commentaries on this issue, see Bodde and Morris, 1967, p. 3, and P. M. Chen, 1973, pp. 10–12.

22. Liang, 1987, pp. 16–18.

23. See Griffin, 1976, pp. 64–108, and Yang and Zhou, 1989, pp. 495–97, for further discussion of the CCP's policy toward the treatment of counterrevolutionaries.

24. Yang and Zhou, 1989, pp. 500–501.

25. During the Cultural Revolution, the term *historic counterrevolutionary* was created to distinguish those who inherited the counterrevolutionary title because of their past association with the Nationalist government or because of their parents' status within the propertied class from those active counterrevolutionaries who were criminal because of their personal political stand or acts against Communism or Marxism.

26. See Yang and Zhou, 1989, p. 487, in which they quote from a court document of the Republic of China that "Communists should be treated as counterrevolutionaries"; and that "those members of the Communist Party who engaged in only propaganda activities shall be punished according to the Statute of Punishment for Counterrevolution" (Republic of China court document, Jiezi 16 and 21, 1928). For the text of the original statute enacted by the Nationalist government in the 1920s, see "Counterrevolutionary Statute of the Nationalist Government," 1928.

27. During this period both the Communists and the Nationalists used counterrevolution to attack their counterparts. See Yang and Zhou, 1989, p. 487, for more references. For the Chinese attitude toward purging political opposition and the Nationalist government's measures against the Chinese Communists, see Moody, 1977, pp. 25–37.

28. The Chinese Soviet Republic was formed along the border of Jiangxi and Fujian Provinces in 1927 and endured until 1934, when Mao Zedong and his Red Army troops were forced by the Guomindang's military campaign into the 25,000-li Long March. The Long March began in October 1934 and ended in Yanan, in Shanxi Province in October 1935, with only 10 percent surviving out of the 80,000 troops who originally left Jiangxi with Mao. See Griffin, 1976, pp. 12–13; Kun, 1934; and Spence, 1990, pp. 403–10, for additional references.

29. *Tuhao* ("local tyrants") is a term used in rural areas of the southern provinces of China.

30. Kun, 1934, p. 18.

31. Article 1 of the Land Reform Law of the Chinese Soviet Republic mandated that:

> All the lands of the feudal lords and the landlords, the militarists and the tuhao, gentry and other big private landowners, shall be subject to confiscation without any compensation whatever, irrespective of whether they themselves work their lands or rent them out on lease. The Soviets must distribute the confiscated lands among the poor and middle peasants. The formal owners of confiscated lands shall not be entitled to receive any land allotment. (Kun, 1934, p. 25)

Also see Spence, 1990, p. 374, for a detailed classification of the peasant classes during the Land Reform Movement in the Chinese Soviet Republic.

32. Mao Zedong vividly documented the details of the peasants' movement on March 27, 1927, in his famous work, "Report on an Investigation of the Hunan Peasant Movement" 1972d, pp. 31–43.

33. In addition, the Nationalist governmental source estimated that as many as 186,000 people were slaughtered, 2,100,000 fled from the Chinese Soviet Republic region, 100,000 houses were burned, and as much as $630,000,000 in property was damaged and confiscated (Griffin, 1976, p. 18).

34. Yang and Zhou, 1989, p. 495.

35. Leng, 1967, p. 3.

36. See Griffin, 1976, pp. 28–32, for the purge against political opposition within the Party, and Moody, 1977, pp. 37–38, for the early Communists' attitude toward political opposition.

37. Griffin, 1976, p. 19.

38. Ibid., p. 23.

39. See Yang and Zhou, 1989, p. 496, for the text of the statute in Chinese.

40. See P. M. Chen, 1973, pp. 57–58 and 144; Bodde, 1973, pp. 32 and 228; and Leng, 1967, pp. 31 and 60, for further discussion of judicial judgment by analogy and the legal status of analogy in imperial law as well as in Nationalist and Communist law.

Application of analogy in punishing crimes which are not defined by the law has been a major characteristic of the Chinese legal tradition since the imperial dynasties. Although scholars have realized that analogy also appeared in the early version of the penal law of the former USSR—which was done away with after the 1958 reform—and that there was generic similarity between China's 1979 penal law and the early version of the Soviet criminal law, analogy was not a legal concept that the Chinese adopted from the former Soviet Union; on the contrary, the Chinese were known to have used analogy in disposing of criminal cases for more than two thousand years. The coincidence of its appearance in the early Soviet penal code does not prove that analogy in Chinese Communist law was a result of the Soviet influence. Ironically, as recognized by Berman et al. (1970), many characteristics of the Soviet law, perhaps including the usage of analogy, might have been influenced by the Chinese law. For further discussion on this issue, see Berman et al., 1970, pp. 313–27; Berman et al., 1982, pp. 238–58; Ginsburg, 1970, pp. 328–36; Giovannetti, 1984, pp. 382–401; and Rickett, 1982, p. 112.

41. The tradition that an internal party organ functions as a judicial body paralleling the judiciary of the Communist government in rendering criminal penalties against politically undesirable conducts of Party members apparently began as early as the Soviet Republic era. Echoes of this tradition can be found in the operation of the DIC in the present-day PRC.

42. Kun, 1934.

43. This quotation appeared in a report from the Hubei-Human-Anhei Soviet District dated December 1, 1931 (see Kun, 1934, p. 10). The same source reported that more than a hundred politically undesirable people were expelled from the Party and several hundred people were censured in just one Soviet Republic region (ibid., p. 11).

44. The statute was drafted and circulated among Soviet Republic officials and the rest of the organization on December 9, 1931, and was finally promulgated by the Central Executive Committee of the People's Congress of the Soviet Republic on April 8, 1934 (Griffin, 1976, Appendices A and B, pp. 155–67).

However, the statute was actually effective for regulating the treatment of counterrevolutionaries for only a sixth-month period because the Chinese Soviet Republic was crushed by the Guomindang's military expedition, and the Red Army, along with the CCP's leaders, retreated from the Soviet Republic territory to begin the Long March to the northern region of China in October 1934 (Spence, 1990, pp. 403–10).

45. Acts aimed at sabotaging the economic order of the Soviet Republic, such as counterfeiting Soviet Republic currency and government bonds, were classified as counterrevolutionary crimes (Griffin, 1976, p. 164).

46. Shan/Gan/Ning refers to the northern provincial region of Shanxi, Gansu, and Ningxia. Jin/Cha/Ji refers to the provinces of the northern Yellow River region—Hebei, Henan, Shanxi, and Inner Mongolia. See Spence, 1990, p. 461, for the geographic division during the 1930s and 1940s.

47. Griffin, 1976; Spence, 1990.

48. Spence, 1990, p. 463.

49. Griffin, 1976, Appendices C–L. The Organic Regulations of the High Court of the Shan/Gan/Ning Border Region were promulgated on April 4, 1939; see ibid., p. 68.

50. See ibid., pp. 67–73, for details on the structural organs of the judicial system and their functions during the Yanan era.

51. Confession and self-surrender were the trademarks of the Chinese legal tradition in imperial societies. See Chapter 2 in this book for a general description of these practices in traditional China and Chapter 6 for their implications in the PRC. Also see Borowitz, 1977, pp. 522–28; Bodde, 1973, pp. 231–36; and Rickett, 1971, pp. 797–800, for their implications in imperial China. See also Cohen 1968, pp. 392-94, and Rickett, 1971, pp. 801–14, for their validity in Communist China.

52. These committees were not as powerful as their counterparts in the Soviet Republic Era. They no longer had the authority to interrogate, arrest, try, or execute counterrevolutionary offenders (Griffin, 1976, p. 71).

53. See Kaminski, 1982, pp. 8–9, for a continuation of this model of recruitment in the judicial system of the PRC.

54. According to some reports released by the government, between 1950 and 1951 some 40,000 people were arrested and accused of counterrevolutionary crimes in Shanghai; 52,620 "bandits" were caught, 89,701 were arrested, and 28,332 were executed in Guangdong (Spence, 1990, p. 535).

55. Ibid.

56. The Three-Antis Campaign (*san-fan yun-dong*) was directed against corruption, waste, and bureaucratism. The Five-Antis Campaign (*wu-fan yun-dong*) was aimed at bribery, evasion of taxes, embezzlement and theft of state property, fraud in production, and theft of state economic information.

57. For the Party's policy regarding the intellectual freedom of speech and expression, see Goldman, 1981, pp. 9–10, who pointed out the Party's contradictory attitude toward the intellectual class, whose members, on the one hand, were extolled for their role in the modernization of science and technology and, on the other, were suppressed for their independent and critical thinking toward Party policy. This dilemma resulted in a cyclical policy toward the intellectual class. At one time, their expression was encouraged under the "hundred flowers policy"; and at another time, they were attacked for their rightist, inconsistent, or anti-Marxist attitude.

58. Spence, 1990, pp. 569–73.

59. Such as the Shanghai Committee to Increase Production and Practice Economy (ibid., p. 537).

60. Yan and Gao, 1986.

61. This category of counterrevolutionary activity was also called historic counterrevolution, to distinguish it from active counterrevolution, which was a conduct or an expression against Communist policy.

62. For a comparison of the Party's policies toward the treatment of political losers during the campaign against Lin Biao and during the trial of the Gang of Four after the Cultural Revolution, see T. Wu, 1983.

63. See Rosen, 1981, pp. 3–121, for Li Yizhe's debate on the freedom of speech under the modernization program. See also Seymour, 1980, for China's human rights movement in 1978–79.

64. See Chan et al., 1985, and Z. T. Li, 1985, pp. 163–76.

65. Hundreds of the participants who were involved in the street violence and barricades against the People's Liberation Army were detained, interrogated, tried, and sentenced to prison or death. In addition, two prominent intellectuals were sentenced to thirteen years in prison solely because of their dissident expressions and critical speeches and writings against the then-current Party policies and in support of the student movement. See *Collection of*

Laws, Statutes and Decrees of the People's Republic of China, January–December 1989, pp. 785–813, for the official version of the accusation.

66. *China: Daily Report*, "Lawbreakers Involved in Riot Sentenced," F.B.I.S., January 7, 1991, at 15.

67. *Jiefang Ribao*, December 5, 1989, in F.B.I.S., January 10, 1990.

68. Thirty thousand Chinese yuan equals US $4,000.

69. *Jiefang Ribao*, December 5, 1989, in F.B.I.S., January 10, 1990.

70. H. Chiu, 1992.

71. Articles 44, 48, and 51 of *The Criminal Procedure Law of the People's Republic of China*.

72. The Constitution of 1982, Article 35 and Preamble, pp. 952 and 946.

73. See *Dennis v. the United States*, 341 U.S. 494 (1951), for the judge's opinion. Although the case was decided during the McCarthy era, the decision has not been challenged since.

74. "Concepts of Law in the Chinese Anti-Crime Campaign," 1985. Policy has been much preferred to the law for curbing undesirable conducts in socialist China. Many offenders were punished not according to the law but according to the Party's policy. The best example of a widely utilized penalty against those who violated policy is the punishment against couples who had more than one child. See Deng Liquin's speech on the relationship between the law and the Party's policy, 1987, pp. 665–70.

75. See Yang and Zhou, 1989, pp. 500–515, and "Lin Yun on Counter-Revolutionary Offenses and Capital Punishment," 1979, pp. 16–17, for additional references.

76. Bodde, 1973, p. 4. He suggested that civil law in Chinese imperial society literally did not exist because of the strong penal emphasis of law. The law in imperial China was interested only secondarily in defending the rights—especially the economic rights—of individuals or groups against other individuals or groups and not at all in defending such rights against the state.

77. Deng Liquin, 1987, p. 668.

78. The right to strike was a constitutional right of Chinese citizens at that time. See Article 45 of the Constitution of 1979, in *Laws and Regulations of the People's Republic of China*, 1982, p. 14.

79. Wei Jingsheng's influence on the Chinese democratic movement was due, in part, to his role as a pioneer in the pro-democracy movement and, in part, to his idea, inspired in the title he chose for his Democratic Wall poster of December 5, 1978: "The Fifth Modernization." In the poster he proclaimed that unless China embraced a fifth modernization—democracy—the other four modernizations would be "merely another promise." This was obviously a gauntlet flung in the face of the CCP hierarchy—including Deng Xiaoping himself, who declared the four modernizations to be a sufficient basis for modernizing China. For further discussions of Wei Jingsheng, see Chan et al., 1985; Goldman, 1981, p. 240; Zhi Liu, 1986, pp. 185–87; and Spence, 1990, pp. 659–66.

80. Wei Jingsheng was officially convicted of providing military secrets to a foreign journalist, a crime of counterrevolution, and was sentenced to fifteen years in prison. He served the full term and was released in 1994. In February 1996, he was arrested and subsequently convicted for attempting to overthrow the Chinese government under Article 92 of the Criminal Law and sentenced to prison for fourteen years ("Legal Expert, Gao Ming-Zuan, Interviewed on Wei Jingsheng Case," 1996).

81. See Gan, Lin, and Shen, 1987, p. 50. For the CCP's role in China's legislation, see Hsia and Johnson, 1986, pp. 1–33, and Stahnke, 1967, pp. 506–525.

82. See "The Law of Demonstration and Assembly of the People's Republic of China," in *Collection of Laws, Statutes and Decrees of the People's Republic of China, January–December*

1989, pp. 99–107, and "Adoption and Mandate of the Law of Demonstration and Assembly of the PRC in Shanghai," in *Collection of New Laws of the PRC*, 1990, vol. 1, pp. 292–98.

83. "The Law of Demonstration and Assembly of the People's Republic of China," in *Collection of Laws, Statutes and Decrees of the People's Republic of China, January–December 1989*, Article 12.

84. Ibid., Articles 8 and 15.

85. The Chinese Constitution contains a section on citizens' obligations to their country, their Party, their fellow citizens, and their community that they have along with their rights.

86. "Revision of Criminal Procedure Law at Seventeenth Session of Standing Committee of the 8th National People's Congress," *People's Daily*, December 21, 1995; "Revision of Criminal Procedure Law and Law on Administrative Penalty," *World Journal*, March 17, 1996.

CHAPTER SIX

The Principle of Voluntariness in Chinese Law and Morality

INTRODUCTION

THE CHINESE practice of either voluntary or coerced confession has drawn heavy criticism from comparative legal scholars, who claim it denies the basic legal protections of due process and presumption of the innocence of the accused in criminal matters. Under the Chinese system, a verdict is often decided prior to trial by authorities who dispense with the formally established procedural rules at the whim of judges, government administrators, and Party officials. Repugnance toward the inquisitorial nature of the Chinese judicial process runs especially high when self-surrender (*zishou*) and confession (*tanbai*)—obtained by the extensive use of psychological coercion and physical torture—hold the spotlight of jurisprudential criticism outside China, even though the Chinese themselves seem to be, to some degree, comfortably inclined toward this type of "self-incriminatory" justice.[1]

This chapter attempts to provide an understanding of some of the possible reasons why the principle of voluntariness is considered legitimate and morally valid in the administration of justice in China. As documented in the Chinese classic literature, arts, folklore, and court records under the imperial system, the authorities had always attached great significance to self-surrender (*zishou*) and confession (*tanbai*) in the codified law as devices for administering social justice and ordering their society. The penal law of the PRC has largely preserved this traditional provision as a means of allowing humanitarian leniency to those who choose to comply with the authorities.[2] Therefore, this chapter first examines the transformation of the imperial law of voluntary surrender and confession into its contemporary legal status in the Chinese social context.

It is well known that the slogan "lenient treatment for those who confess (*tanbai congkuan*) and severe punishment for those who disavow the accusation (*kangju congyan*)" is the typical administrative model of justice in China. The elements of a culture—including its laws—always prolong the social norms with a certain degree of continuity and preserve the moral content which is endorsed by the social mainstream. China is no exception. Nevertheless, the continuity of norms and the preservation of social morality are not simply a replication of history but rather a selective process to meet the needs of each successive generation. The social purpose of implementing the law of voluntariness in criminal proceedings might vary in terms of its utilitarian value to suit the mood of the ruling and the ruled toward disorderly social conducts.

But it should be pointed out that the voluntariness principle as a social control faculty in modern Chinese society is unique, not because it was transformed into codified law and systematically administered by the authorities in criminal proceedings,[3] but, rather, because of its inherent connection with the intensified socialist moral persuasion and thought control valued by the Chinese Communists. Karl Marx, indeed, might have addressed the important power of the cultivation of political ideology in the proletarian revolution against capitalist forces, as do the Chinese Communists. But it takes a bit of investigation to learn that moral persuasion was definitely indigenous to Confucian moral cultivation. To be sure, "few societies have been as self-consciously moral as the Chinese."[4]

An examination of the moral justification for self-surrender and confession in Chinese society is the second task of this chapter, which also examines the content of the so-called socialist morality which is advocated by the authorities. This chapter considers whether China's socialist morality in defining social disorder and deviance varies remarkably from its traditional morality and from its counterparts elsewhere in the world.

Furthermore, several scholars have recognized that the self-surrender and confession law is moralistic because it incorporates the Confucian traditions of humanitarianism and moral education into the reform of those officially defined as socially undesirable and legally offensive.[5] But the officially mandated moral persuasion affecting individuals is not limited to crime detection and court procedures; it is also carried out during the postsentencing stage in correctional institutions and rehabilitative facilities. Undoubtedly, the Chinese correctional system stands apart from its counterparts elsewhere in the world. The third section of this chapter characterizes the uniqueness and effectiveness of the Chinese correctional system, which continues to enforce the voluntariness principle.

VOLUNTARINESS IN TRADITIONAL CHINESE LAW

According to newly discovered archaeological evidence, as early as the Qin Dynasty (221–207 B.C.), *zichu* ("self-submission") appeared in legal texts which were written on 1,155 bamboo strips.[6] In the fourth volume of documents, entitled *Answer to Questions about the Qin Law*, the text on the strips noted that

> An absconder who fled with stolen goods surrendered voluntarily. Should this be adjudicated as a theft? If he voluntarily surrendered, it should be treated as a crime of abscondence; if the absconder was captured, it should

> be treated as a theft; if the punishment for theft is lighter than that for abscondence, it shall be treated nevertheless as a crime of abscondence.[7]

This was the earliest recorded instance in which voluntary surrender was officially recognized as a mitigating factor in adjudication.

Later, *zichu* was transformed into *zigao* ("self-reporting") under Han law (206 B.C.–220 A.D.). In addition to mandating mercy for those who voluntarily surrendered and confessed before official acknowledgment, Han law also put more restrictions on the application of the voluntary confession clause for certain types of cases. Masterminding a criminal conspiracy, for example, could not receive a penalty reduction even if the offender came forward of his own volition to confess.[8] During the Southern Dynasty (420–589), offenders could receive a lenient punishment or even a total remission of their penalty if they surrendered and confessed their crimes within a reasonable period of time, for example, within a hundred days after official discovery of the crime.[9]

The Tang Code (652)[10] provided even more detailed statutory clarifications of penalty reductions or remission for offenders who confessed voluntarily according to the seriousness of their offenses. For instance, if a robber confessed to a crime in which the victim was physically injured, he was entitled to a pardon only for the crime of robbery but not for the crime of aggravated assault. Confessing to a property owner for stealing goods was considered the same as confessing to the court authorities under the condition that the stolen goods must be returned to their owner.[11] All offenders were expected to surrender to the authorities and confess within a hundred-day grace period. If they did not do so and were captured within this grace period, they could not be treated as if they had deliberately concealed their crime. They would be tried not for the original crime but only for the crime of abscondence if they confessed their original crime to the authorities after being captured, with the possibility of a reduction in penalty; otherwise, they would be tried for both the original crime and the crime of abscondence after the hundred-day grace period had expired.[12]

The clause of self-surrender and confession was adopted in each successive imperial penal code, even in the 1910 New Penal Code of the Great Qing (*Da Qing Xin-xing-lü*), which introduced Western legal concepts—such as legal defense—to the Chinese system for the first time. In addition, later imperial law showed greater concern for official responsibility in verifying the truthfulness of a confession in legal proceedings. If an offender confessed to only a fraction of the crime he had committed—for instance, he admitted to stealing only $100 of the $120 he actually stole—he was entitled to a penalty reduction only for that portion of the crime; if he came forward to confess a crime he had not committed at all, he would be punished for perjury. What is more interesting is that a false confession might sometimes be considered excusable under the rule of Confucian filial piety and familism, such as when the parents, older brothers, or husband ordered a defendant to confess to the authorities in order to cover up another family member's deed.[13] The investigative officers were also held liable if they failed to verify the truthfulness of a confession which resulted in a lighter or heavier penalty than the offender deserved according to the actual crime committed.[14] All the evidence suggests that voluntariness in surrendering and confessing to a crime had a very important impact on determining the nature and severity of criminal penalties.

However, the most interesting part of self-surrender and confession was that imperial law also legalized torture—ranging from whipping and beating with a bamboo strip or wooden stick to twisting the ears, squeezing the fingers or ankles with wooden compressors, and breaking the kneecap, etc.—to obtain confessions from principal and secondary suspects and witnesses and even victims. The imperial lawmakers seemed to believe that if the torture were properly administered by the court, the wrongdoer would eventually reveal the truth. Rather than looking into possible due process procedures, which would provide a legal forum for both the accuser and the accused to exhaust reasonable doubt, Chinese imperial law placed enormous responsibility on individual judicial officers to eliminate reasonable doubt. It would be naive to speculate that the authorities did not realize that false confessions may have resulted from cruel torture. Instead, they traditionally had more faith in the personal qualities and skills of the judicial officers than in technically and procedurally oriented due process to prevent such misfortunes.

Lawmakers under the imperial system went to great lengths to emphasize the importance for individual defendants to realize their immorality within a reasonable period of time and to have a chance to change their minds and repent. Obviously, detecting crime and punishing wrongdoers were not regarded as the ultimate goals of the criminal justice system. Rather, rehabilitating wrongdoers with certain rewards and allowing a reasonable time interval for a change of heart and moral repentance took priority in lawmaking and adjudication in the imperial society. Indisputably, the ultimate goal of the judicial process at that time was not finding the *legal guilt* of crime by using legally admissible evidence against defendants but, rather, discovering the *factual guilt* and making the offender morally shameful and remorseful. By the same token, penal sanctions were reserved as the last resort for those who rationally chose to defy social conformity.

But this humanitarian amnesty of voluntariness was not without its limitations. During most of the imperial dynasties, certain types of criminal offenders were consistently excluded from judicial amnesty regardless of whether they voluntarily surrendered and honestly confessed or were captured by the authorities. For instance, the unauthorized practice of astronomy could not be pardoned by confession because of the fear in the officials' minds that the astronomer's prediction of the emperor's death and of a dynastic transition might incite a popular rebellion.[15] Crimes punishable by the death penalty or exile for life were generally not eligible for any penalty reduction or remission. The so-called ten abominations[16] were certainly excluded from consideration for adjudicatory immunity even if the offender had chosen to comply with the authorities by confessing to the crime for which he or she was charged. An old Chinese proverb—"defiance against the authorities and inciting disorder" (*Fanshang zuoluan*)—indicated that rebelling against the authorities was considered a most heinous crime, punishable by the most severe penalty. Coincidentally, the complete language of the self-surrender and confession clause was retained by the emperors and their successors, with consistent emphasis on moral repentance and factual admission.

THE PRINCIPLE OF VOLUNTARINESS UNDER COMMUNIST LAW

In observing the imperial legal tradition and the penal code of the Nationalist government,[17] the Chinese Communist government also preserved the statute of voluntary surrender and confession in the penal law,[18] although some principles and provisions underwent considerable changes. As early as the 1930s, the Chinese Soviet Republic government made a distinction between two types of voluntary surrender: (1) before the crime was discovered by the authorities and (2) after the suspect was known to the authorities but had not yet been arrested and when he cooperated in the criminal investigation under the Statute of the Chinese Soviet Republic Governing Punishment of Counterrevolutionaries.[19] The first type was called *zishou* ("self-surrender"), and the second was referred to as *zixin* ("self-reform"). Although in both cases persons who surrendered were entitled to leniency in sentencing, the latter group was considered to have gone a step further because of their greater willingness to help the authorities and their meritorious acts in solving the case.

Nevertheless, unlike the imperial legal tradition, in which the time interval between the commission of the crime and voluntary surrender had always drawn considerable attention from lawmakers, the Communist lawmakers were less concerned with the time factor in the offender's surrender and confession. Rather, they were more interested in categorizing the offender's eligibility for penalty reduction according to the nature of the criminal conducts. For example, the Separate Statute of the Shansi-Chahar-Hopei Border Region Concerning Voluntary Surrender and Confession of Traitors, promulgated in 1938 during the Anti-Japanese War, categorized five types of traitors with eleven meritorious conducts—including defecting from or sabotaging the Japanese bandits or helping the Chinese resistance forces—as being eligible for penal amnesty.[20] In order to disband the pro-Japanese forces effectively, a differential treatment policy was issued by the Communist government that incorporated the voluntary surrender and confession statute: "principal offenders must be severely punished; coerced participants will be exonerated; and offenders with meritorious service will be rewarded."[21]

Like their predecessors before the 1949 revolution, the Communist government has adhered to the tradition of voluntariness in dispensing rewards and punishments for those officially identified as criminals. In the earlier campaigns against the class enemies, such as in the Five-Antis Campaign in 1951, prominent business figures in the cities were forced to undergo group criticism sessions and to confess their past economic crimes—such as fraud, extortion, and malfeasance—as part of the government's efforts to transform private industries into the state's hands.[22] It should be pointed out that voluntary surrender, confession, and self-criticism are not measures limited merely to criminal cases but are also powerful weapons used in political campaigns—as in the Anti-Rightists Movement—to purge those who dare to express anti-Marxist, anti-Communist, and antisocialist sentiments and opinions.[23]

After the Cultural Revolution, when lawmakers began to draft the first penal law of the PRC in 1977, they preserved the phrase "surrender must occur before the crime is known to the authorities" in the twenty-second draft. But it was withdrawn from the thirty-third draft—the one eventually promulgated by the National People's Congress in 1979—and replaced with "surrender after the crime was committed."[24] Article 63 of the Criminal Law of 1979 states[25]

> Those who voluntarily surrender after committing a crime may be given a lesser punishment. Those among them whose crimes are relatively minor may be given a mitigated punishment or be exempted from punishment; if their crimes are relatively serious, they may also be given a mitigated punishment or be exempted from punishment if they demonstrate meritorious service.[26]

The change in wording indicates that modern lawmakers were more interested in the essence of voluntariness in an offender's surrender and confession than in their timing and left the temporal restriction on surrender to the discretion of the local governments and judiciary. In other words, this provision serves only as a general guideline to encourage offenders to surrender and confess by promising a tempting reward for such voluntary acts without putting any specific restrictions on the time interval between the commission of the crime and the offender's surrender or on a commensurate degree of penalty reduction. Decisions regarding sentencing reduction or remission and the degree of leniency are subject to judicial discretion and to the crime control policies set up by local authorities according to their agenda for maintaining political and economic order.

Moreover, in an attempt to provide more practical guidelines for implementing the self-surrender provision, the lawmakers have made a further clarification about the circumstances of *zishou* (self-surrender) and *tanbai* (confession). According to a Chinese jurist's clarification, *zishou* and *tanbai* might not qualify for judicial leniency unless they occur (1) before the crime is known to the authorities, (2) after official discovery of the crime but before the suspect is identified, (3) while the offender is in police custody for another, totally unrelated event, and (4) when the police suspect a person but have no warrant to make an arrest.[27]

To further distinguish surrenders based on the temporal order of crime occurrence and crime discovery, *touan* (turning oneself in to the authorities) is cited for those individuals who turn themselves in after the crime becomes known to the authorities and the investigation has begun and for those who know they are wanted by the police. Generally speaking, if an arrest warrant is issued and the offender knows that he or she is wanted by the police and thus turns himself or herself in, the action is legally classified as *touan* rather than *zishou*. Under *touan* individuals in general neither qualify for the statutory definition of voluntary surrender and confession nor are entitled to judicial leniency. However, they may still be eligible to receive lenient treatment if they choose to cooperate totally with the authorities, honestly admit the facts of their crime, demonstrate sincere remorse, and perform meritorious service at the behest of the authorities.

In this regard, several early statutes provided plausible evidence for the importance of self-initiated surrender and the spontaneity of the confession and distinguished between the mere admission of a crime and the morally conscious confession of one's wrongdoing. Article 9 of the Temporary Statute on Punishing Crimes of Sabotaging Land Reform in the Jin-Ji-Lu-Yu Border Region (Shanxi-Hebei-Shandong-Henan), for instance, provided that "anyone has the right to reveal crimes enumerated in this statute. Persons who voluntarily reported and confessed to crimes which have not been revealed by others are entitled to a remission or reduction of their penalty under this law."[28] "A person who voluntarily surrendered but did not confess completely is punishable for the proportion of the disclaimed crime."[29] The Statute on Punishing Counterrevolution in the PRC specified that only those counterrevolutionaries who "(1) spontaneously, sincerely, and voluntarily surrendered to the People's Government and penitently confessed and/or (2) sincerely want to expiate by performing meritorious service to atone for their crimes are entitled to a lenient, reduced, or remitted penalty."[30] Clearly, the disposition of judicial leniency and amnesty are actually conditioned on an offender's willingness and spontaneity in cooperating fully with the authorities and in making a bona fide confession of moral or political wrongfulness.

We must keep in mind that under the Chinese tradition of a politically oriented judiciary, commission of a crime is regarded as not merely a violation of law but also an antagonistic rebellion against the state authorities. Voluntary surrender and confession undoubtedly hold symbolic meaning as evidence of the offender's initiative in complying with the authorities and in reemerging into the social mainstream and thus ought to be rewarded.[31] Nevertheless, an offender is not rewarded simply for admitting to the facts of the crime but for submitting himself or herself to the authorities' control so that the officially endorsed ethos can be maintained. By the same token, offenders who surrender under an official warrant and/or simply admit the facts of their crimes neither qualify for an exemption in adjudication nor are entitled to any consideration for judicial leniency.

It thus seems that the voluntary surrender and confession statute focuses merely on the offender's conscious desire to surrender rather than on the physical fact of the surrender. In other words, an offender's volition and spontaneity to submit himself or herself to the authorities are the essence of the statute. Physically turning oneself in as a result of compelling reasons or constraint from the authorities, such as an arrest warrant, is not generally considered as voluntary surrender except in the case where an offender has turned himself in under family pressure or constraints—that is, his parents ordered him to surrender.

To a certain degree, this exception contradicts the Confucian morality that family members should conceal each other's crimes. The Communist government encourages family members to report one another's crimes to the state authorities, which reflects its perplexity in dealing with family relationships. On the one hand, the Communists apparently departed from the Confucian tradition of family loyalty and filial piety by stressing the importance of the state authorities.[32] Although the family still plays a strong part in socialization and informal social control in China, the Communist government has degraded somewhat the value of the individual family unit and signifies that people as a whole in the socialist society should appeal to the higher loyalty of the state. On the other hand, the familist tradition, especially blood relationships within the family rather than individual performance, still plays an important role in class division and social, economic, and political disenfranchisements.

VOLUNTARINESS VERSUS COERCED SELF-INCRIMINATION

Since the promulgation of the Criminal Law of the PRC in 1979, the principles and practical guidelines for implementing the self-surrender clause have undergone major changes and, at the same time, raised a number of crucial questions concerning the truthfulness of the offender's confession and the validity of the promised rewards. There is little doubt that the law is self-incriminatory in nature. Nevertheless, morally speaking, if the law indeed attempts to encourage people to be honest and conscientious about their criminal wrongdoing, then such an attempt is morally justifiable. However, the problem lies not in the self-incriminatory nature of the voluntary surrender and confession law but rather in the legal procedures and mechanisms provided to safeguard the original attempt of the law. What the law intends to achieve might not always be the actual result. To be sure, if the voluntary confession becomes a standardized requirement for adjudication and conviction, the original intention of this law—being honest about one's wrongdoing and spontaneous in expressing one's shame over the misconduct—will be undermined if there are no basic legal procedures to assure spontaneity and truthfulness. For the Chinese legal system, self-confession is not just a procedural preference of law but literally a process of personal purification following moral impurity.

The legal encouragement to be honest about one's conduct is often undermined in reality for several reasons. First, voluntary confession has been utilized as a major weapon and an indispensable tactic for law enforcement agencies to crack down on various crime problems in China with unprecedented intensity. As a normative approach to combating crime problems, the Chinese judicial system, in cooperation with law enforcement agencies and municipal governments, periodically issues warrants to urge offenders to come forward to report their criminal wrongdoing. For instance, in 1982 the standing committee of the National People's Congress launched a nationwide campaign to urge offenders to surrender voluntarily by enacting a Resolution on Punishing Those Offenders Who Seriously Threaten the Economic Order.[33] On September 2, 1983, the same committee passed another resolution on Rigorously Punishing Those Offenders Who Seriously Disturb the Social Order.[34] Within twenty days after this resolution was made public, 31,000 offenders nationwide had surrendered voluntarily. This same type of decree was also issued by several municipal governments in the summer of 1986. During the first two months of that anticrime campaign, a total of 15,272 offenders had turned themselves in. With the information gathered from the offenders' confessions, the law enforcement agencies were able to solve 5,279 crimes reported to the police, clear an additional 1,903 cases either backlogged from or unsolved in previous years, and recover $388,000.[35] Undoubtedly, the voluntary surrender and confession decree provided considerable help for the government in cracking down on crime effectively and efficiently (see Table 6.1). Literally, it has become an aggressive tactic in every anticrime campaign.

On August 15, 1989, the People's Supreme Court and the People's Supreme Procurate jointly issued a Public Notice on the Statutory Limitation of Voluntary Surrender and Confession for Those Involved in Crimes of Embezzlement, Bribery, and Trading Fraud (cited hereafter as the Public Notice) due to increased public complaints about the widespread epidemics of these crimes that had severely disrupted the progress of economic reform and the newly transformed market-oriented economic order. Offenders were urged to come forward to confess within seventy-six days.[36] The result was overwhelming (see Table 6.2). According to an official report released in October 1990, nearly 36,000 offenders had voluntarily surrendered after the Supreme Court and the Supreme Procurate issued the Public Notice in August 1989. The immediate recovery of cash surrendered by the offenders totaled more than $111 million (633 million Chinese yuan). By the end of June 1990, 81 percent of the cases (45,000) investigated by the law enforcement agencies and the state prosecutor's offices, including both self-surrendered and captured, had reached judicial conclusion.[37]

Table 6.1
Number of Offenders Who Voluntarily Surrendered in Beijing by Type of Offense, June 1–August 20, 1986

Offense	Number of Offenders Who Surrendered
Murder	3
Rape/Sexual Assault	271
Robbery	158
Aggravated Assault	240
Arson	7
Theft	3,962
Narcotics	4
Fraud	277
Hooliganism	606
Other	9,744
Total	15,272

Source: Gan, Yupai, ed., *Special Edition on Criminal Law* (*Xing-fa-xue zhuan-lun*), p. 381. Beijing: Beijing University Press, 1989.

Table 6.2
Numbers of Offenders Who Surrendered within the Statutory Limitation

	8/31/89	9/15/89	10/15/89	10/31/89
Number of Offenders Who Surrendered	1,082	5,674	13,640	36,000
Cash Surrendered (US$ in millions)*	1.1	6.7	15.0	111.2

* The amount of money in this row indicates only the total cash surrendered by the offenders when they turned themselves in to the authorities; it does not reflect the total amount of money taken by the offenders during their alleged criminal activities.

Source: People's Daily, August 31, September 20, and October 17, 1989, and October 13, 1990.

From the official reports on the criminal investigations and trials we know that an offender's confession not only is considered essential evidence for reaching a legal conclusion but is also treated literally as a prerequisite condition for the verdict. The police and state procurators are required, first, to determine if the case is one of *zishou* (self-surrender before the official discovery of the crime or the suspect) or *touan* (surrender due to police pursuit) and, second, to verify the thoroughness and truthfulness of the confession. The state procurate is required to introduce the details of the defendant's spontaneity of surrender and confession to the court and to recommend a lesser sentence accordingly if the offender is judged to be a true confessor. Consequently, about 10 percent of the offenders receive amnesty in the form of nonadjudication when they voluntarily confess all the crimes they had committed and surrender their monetary profits from their alleged crimes of embezzlement, extortion, bribery, or trading fraud.[38]

But the more immediate question is how can the authorities be sure that an offender does not admit to more or less crime than he has actually committed? Contrary to the Western system, which bases truthfulness on the establishment of legal guilt through due process, the Chinese judicial system relies on the credibility of the judicial authorities by emphasizing factual guilt. In other words, it relies heavily on the judicial officers' accountability in affirming the truth of the confession and in determining the offender's sincerity in his repentance. That is to say, justice and truthfulness are guarded by the individual skill or perceptiveness of judicial officers in assessing the accuracy of a confession rather than secured by a designated adversarial process. To assist the authorities in discovering the truth and redistributing appropriate punishments and rewards, local and state governments and legal organs have set up various *jiefa jianju* ("crime-reporting") hotlines to gather information on the crime activities under investigation. The burden of proof is on the individual offender to convince the authorities that he has told the whole truth—no more, no less.

Furthermore, although the use of physical torture or coercion, including illegal detention, to obtain a confession is legally prohibited in China today,[39] evidence from various sources indicates that confessions coerced by means of physical torture and psychological intimidation remain a common and serious problem in the Chinese legal system. The problem, according to various reports from China, is far greater than isolated incidents; it is a widely acknowledged epidemic among law enforcement personnel. International human rights organizations, for instance, have alleged that Chinese prisoners or detainees are often mistreated with physical beatings, restraint, discomfort, or solitary confinement.[40]

The Chinese officials themselves have also admitted the existence of coerced confession through illegal means in their legal system. Government officials have admitted that during the first three months of 1990, government agencies received more than 9,500 complaints involving infringements on citizens' rights, the coercion of confession by torture or illegal detention, and the perversion of justice by means of bribes. Of these cases, 490 involved deaths and serious injuries of detainees or prisoners, a 60 percent increase over the previous year.[41] The Ministry of Public Security's internal investigation of 4,887 cases involving police violations of defendants' rights in 1987 reported that the rate of such violations consistently remained at the level of 7.6 per 1,000 police officers each year.[42] There is reason to speculate that the incidents revealed here are only the tip of the iceberg.

Although it is difficult to estimate accurately the extent and prevalence of confessions coerced by the police in the course of their criminal investigations, the data presented here indicate at least two important aspects. First, using physical torture or punitive measures to coerce an offender's confession is a persistent problem that essentially undermines the truth-finding mechanism of confession and the fair disposition of criminal punishment; and, second, officials have taken the initiative to crack down on such incidents by increasing training, education, and internal discipline. Evidently, referring to the traditional fashion of police interrogation tactics and the lawless state during the turmoil of the Cultural Revolution, even the official Chinese legal press has publicly acknowledged that

> the problem is extremely serious in certain areas and units, indeed it has virtually become a "chronic disease," giving the masses the false impression that if one merely enters a public security bureau one will inevitably be beaten up. How has it ever been possible for the extracting of confessions through torture to become such a "chronic disease"? In my view, the fundamental reason is the influence of feudal vestiges and the leftover tendencies from the Cultural Revolution.[43]

Official efforts to reduce such incidents further have encountered loopholes in the penal law and the criminal justice policy, which is geared toward maintaining order. The mass media frequently report citizens' complaints about the police illegally detaining suspects, obviously without any probable cause. For instance, as one aggressive tactic used during anticrime campaigns, police often round up masses of so-called "disruptive elements"—such as those who have had a criminal conviction, have received a suspended sentence or parole, have been involved in an earlier criminal investigation, or are reputed to be bad elements in the community—and lock them up in jail for an indefinite period of time for the purpose of investigative screening and peacekeeping.[44]

As cited in an Amnesty International report, the leadership in the Qiqihaer municipality of Heilongjiang Province "encouraged everyone to get stuck in and work boldly but some police officers wrongfully interpreted this to mean that they could move in with fists and feet." As a result, "in the criminal investigation section, the infliction of beating and corporal punishment upon offenders was fairly generalized."[45] As a matter of fact, the law gives police the discretion to detain any person for an indefinite period before he or she is actually identified as a crime suspect.[46] Undeniably, it is largely attributable to a loophole in the law. Arbitrary detention serves not only the ongoing criminal investigation but also the purpose of "temporary incapacitation."

In addition, this traditional style of law enforcement—under which crime suspects, witnesses, and even victims of crimes could be detained by the authorities for an indefinite period for the convenience of the ongoing criminal investigation—is profoundly inveterate among law enforcement personnel and local cadres. Interrogating suspects in police custody to obtain their confessions through intimidation, coercion, or even torture has been a traditional form of judicial work which was supported by the law and the state authorities. For example, one ex-prisoner's firsthand experiences with the police during two periods of detention in Shanghai are indicative of the police officers' attitudes toward arbitrary detention and an offender's presumed guilt. When he asked the officers what charges they had against him, they said, "You know in your head why you are here . . . you better tell the truth; the police station is not a place where you can question police but a place where suspects are questioned"[47]—their common response to detainees.

Coerced confession through illegal detention, intimidation, and torture is especially prevalent in local police forces. Police often trick detainees by promising to dismiss the charges if they confess to the crimes they are accused of. In fact, as discussed earlier, a suspect's confession made while in police custody neither qualifies him for *zishou* nor entitles him to a penalty reduction under the courts' interpretation of the voluntary surrender and confession statute. Coercing detainees to comply with the authorities is the ultimate goal of police investigation.

Political interference with justice matters often further opens the door for abuse of police power in the illegal detention and interrogation of crime suspects.

> Some illegal detentions were decided during an administrative meeting of local cadres; others were carried out after a nod of assent or with the tacit support of the head of the higher level of administration. In many cases, some cadres would give orders to police officers; some would participate in the back-room planning; some would personally tie up and beat the suspects, while others would take part in the interrogation.[48]

Consequently, ignorance of and bypassing the legal procedures on the part of the local cadres and law enforcement personnel frequently lead to wrongful accusations and convictions. The courts often have to throw out confessions obtained by the police because of obvious inconsistencies or the lack of sufficient evidence.[49]

VOLUNTARINESS AND THOUGHT REFORM IN PENAL INSTITUTIONS

China has one of the oldest penal institutions in the world. According to ancient legal documents, China began to use penal facilities to confine those found guilty of crime as early as 770 B.C.[50] As Western penologists have observed, Chinese penal institutions are not so much retributive or punitive, as in the West, but rather rehabilitative and self-sufficiency-oriented.[51] In an overview of the penological literature on the Chinese correctional system, perhaps nothing has drawn as much attention from the West as China's practice of rehabilitating offenders through thought and labor reform.[52] Consistent with the philosophy of moral self-internalization and self-discipline, voluntariness continues to be an important component in the thought and labor reform of offenders in China's penal institutions. The importance of an individual's willingness to atone for one's misdemeanors and thus surrender oneself to the social mainstream typically reflects the Chinese moral attitude toward those who are socially undesirable, deviant, and offensive to the social morality and rules of law. Winston Churchill once said that "the mood and temper of the public in regard to the treatment of crime and criminals is one of the unfailing tests of the civilization of any country."[53] Perhaps understanding the Chinese mood and temper with regard to the treatment of crime and criminal offenders by examining the moral and cultural grounds of voluntariness in corrections is the key to assessing fairly the social impact of thought and labor reform.

The Chinese correctional system consists of two components—the labor reform system (*laogai*), which confines adjudicated and convicted offenders, and the labor education system (*laojiao*), which is the civil disciplinary or administrative incarceration of those alleged offenders who were not adjudicated due to insufficient evidence. In defining the labor reform system's functions, the Statute of Labor Reform of the People's Republic of China states that "labor reform must combine with education of political thought so the forced labor will gradually transform to voluntary work and thus achieve the goal of remodeling inmates to new men (article 25)."[54] The same goal is also identified by the Trial Methods for Labor Education of 1982:

> [F]or those who are in labor education, [we] must implement guidelines of education, help and reform with emphasis on education and persuasion first and production and work second. Under restricted management, [they] shall become people who are self-disciplined, patriotic, [and] productive, [who] respect public morality and love to work with knowledge and working skills through deep and thorough efforts of political thought reform, vocational training, and working practice.[55]

Apparently, political education and labor are regarded as two parallel vehicles which essentially serve the purpose of rehabilitation.

Contrary to the Western idea of original sin, which is deeply rooted in the Judeo-Christian belief about human nature, Chinese society has largely accepted the Confucian belief in the intrinsic goodness and ability of man to pursue good virtues. Crime is viewed primarily as a result of bad influences from the social environment upon individuals—influences that can be changed through education and persuasion. The society, community, or group—such as the family—largely bears accountability for the individual's moral failure and behavioral defect. Generally speaking, Chinese society has relatively stronger faith in its ability to reform offenders, whether or not individuals are willing to conform themselves to the social morality. Therefore, rehabilitation is not what it is commonly understood to be in Western society—an alternative or option available to criminal offenders—but rather a mandatory process supported by mass sentiment and delegated to penal institutions on behalf of the entire society. Indisputably, the correctional process, through thought and labor reform, is forced upon individual offenders regardless of their personal willingness and faith in the reform. There is an apparent clash between the societal volition to reform those deemed to have deviated from social norms and the individual's choice to be deviant. According to the notion of Western penology, forced reform is undoubtedly an infringement on an individual's freedom to choose no matter what the consequences will be. But to the Chinese, because crime is regarded not only as the mischief of an individual but also as the failure of the group with which he or she is associated, the group or society at large is also determined to help the individual for both his own and the society's good, even though the individual might or might not appreciate such efforts. We must remember that China has always been a society oriented toward the collective interest, in which individual choice and freedom are traditionally regarded as morally inferior or even insignificant to the collective volition. Therefore, the rehabilitation of offenders is deemed not as an option for individual offenders but rather as society's inherent responsibility to rescue those people from drifting into moral malignancy.[56]

Furthermore, contrary to the common interpretation that voluntariness serves only as a means to attain the conviction and incarceration of those individuals identified by the authorities as undesirable and offensive, voluntariness is actually deemed not just as a means but as the ultimate goal of the justice system. The Chinese correctional authorities identify their ultimate goal as that of inspiring an offender's willingness to work and to comply with social morality, though the process may begin with compulsion through forced labor and thought reform. As stated by the Chinese correctional authorities in 1952,

> in the process of forced labor work upon offenders, [we] must spontaneously impose vigorous discipline and frequent education . . . to inspire the offender's consciousness of self-reform through work and to [enable him to] become a new person. . . . To reform an offender through labor work, it first must be mandatory so he can be changed spiritually from semi-voluntary reform through working to complete voluntariness. This is a process of struggle from compulsion to voluntariness.[57]

There is little doubt that making a living through one's diligent and honest work is highly valued by the Chinese cultural tradition. To teach offenders such a value system is one of the primary functions of the penal institutions. Although working skills are universally considered to be necessary in enhancing one's ability to work during the postrelease phase, an individual's willingness to work is regarded by the Chinese as even more vital because inmates will eventually return to the environment where they once had failed to conform to the social mainstream. Whether they can resist the bad influences of their environment is determined not by their ability to work but by their habits and willingness to work. As vividly described by the Chinese correctional authorities, "without such voluntariness to repent for one's past mischiefs and willingness to work, the rehabilitation of offenders would be like offering water without a source and planting trees without roots."[58]

Finally, in line with the judicial system's initial attempts to encourage offenders to be honest and repentant about their crimes, the correctional institutions continue to pursue such goals through self-criticism and voluntary confession. The correctional authorities systematically launch thought reform with enormous intensity and on a large scale. This reform comprises seven programs: (1) political education, such as the four principles of adherence; (2) legal education, including understanding the law and the causes and consequences of crime; (3) moral education about the goals of one's life and the means used to achieve them; (4) education regarding the importance of work and discipline; (5) education about government policies on the future and remedies during the postrelease phase; (6) academic education at the high school and college levels; and (7) work skills training.[59]

Participation in all these programs is mandatorily enforced regardless of the type of offenses of which an offender was convicted. Punishments and rewards are utilized as enforcement agents by the authorities through the parole and sentencing reduction system. Primarily, an individual's eligibility for parole or a reduced sentence is decided not by an inmate's "good-time credits"—as occurs in the United States—but rather by whether he demonstrated (1) repentance during his incarceration and (2) a sense that he would not harm society again.[60] Apparently, simply obeying the rules of a correctional institution and participating in a reform program are insufficient to qualify for parole or a reduced sentence. It is obviously a goal of the Chinese correctional system to bring about a change of heart and mind among criminal offenders.[61] Thus, voluntariness in the correctional process is more or less a goal of reform rather than a means to justify an individual's incarceration.

THE MORAL LEGITIMACY OF VOLUNTARINESS IN CHINESE CULTURE

An interesting issue closely related to the implementation of the voluntary surrender and confession law is how the Chinese people perceive the moral legitimacy and social justification of this self-incriminatory law. In the previous discussion, we have seen that voluntariness has numerous meanings in Chinese society. First, it is a vehicle for individuals to internalize a morally approved value system.

For example, a unique—but at the same time controversial—characteristic of Chinese police work is the so-called "study sessions" held for crime suspects who are in police custody as part of either an ongoing investigation or a campaign to incapacitate disruptive elements temporarily. All suspects, whether they surrendered or were captured, must participate in endless study sessions to morally realize the seriousness of their criminal wrongdoing and the wrongfulness of their greed, brutality, lack of compassion, selfishness, and so on. Although the penal law has never mandated that offenders must atone for their moral faults for the case to reach a legal conclusion, the Chinese legal system actually pursues the moral repentance of offenders while implementing the voluntary surrender and confession law.[62] The purposes of participating in the study sessions are frequently twofold: On the one hand, the police present their version of the facts of the crime to the suspects and insist on the latter's admission; on the other hand, the interrogative staff repeatedly inculcates official opinions and value systems about what is right, what is wrong, why it is wrong, and how it can be corrected. If the former purpose can be seen as an official, legal duty of the police investigation, then the latter is a completely moral inculcation that is not mandated by the law.

But why do we so often observe that nearly all the personnel in the Chinese legal system—from the police investigators to the prosecutors, the trial judges,[63] and the correctional officers[64]—spontaneously and persistently impose such moral persuasion and political education upon offenders? Perhaps this type of moral persuasion is unique to the Communist legal system or maybe it is the continuation of the Chinese tradition, which emphasizes a moral internalization that devolves from the entire society to the legal system. Contrary to Western culture, in which individual rights and mental independence are highly respected, Chinese society—throughout its history—has valued overwhelmingly the individual's obligation to his fellow men and the psychological interdependence between the individual and the group. All individuals, especially those in positions of authority, are obligated to scrutinize their moral well-being as well as their fellow men's moral purity. In a purely ethical sense, the judicial officers' duty to persuade criminal offenders morally is self-defined, self-contained, and spontaneously performed even though there is no official requirement for them to engage in such persuasive activities. Every person in Chinese society has the responsibility to persuade others morally by telling them what is right and what is wrong, including law enforcement and judicial personnel. Perhaps it is fair to say that justice officials have an even stronger sense of responsibility and moral consciousness because of their official role of order maintenance in Chinese society.

Second, self-confession, or self-criticism, is important in alleviating the antagonistic relationship between the insurrectionist elements and the authorities. It symbolizes the desire of rebelling individuals to become reintegrated into the community. For the Chinese people, criminal conduct implies more than just breaking the rules of law; such conduct is often regarded by society as an insurgent act against the state authority and as a retrogradation of the normal relationship between the ruler and the ruled. Therefore, an offender's voluntary surrender and confession serve a symbolic meaning in initiating a process of alleviating the disruption and integrating himself back into society. The social meaning of an offender's initiative to surrender and confess is just as important for the authorities as it is for the offender himself. For the former, when the rules of law are violated by individuals, their dignity is also threatened and must be restored, either by punishment of the violator or through the violator's initiative in submitting himself to the authorities—in a sense to save the face of the authorities. For individual offenders, spontaneously surrendering themselves to the authorities would, first, entitle them to judicial leniency or a possible pardon for the crime committed and, second, show their willingness to comply with the social disapproval about law breaking. Psychologically speaking, self-confession is just as beneficial for the offenders themselves as it is for the authorities' pride.

Third, self-confession is undoubtedly an instrument by which the authorities implement mandatory thought reform and political correction. Although self-confession is legally defined as a voluntary act, it often becomes procedurally indispensable in the course of the police interrogation, the adjudicatory process, and corrections. For instance, participating in study sessions while in police detention is mandated regardless of whether the offender chose to confess or proclaimed his innocence. In other words, in addition to confessing to his past misdeeds, an offender must also confess to the sinfulness of his criminal conduct and criticize himself. Apparently, moral persuasion, or thought reform, not only is prevalent throughout the system but is also coerced regardless of the offender's willingness. Offenders are frequently forced to participate in endless political study sessions and to consider the official version of the facts of their crimes as well as political opinions on the right or wrong of their alleged criminal violations as presented to them by the authorities.[65] On the one hand, the law perhaps intends to encourage the spontaneity of an offender's confession; on the other hand, the legal system not only necessitates confession according to the official version of the facts but also often coerces offenders into repenting to prove the spontaneity of their confession. Therefore, a voluntary confession may not be voluntary at all.

It is true that thought reform in both the Chinese legal system and Chinese society as a whole is ubiquitous and compulsory.[66] It is equally true that reforming people—making "new men"—is regarded as an important mission of the Chinese Communist government. To some Western observers, coerced thought reform is, no doubt, a violation of the right to choose a moral rationale freely.[67] But this criticism is as much politically prejudicial as it is culturally superficial. It is indisputable that the Communist government is a totalitarian state which imposes political corrections. But, coincidentally, forced moral persuasion has also been long honored by a Chinese tradition which has little connection to the Communist ideology. Morally, the Chinese people as a whole do not view such coerced participation in study sessions as a violation of an offender's rights. Rather, if a person is accused of doing something wrong, he has both the social and legal obligation to help the authorities clear his name regardless of whether he has actually committed a criminal act. Socially, the Chinese people also anticipate that the legal authorities take responsibility for reeducating, reforming, and exhorting those who either rationally choose to defy the social mainstream or mistakenly commit a moral fault when other social agencies—such as the family, school, peer group, or guild—have failed to redirect them.[68] No matter how Western commentators view the Chinese style of thought reform politically and ethically—either as "totalism of human change,"[69] "brainwashing,"[70] or "thought control"[71]—all agree that it seems to be an "all-powerful, irresistible, unfathomable, and magical method for achieving total control over the human mind."[72] After all, it may not be so much justice with Communist style as it is justice with Chinese characteristics. Although we have no empirical data that quantitatively measure the effectiveness of such coerced thought reform, we do know that its long practice in Chinese history provides cultural comfort, enabling the society to tolerate this type of coerced thought reform for criminal offenders. For the Chinese, thought reform is a means not just for adjudicating those accused of criminal wrongdoing by the authorities but also for changing the hearts and minds of the accused.

FINAL REMARKS

To summarize, the voluntary surrender and confession clause in Chinese penal law and in the statutes of corrections not only has its historical roots in the imperial tradition of law and adjudication but also carries social and moral legitimacy among the Chinese people. Theoretically, the principle of voluntariness intends to encourage honesty and spontaneity among offenders by promising a tempting reward to those who choose to cooperate with the authorities in restoring social peace and order. The societal view on crime and law violators gives the authorities additional moral legitimacy to take measures to coerce confessions and press for repentance. It is important to keep in mind that Chinese law is largely moralistic in nature. Its implementation often yields to public pressure and, therefore, may be skewed toward social peace and order at the expense of individual rights to freedom of choice, which are viewed as the essence of human rights in Western culture. The call for voluntary surrender and confession becomes compulsory due to social pressure and the traditional view of rights and the duties of individuals and government officials. Essentially, voluntariness in Chinese law, which to Western jurists may be totally unacceptable because it goes against the concepts of presumed innocence and due process, is nevertheless regarded by the Chinese as the ultimate goal of social justice. With that goal in mind, of encouraging offenders to repent and to be reintegrated into the social mainstream, it is not too difficult to understand why "voluntary" surrender and confession under the Chinese legal system may not be voluntary after all.

NOTES

1. For major criticisms of self-surrender and self-confession, see Bassiouni, 1971, p. 189; Cohen, 1968, pp. 341–42; and Rickett, 1971.

2. See Article 63, Section 3, on voluntary surrender in *The Criminal Law and the Criminal Procedure Law of the People's Republic of China*, 1984, for the textual content.

3. The People's Republic of China is not the only Asian country which has a provision for voluntary surrender and confession in its criminal law. Taiwan and Japan, among others, also have adopted this principle in their penal laws. For example, see the *Criminal Code of Japan*, 1954, Section 7, Article 42.

4. Wilson, 1981, p. 1.

5. For a comprehensive discussion of the importance of moral persuasion in Chinese society, see Lifton, 1989; Rickett, 1971; Rickett and Rickett, 1981; and Yu, 1964.

6. These bamboo strips were found in December 1975 in the coffin of tomb no. 11 located in the Shuihu di area of the Xiaogan District in central Hubei Province. The texts belonged to Xi, a prefectural clerk of the Qin Dynasty (Hsi, 262 B.C.–?), and comprised adjudicatory records, including penal rules and administrative journals. For an annotated translation of the texts of all the strips, see Hulsewé, 1985.

7. Gong, 1989, p. 371. This quotation is translated from the original Chinese text. For another English translation, see Hulsewé's translation, 1985, p. 173. For a further discussion of self-surrender and confession in Qin law, see Pu and Zhou, 1987, pp. 58–59.

8. "Xingfa Zhi" in *Han Shu*, 1962, edition with punctuation.

9. McKnight, 1981, p. 43.

10. The Tang Code was promulgated in 653. It was originally called *Tang Lü* and later changed to *Tang Lü Shuyi* during the Song Dynasty (960–1279). This title is still in use today. This code contains twelve volumes with 502 items. See W. Johnson, 1979, for an introduction to and translation of the original texts.

11. Ibid., Article 39.

12. Ibid., Articles 13–15.

13. Bodde, 1973, pp. 511–12.

14. As a matter of fact, the Qin legal bamboo strips had already recorded various penalties for officers who failed to verify the truthfulness of an offender's confession. See the translation of strips nos. 35–39 in Hulsewé, 1985, pp. 130–31.

15. The Tang Code, Article 37. See also Needham, 1956b, p. 193.

16. The ten abominations, which varied slightly from dynasty to dynasty, were first categorized by the Northern Qi State (550–557) as the following, in order from most to least severe:

1. plotting rebellion;
2. plotting sedition against the authorities;
3. treason;
4. violent crime against family members;
5. slaughtering more than three people from the same family, or killing and dismembering a body for superstitious reasons;
6. sacrilege against the emperor, an ancestor, or clan property;
7. impiety against the paterfamilias or senior family members;
8. murder or assault of relatives or husband, or disclosing a husband's or family member's crime to the authorities;
9. killing officers, masters, teachers, or superiors, or a widow's impiety such as her absence from her husband's funeral or remarriage during the mourning period; and
10. incest.

For further discussion of the statutory texts of and punishments for the ten abominations, see P. H. Chen, 1979, pp. 4, 47, and 62; W. Johnson, 1979, pp. 17–18; C. Kim, 1982a, p. 336; McKnight, 1981, p. 60; and Shen, 1985, pp. 41–44 and 183–87.

17. See Griffin, 1976, pp. 184–84, for the translation. This statute was originally promulgated by the Nationalist government in November 1937 and later adopted by the Communist government, with an introduction by the Shansi-Chahar-Hopei Border Administrative Committee, on January 15, 1941.

18. For a discussion of the early application of self-surrender and confession by the Chinese Communist government from 1930 to 1970, see Rickett, 1971, pp. 803–13.

19. For the textual content of the statutes of the Chinese Communist government, see Griffin, 1976, Appendices A, B, and G, pp. 155–67 and 181–83.

20. Ibid., pp. 181–83.

21. Pu and Zhou, 1987, p. 522.

22. For further discussion of these self-criticism sessions during the Five-Antis Campaign and the results of this movement, see Spence, 1990, pp. 535–40.

23. See ibid., pp. 563-70, for a detailed discussion of the Anti-Rightists Movement and the campaign against the intellectual class in the 1950s.

24. Gao, 1987, p. 100.

25. This clause is called zishou ("self-surrender"). Although the word tanbai ("confession") did not appear in the text of the penal law, it is a step that naturally follows the surrender of the offender.

26. *The Criminal Law and the Criminal Procedure Law of the People's Republic of China*, 1984, p. 27.

27. Gan, 1989, p. 379.

28. The Temporary Statute on Punishing Crimes of Sabotaging Land Reform in the Jin-Ji-Lu-Yu Border Region (Jin-ji-lu-yu bian-qu po-huai tu-di-gai-ge zhi-zui zhan-xing tiao-li), January 15, 1948. See Pu and Zhou, 1986, pp. 523–24, for further discussion of the implementation of this statute in the 1940s.

29. The Temporary Statute on Punishing Traitors Who Collaborated with the Japanese (Hanjian) in the Shuwan Border Region (Shu-wan bain-qu cheng-zhi pan-guo-zui-fan zhan-xin tiao-li), December 1945. See ibid.

30. See Article 14 of the Statute on Punishing Counterrevolution in the PRC (Zhonghua renming gongheguo chengzhi fangeming tiaoli), February 21, 1951.

31. It should be pointed out that the penal law of the PRC provides no specific restrictions on sentencing reduction for those who voluntarily surrender and confess to the crime. Therefore, all criminal offenders, even those whose crimes are subject to life imprisonment or the death penalty, theoretically are eligible for judicial leniency.

32. The concept of *nation* in the Chinese language means "the family of the country." Traditionally, the country was considered as an enlarged family unit in which the emperor and governmental authorities are the parents who maintain order, and the citizenry are the children who serve and obey orders from the top.

33. "Chinese Legal System," *China Legal Daily* (*Zhongguo Fazhi Bao*), April 16, 1982.

34. *Hebei Law Review* (*Hebei Faxue*), no. 2, 1984.

35. Gan, 1989, p. 381.

36. If we pay a little more attention to the temporal frequency of anticrime campaigns in China, we notice that summer is always the peak period for law enforcement agencies and the judicial system to make massive moves on criminal elements. The massive arrests of alleged offenders or the large scale of self-surrender warrants frequently occur before October 1, the national holiday commemorating the anniversary of the People's Republic of China. The seventy-six-day period is precisely calculated from August 15 to October 31, 1989.

37. "Prosecutory Priority in Next Year: Advancement of Anti-Embezzlement, Corruption, and Bribery," 1990.

38. Ibid.

39. According to Article 136 of *The Criminal Law and the Criminal Procedure Law of the People's Republic of China* (1984, p. 48):

> The use of torture to coerce a statement is strictly prohibited. State personnel who inflict torture on an offender to coerce a statement are to be sentenced to not more than three years of fixed-term imprisonment or criminal detention. Whoever causes a person's injury or disability through corporal punishment is to be handled under the crime of injury and given a heavier punishment.

Article 32 of *The Criminal Law and the Criminal Procedure Law of the People's Republic of China* contains the same restriction (1984, p. 124).

40. Asian Watch Committee, 1990, pp. 25–40.

41. Schweisberg, 1990.

42. *People's Daily*, October 5, 1988. The Ministry of Public Security was satisfied with this rate. Of course, the figures given by the public security officials were only for those cases serious enough to warrant an official investigation, such as torture resulting in death or physical disability. We have neither data on the prevalence of unreported and dismissed cases nor other sources of information to verify the official version of the statistics.

43. *China Legal Daily*, May 31, 1985; cited in Asian Watch Committee, 1990, p. 33.

44. For example, nearly a thousand people were detained after the crackdown on the pro-democracy movement on June 4, 1989. Gao Xin, a newspaper editor, was detained 185 days by the police under suspicion of plotting counterrevolution and then released without any charges, even though the law requires that a suspect must be interrogated within twenty-four hours and released immediately if there is no probable cause to warrant a valid indictment (see Articles 44, 50, and 51 of *The Criminal Law and the Criminal Procedure Law of the People's Republic of China* for additional references). Police simply told him that the investigation had been completed and he was free to go (reported in *China Morning Post*, September 23, 1989). For the names of the 903 people arrested and/or detained for investigative purposes after June 4, 1989, see also *China Spring*, 101 (1991): 1–16.

45. Amnesty International, 1987, p. 5.

46. Article 41 of *The Criminal Law and the Criminal Procedure Law of the People's Republic of China*, 1984, p. 127. In China the public security bureaus (police) have discretion that is considerably broader and greater than that of American law enforcement agencies. For example, police in China can imprison a crime suspect even if they lack sufficient evidence to warrant an official arrest and prosecution. In another case, police, with the approval of a supervisory committee, also have the power to incarcerate misdemeanants or crime suspects in labor reform camps for as long as three years without going through the adjudicatory process, although this type of penalty is officially called an administrative rather than a criminal penalty. No doubt so much police discretion provides alternatives for the police to sidestep legal procedures in those cases where they believe the offender is guilty of a crime but cannot gather sufficient evidence to secure a prosecution.

47. "It Is Worrisome When the Country Does Not Follow the Law," *China Spring*, 3 (1991): 37–39.

48. *Democracy and Legal System*, 1986.

49. Ibid.

50. Shen Jiaoben, a prominent jurist in the Qing Dynasty, documented that the earliest prison, called *xiatai* and considered no harm to prisoners, was established during the Xia Dynasty. During the Zhou Dynasty, *xiatai* was renamed as *ling-yu*. *Ling* confined people and forced them to be introspective about their wrongdoing. *Yu* means to change the heart of a

person from wickedness, which is the reason for misdeeds, to benevolence. See Shen, 1988, pp. 234–35.

51. Allen, 1987a, pp. 78–79; and E. H. Johnson, 1984, pp. 143–44.

52. Ironically, criticism of China's procedures for rehabilitating offenders through thought reform and labor was as loud as the plaudits from Western penologists. On the one hand, Western observers were impressed with China's efforts at moral cultivation to help inmates internalize social norms and introspect their past mischiefs. On the other hand, coerced participation in self-criticism and study sessions has the connotation for many Western penologists of political "brainwashing" associated with the Communist dictatorship. In a similar way, the economic productivity and self-sufficiency of Chinese penal institutions, on the one hand, generate a considerable temptation to those nations which face tremendous economic burdens and total failure in their efforts to reform criminal offenders; on the other hand, forced labor for profit brings back painful memories of the exploitation of prison labor once facilitated by the Western penal system.

53. Quoted by Neier, 1976, p. 135.

54. Statute of Labor Reform of the People's Republic of China, September 7, 1954, in Wang et al., 1989, pp. 1577–82.

55. Trial Methods for Labor Education, January 21, 1982, in Wang et al., 1989, p. 1583; my translation.

56. As Rickett and Rickett pointed out, "as for the Chinese people as a whole, the only force exerted on them is the pressure of public opinion" (1981, p. 325). Perhaps this pressure exists in every society. Nevertheless, no one has given as much weight to social conscience as the Chinese do in dealing with those individuals who are judged as not conforming to social norms.

57. *Report to First National Conference of Corrections*, 1952, in K. T. Li, 1986, pp. 72–73. This general belief certainly reflects Mao Zedong's philosophy that society must take an aggressive and forceful approach to thought reform, either in general or directed at criminals in order to strengthen the moral mentality of the working class. Mao once said that "truth, virtue, and beauty are always struggling with falsehood, evil, and ugliness in order to survive and advance." See Mao, 1970, vol. 5, p. 390.

58. Xiu et al., 1983, pp. 34–35.

59. See K. T. Li, 1986, for a more detailed discussion of these seven programs.

60. Section 2 of The People's Supreme Court's Memorandum on Procedure and Criteria in Granting Sentencing Reduction and Parole, February 2, 1988, in Wang et al., 1989, pp. 158–59.

61. Undeniably, the determination of one's sincerity about repentance and an assessment of one's probability of recidivism are subjective. It is up to the individual correctional officers and the members of the parole board to decide, based on oral and written confessions regarding one's past misdeeds—whether known or unknown to the authorities—and a self-assessment of the roots of one's criminal conduct.

62. For the official Chinese interpretation of the essential principles of the self-surrender and confession law, see Gong, 1989, pp. 370–418.

63. Many observers of the Chinese legal system have noticed that a trial judge in the Chinese judiciary often makes a general statement of socialist morality before the verdict is announced. The statement often includes criticism of the offender's misconduct as well as expressions of social disapproval and disappointment on behalf of the offender's family and the government.

64. Correctional officers' duty regarding moral persuasion is discussed in this chapter.

65. For many Western commentators this type of political study represents psychological torture, especially if the offenders are political prisoners. But for other commentators, the political study session reflects the longstanding Chinese tradition of moral internalization, especially for those who are deemed to be confused, deviant, or too morally weak to control their behavior. For a discussion of thought reform, see Rickett and Rickett, 1981. For further discussion on the study sessions for alleged counterrevolutionaries following the pro-democracy movement in 1989, see Asian Watch Committee, 1990, p. 35. For the psychological impact of coerced thought reform, see Lifton, 1989.

66. Compulsory thought reform in the Chinese prison system was discussed extensively by Rickett and Rickett, 1981.

67. See Rickett and Rickett's discussion of the Western interpretation of a person's free will in choosing the moral rationale (1981, pp. 323–25).

68. Our discussion here focuses exclusively on common criminal offenders. Political offenders constitute a different issue, which has been discussed in Chapter 5.

69. In Lifton's opinion (1989, pp. 438–61), the general approach to human changes includes four agencies: coercion, exhortation, therapy, and realization. These agencies are by no means mutually exclusive, however; each conveys a distinct message, a specific goal, and an appeal to a particular aspect of human nature. The totalist model of human change—such as the Chinese Communist model—utilizes all four agencies but leans heavily toward the first two.

70. "Brain-washing" was first used by Edward Hunter (1951) as a translation of the Chinese colloquialism *xi nao* (literally "wash the brain").

71. W. C. Jones, 1977, pp. 219–26.

72. See Lifton, 1989. In comparing moral persuasion in the judicial system—including both police investigative and court adjudicatory processes—with thought reform in the prison system, the latter is much more systematic and intensive. However, it should be pointed out that the reform of an offender's thoughts in Chinese society is a continuous mission of the criminal justice system and the social responsibility of every officer of the legal system, including the defense attorney.

CONCLUSION

Chinese Law under a Socialist Mantle

IN CONTEMPORARY social control theories many scholars have blatantly demonstrated their contempt for the state's proactive role in ordering human behavior and shaping the political order. For decades social control theorists in the West have constrained their political thrust and thus become less structurally and more social-psychologically centered around the individual socialization process. That is, they have become more concerned with the socialization process, by which individuals are induced into becoming, on the one hand, somewhat willing participants in social conformity or, on the other hand, deviants against established societal rules. For these theorists, the state comes to play a role in the drama of social control only if the individual's "informal" control faculties have failed to conform with the standardized rules and have broken away from the established boundary of social norms.

The state's role in social control is more or less like a reactive bouncer, pushing and punching drifters back to where they are supposed to be. Under this model of social control, the "official"—or "formal"—control is viewed either as compensating for the individual's failure to participate willingly in the social order or as repressing the disadvantaged. For Western societies such as the United States, the admiration of individualism and the ubiquity of privatization, of course, hint at the diminished or minimized direct role of the state in the social control mechanism.[1] Therefore, such an individualism-centered, social-psychological approach in understanding social deviance and its control is a natural reflection of its very own culture.

The state in China, on the contrary, has demonstrated a strong will in ordering Chinese society. Under this model, the state's obligation to preserve social harmony and conformity goes far beyond the conventionally defined state's role in controlling the behavior of individuals. Instead, the role of the state in China has long extended from behavioral conformity to "mind uniformity" through the state's penetration into social fabrics such as the family, school, media, political parties, and various associations and organizations. Minimized economic privatization in socialist China has been, no doubt, a crucial reason for the direct and proactive role of the state in ordering the Chinese people and society. Unfortunately, this unique model of social control is often judged as being culturally inferior and politically incorrect because such a model is associated with socialist authoritarianism and is directly against individualism—highly honored and respected in the Western culture.

This study, as outlined in Chapter 1, began by characterizing law and morality in the Chinese tradition. China's struggle for legalization began during the seventh century B.C., during the so-called "Greatest Intellectual Contention" between the Legalist and the Confucian schools. The Legalists' premise—"ruling by law"—was surprisingly close to the notions developed much later by the school of positivist law in the West. Unfortunately, the vast bureaucratic government structure invented by Legalism did not prevent the ouster of its own architects. The Confucian notion of *Li*—moral code—was far more flexible, humanitarian, naturalistic, and amicable than the formality, rigidity, and cruelty of law advocated by the Legalist school.

Following the Confucianization of law during the Han Dynasty, *Li* seemed to belittle the Legalist attempt at positivist law. It was said that China then entered a realm of "government by man"[2] because *Li* was more or less a moral code, not law, and because it was only "enforced by society," not by the government.[3] It is true that Chinese traditional law had a strong moralistic character. The Confucian moral code was incorporated into the formally written law under the notion of *chunqiu jueyu* and was vigorously enforced by both the society and the government.

The core notion in understanding Chinese traditional law and morality is familism. Clan/family law worked hand in hand with state law to make people conform to social norms of behavior and to internalize familial values, such as respecting patriarchal authority, admiring seniority,[4] and obeying political superiors. A person's obligations to his or her family, clan, guild, or community were regarded as natural and superior to individual rights and freedoms. With such moral cultivation, "Chinese well habituated to the family system have been prepared to accept similar patterns of status in other institutions, including the official hierarchy of the government."[5]

Chapter 2 dealt with general characteristics of criminal penalties and official control in traditional China. Self-surrender and confession, differential treatment of offenders, collective punishment, and suppression against political deviants best exemplified the state's strong will and familial rules in rendering punishment against undesirable behaviors and thoughts. The most striking feature of those official measures against deviance was the Confucian discovery about the importance of the mental faculties of men in directing and controlling their acts. For Confucius, a person's will was not free and could be constrained through hierarchically designated social bonds, morally internalized obligations, and kinships; and the state vigorously enforced standardized rules. Behavioral conformity and thought uniformity were not free choices left to an individual's decision but, rather, constituted a vigorously coerced social order and represented the state's active participation in moral cultivation and behavioral and mind control.

Undeniably, old ideas and attitudes about the state's authority and the role of law continue to exert their influence in social control, even in post-Maoist China. Chapter 3 examined this continuity of the old ideas and values regarding political superiors, the state, the judiciary, and the role of law. Despite the radical changes in political ideology following the 1949 socialist revolution, Chinese tradition persistently exerted its influence on Mao's revolutionary agenda. Although Mao rebelled against the humanitarian character of Confucianism, he openly expressed his admiration for the violent and brutal suppressive functions of law and the legal machinery that were once zealously advocated by the Legalists. Unfortunately, he did not move in the direction of positivist law as an admirer of Legalism. Instead, he inherited more from Confucianism. Primarily, he carefully and zealously guarded the superior power of the Communist Party over all facets of China's affairs.[6]

Therefore, judicial power became just a subsidiary instrument of the Communist Party's political power in achieving the solidarity of the global Communist utopia, even though judicial independence was constitutionally guaranteed. Of course, this normative and routine interference of political power with the judiciary would have been impossible without constitutional and organizational protection. The minimized judicial independence in China was a direct result of the Party's political manipulation in establishing its unshakable leadership in the Constitution, recruiting judicial officials exclusively from the Party, and upholding the supremacy of Party policy over the law. China may appear to have a system of Marxist-Communist totalitarianism. But what China has practiced is also a continuation of Chinese authoritarianism. Without essential changes in the judicial structure and without the removal from the Constitution of the clause regarding the one-party ruling status of the Communist Party, the modernization of law and the legal system in China is but a mirage.

The remaining three chapters approached the state's active participation in planned and programmed social control through a legal analysis of three issues that best exemplify the convergence and divergence of Chinese tradition and Marxism-Maoism. The discussion began by examining class division and equality before the law in Mao Zedong's philosophy regarding the individual in relation to the family, the Communist Party, and the state authority. As is pointed out in Chapter 4, the arbitrary division of political-social classes in China not only served as a political instrument for reshaping social relationships for the purpose of building a new society; it also set a general tone for implementing "differentialism" in official control to distinguish the ruling and the ruled. The notion of "class" symbolizes a political status rather than a socioeconomic one and has its ideological foundation in the familist tradition. Throughout Chapter 4, we see, on the one hand, the attempt by the new generation of the Party elite to minimize unequal treatment before the law and, on the other hand, its inability to overcome the persistence of the familist and hierarchical traditions deeply ingrained in the minds of the Chinese people.

China's treatment of political dissidents and ideological aliens best exemplifies the state's role in extended social control goals through the stipulation of legal statutes, such as the counterrevolutionary crime clause in Chinese penal law. An examination of the history of counterrevolutionary crime under Communist law and the inherent dilemma in law enforcement grounded the discussion in Chapter 5. As stated at the beginning of the chapter, my intention was not to criticize the political totalitarianism of the Chinese leaders, which is most prominent in this area, but rather to look at the function of counterrevolutionary crime in the Chinese style of social control, that is, the control of both behavior and the mind. Unfortunately, vigorous suppression of political opponents by the state is not unique to the Communist government. Throughout China's history of official control, free will or an independent or innovative mind has always been subject to legal sanctions, even under the non-Communist and non-Marxist regimes.

The vigorous suppression of ideological and political opponents not only aims to prevent rebellious acts against the current political order, but is also viewed as an important part of the state-programmed and -coerced moral internalization of the people. To a degree, the Chinese embody the state's power in behavioral conformity and thought uniformity. While positivist criminologists have introduced biopsychological and social determinism into the etiology of crime and deviance, the Chinese, inspired by Confucius, have realized the important relationship between conduct and the mind and the possible external manipulation of the mind through internalization and coerced brainwashing. These practices are, indeed, a remarkable attempt at social control—if we disregard the political criticism toward China's ongoing measures against political dissidents. Whether China should abandon such legal practices against those who dare to be original and challenge the authorities probably depends on the total acceptance of the idea of free will among the Chinese people.

The issue of voluntariness in Chinese law and morality, which is related to the state's role in social control, centered the discussion in Chapter 6. Specifically, voluntary surrender and confession have been viewed as the boldest faults in Chinese law and the administration of justice. The principle of voluntariness goes directly against the principle of presumed innocence and the idea of due process. But it is the legacy of the Chinese legal tradition and still bears a certain moral legitimacy in defining the self-containment of right from wrong. For legal scholars brought up under the idea of presumed innocence and formally established due process, voluntary surrender and confession are faults in procedure that obviously give the state an advantage over individuals. But for the Chinese, voluntariness serves dual functions in the pursuit of social justice: On the one hand, it serves as a legal means for reaching the legal conclusion of a case; on the other hand, it serves the end of justice—making an effort at personal repentance and a return to the social mainstream. Symbolically, it is not just an admission of a violation of law but also a resubmission to the authorities. Technically speaking, legal guilt is not as important as factual guilt. Obviously, since personal willingness to repent becomes the foremost goal in adjudication, voluntary confession, of course, may not be "voluntary" at all. Very often, even though legally admissible evidence is sufficient to reach a legal conclusion, the defendant's admission of guilt is, nevertheless, a must in the judicial process. Interestingly enough, official efforts to obtain a defendant's admission of guilt do not stop at the guilty verdict; they continue into the correctional phases. Self-criticism and self–thought reform characterize the official intention to change both the behavior and the heart of the individual.

After examining these four legal issues in contemporary Chinese law, we can conclude that there is a remarkable convergence between China's traditional values regarding the state's role and capability in social control and the Marxist-socialist idea about proletarian suppression against the reactionary classes. When some scholars look at the institutional and legislative landscape in socialist China, they quickly jump to the conclusion that the attitude of the Chinese Communists toward law "has no connection with either the Chinese traditional attitude or the system introduced from the West. . . . Chinese communist law . . . is an application in China of a system derived from Communist doctrine and the practice of the Soviet Union."[7] Unfortunately, such scholars fail to see how Chinese traditional values and attitudes toward the role of law and the state have provided enormous moral and psychological preparation to help the Communist state leaders mobilize the social and economic resources for inculcating Marxist ideology and reshaping social relations.

There is no doubt that in a social control process, the individual plays an important role in internalizing norms and merging with the social mainstream. However, exogenous factors—such as the state—can also exert strong influences by either reinforcing official norms or weakening the individual's involvement in internalization. Of course, the lack of an individualist tradition and the minimized privatization in economics and social lives are essential preconditions that allow the Chinese state a strong role in the social control process.

As China moves ahead with economic reform and the modernization of its political and legal system, the state's traditional role in coercing behavioral conformity and ideological uniformity will undoubtedly face greater challenges. There will be more uprisings and more revolutionary attempts. Looking at the future changes in China's system of law and social control, perhaps Meadows was right. There is a distinction between revolution and rebellion: "revolution is a change of the form of government and of the principles on which it rests" and does not necessarily imply a "change of rulers," while rebellion is an uprising against the rulers. Over four millennia of Chinese history have demonstrated that "of all nations that have attained a degree of civilization, the Chinese are the least revolutionary and the most rebellious."[8] "To modernize, in short, China has had farther to go and more changes to make than most countries, simply because it has been itself for so long."[9] China's traditional attitudes toward authority, the state, law, and collective interests will continue to shape the outcome of the administration of law and the operation of social control vehicles, even after the old Communist cadres are long gone from their state posts.

NOTES

1. From a cultural perspective, individualism-centered societies are certainly apt to protect an individual's rights and freedoms against the interests of the state. Furthermore, ubiquitous privatization takes over the majority of spaces and resources. Therefore, the state's

control over individuals and its intrusion into privatized space are far more likely to be subject to regulation and scrutiny. Considering the combined impacts of an individualism-centered political culture and privatized economics, the state in this kind of society, of course, lacks penetration into conventional social control organs such as the family, school, church, guild, and so on.

2. Michael, 1962, p. 126.

3. Ibid.

4. Compared to the West, China, in a way, is still a gerontophilic society.

5. Fairbank, 1987, pp. 31–32.

6. As a matter of fact, both Confucianism and Legalism believed that the ruler has absolute and ultimate power over the government and law.

7. Michael, 1962, p. 135.

8. Meadows, 1856.

9. Fairbank, 1987, p. 7.

APPENDIX

Chronology of Chinese History

Xia Dynasty		2100–1600 B.C.
Shang Dynasty		1600–1100 B.C.
Zhou Dynasty	Western Zhou Dynasty	1100–771 B.C.
	Eastern Zhou Dynasty	770–256 B.C.
	Spring and Autumn Period	770–476 B.C.
	Warring States	475–221 B.C.
Qin Dynasty		221–207 B.C.
Han Dynasty	Western Han	206 B.C.–A.D. 24
	Eastern Han	25–220
Three Kingdoms	Wei	220–265
	Shu Han	221–263
	Wu	222–280
Western Jin Dynasty		265–316
Eastern Jin Dynasty		317–420

Southern Dynasty	Song	420–479
	Qi	479–502
	Lian	502–557
	Chen	557–589
Northern Dynasty	Northern Wei	386–534
	Eastern Wei	534–550
	Northern Qi	550–577
	Western Wei	535–556
	Northern Zhou	557–581
Sui Dynasty		581–618
Tang Dynasty		618–907
Five Dynasty	Later Liang	907–923
	Later Tang	923–936
	Later Jin	936–946
	Later Han	947–950
	Later Zhou	951–960
Song Dynasty	Northern Song Dynasty	960–1127
	Southern Song Dynasty	1127–1279
Liao Dynasty		916–1125
Jin Dynasty		1115–1234
Yuan Dynasty		1271–1368
Ming Dynasty		1368–1644
Qing Dynasty		1644–1911
Republic of China		1912–1949
People's Republic of China		1949–

Source: "Appendix 7: A Brief Chinese Chronology," in *Chinese-English Dictionary* (Revised Edition), p. 1430. Beijing: Foreign Language Teaching and Research Press, 1995.

Bibliography

Abadinsky, H. Foreword to W. F. McDowell, *Police-Prosecutor Relations in the United States: Executive Summary*, p. xii. Washington, DC: U.S. Government Printing Office, 1980.

———. *Law and Justice*. Chicago: Nelson-Hall Publishers, 1990.

Ackerman, B. A. *Social Justice in the Liberal State*. New Haven, CT: Yale University Press, 1980.

Alderson, J. C. "Hong Kong, Tokyo, Peking: The Three Police Systems Observation." *Police Studies* 33:3 (1980).

Alford, W. P. "Zhu Qiwu and the Development of Criminal Law in the People's Republic of China." *UCLA Pacific Basin Law Journal* 2 (1983): 60–64.

Allen, G. F. "Reforming Criminals in China: Implications for Corrections in the West." *International Journal of Comparative and Applied Criminal Justice* 11:1 (1987a): 77–86.

———. "Where Are We Going in Criminal Justice: Some Insights from the Chinese Criminal Justice System." *International Journal of Offender Therapy and Comparative Criminology* 31:2 (1987b): 101–10.

Amnesty International. *China: Torture and Ill-Treatment of Prisoners*. New York: Amnesty International Publications, 1987.

———. *China: Violations of Human Rights: Prisoners of Conscience and the Death Penalty in the People's Republic of China*. New York: Amnesty International Publications, 1984a.

———. *Torture in the Eighties: An Amnesty International Report*. New York: Amnesty International Publications, 1984b.

Anderson, M. *Policing the World: Interpol and the Politics of International Police Co-Operation*. Oxford: Clarendon Press, 1989.

Ansley, C. "Chinese Criminal Law under Manchus and Marxists." *University of British Columbia Law Review* 20 (1986): 165–91.

"Appendix 7: A Brief Chinese Chronology." In *Chinese-English Dictionary* (Revised Edition), Beijing: Foreign Language Teaching and Research Press, 1995.

Asian Watch Committee. *Punishment Season: Human Rights in China after Martial Law*. New York: Asian Watch Committee, 1990.

"The Assembly and Demonstration Law of the People's Republic of China (*Zhong-hua ren-min gong-he-go you-xing shi-wei fa*)." *People's Daily* (overseas edition), October 10, 1989, p. 4.

Baker, B. G. "Chinese Law in the Eighties: The Lawyer and the Criminal Process." *Albany Law Review* 46 (1982): 751–75.

Balazs, E. *Political Theory and Administrative Reality in Traditional China.* London: University of London, 1965.

Barber, B., and P. Watson. *Struggle for Democracy.* Boston: Little, Brown and Co., 1988.

Barlow, D. G., and D. W. Wahner. "Public Order and Internal Security." In F. M. Bunge and R. S. Shinn, eds., *China: A Country Study,* pp. 423–56. Washington, DC: U.S. Government Printing Office, 1981.

Barton, J. H., J. L. Gibbs, Jr., V. H. Li, and J. H. Merryman, eds. *Law in Radically Different Cultures.* St. Paul, MN: West Publishing Co., 1983.

Basler, B. "A Victorian Relic, Flogging, Arouses New Distaste." *New York Times,* January 25, 1989.

Bassiouni, M. C. "The Criminal Justice System of the Union of Soviet Socialist Republics and the People's Republic of China." *Revista de Derecho Puertorriqueno* 42 (1971): 163–93.

Beg, M. H. "Human Rights and Asia." *Santa Clara Law Review* 20 (1980): 319–50.

Bell, D. "Inside China: Conformity and Social Reform." *Juris Doctor,* April 1978, 23–31.

Berman, H. J., S. Cohen, and M. Russell. "A Comparison of the Chinese and Soviet Codes of Criminal Law and Procedure." *Journal of Criminal Law and Criminology* 63:1 (1982): 238–58.

———. "Soviet Perspectives on Chinese Law." In Jerome A. Cohen, ed., *Contemporary Chinese Law: Research Problems and Perspectives,* pp. 313–27. Cambridge, MA: Harvard University Press, 1970.

Bhatia, H. S., and T. Chung, eds. *Legal and Political System in China.* Vol. I (pre-1949 period). New Delhi, India: Deep & Deep Publications, 1974.

Birnbaum, P. "End of the State?" Paper presented at the Hebrew University Political Science Department Seminar, Jerusalem, December 25, 1985.

Blackstone, W. *Commentaries on the Laws of England.* Vol. 4. Oxford: Clarendon Press, 1765–69.

Blaustein, A. P. *Fundamental Legal Documents of Communist China.* South Hackensack, NJ: Fred B. Rothman & Co., 1962.

Bloodworth, D. "The Chinese Antisociety." In D. Bloodworth, ed., *The Chinese Looking Glass,* pp. 113–25. New York: Farrar Straus Giroux, 1980.

Bloom, Alfred H. "Language and Theoretical vs. Reality-Centered Morality." In Richard W. Wilson, Sidney L. Greenblatt, and Amy Auerbacher Wilson, eds., *Moral Behavior in Chinese Society,* pp. 21–37. New York: Praeger, 1981.

Bodde, D. *China's Cultural Tradition.* New York: Holt Rinehart and Winston, 1962.

———. "Chinese 'Laws of Nature': A Reconsideration." In D. Bodde, ed., *Essays on Chinese Civilization,* pp. 299–315. Princeton, NJ: Princeton University Press, 1981a.

———. "Evidence for 'Laws of Nature' in Chinese Thought." *Harvard Journal of Asiatic Studies* 20 (1957): 709–27.

———. *Law in Imperial China.* Philadelphia: University of Pennsylvania Press, 1973.

———. "Myths of Ancient China." In S. N. Kramer, ed., *Mythologies of the Ancient World.* New York: Doubleday Anchor Books, 1961.

———, ed. *Essays on Chinese Civilization.* Princeton, NJ: Princeton University Press, 1981b.

Bodde, D., and C. Morris. *Law In Imperial China: Exemplified by 190 Ch'ing Dynasty Cases.* Philadelphia: University of Pennsylvania Press, 1967.

Bonnichon, A. *Law in Communist China.* The Hague, Netherlands: International Commission of Jurists, 1958.

Borowitz, A. I. "Strict Construction in Sung China: The Case of a Yun." *American Bar Association Journal* 63 (1977): 522–28.

Boudreaux, P. "Booth v. Maryland and the Individual Vengeance Rationale for Criminal Punishment." *Journal of Criminal Law and Criminology* 80:1 (1989).

Bowden, T., and D. S. G. Goodman. "China: The Politics of Public Security." *Conflict Studies* 78 (1976): 1–18.

Bozeman, A. B. "Human Rights and National Security." *Yale Journal of World Public Order* 9:40 (1982): 40–77.

Bracey, D. H. "Like a Doctor to a Patient, Like a Parent to a Child—Corrections in the People's Republic of China." *Prison Journal* 68:1 (1988): 24–33.

———. "The System of Justice and the Concept of Human Nature in the People's Republic of China." *Justice Quarterly* 2:1 (1985): 139–44.

Brady, J. P. "Criminology, Crime and Justice in the People's Republic of China." In E. Johnson, ed., *International Handbook of Contemporary Developments in Criminology*, pp. 107–41. Westport, CT: Greenwood Press, 1983.

———. "Political Contradictions and Justice Policy in People's China." *Contemporary Crises* 1 (1977): 127–62.

———. "The Political Economy of Crime and Punishment in China." Paper presented at the annual meeting of American Society of Criminology, Atlanta, November 1986.

———. "A Season of Startling Alliance: Chinese Law and Justice in the New Order." *International Journal of the Sociology of Law* 9 (1981): 41–67.

Bredemeier, H. C. "Law as an Integrative Mechanism." In W. Evans, ed., *Law and Sociology*, pp. 74–90. New York: Free Press of Glencoe, 1962.

Brewer, John D., Adrian Guelke, Ian Hume, Edward Moxon-Browne, and Rick Wilford. "The People's Republic of China." In J. D. Brewer, A. Guelke, I. Hume, E. Moxon-Browne, and R. Wilford, *The Police, Public Order and the State: Policing in Great Britain, Northern Ireland, the Irish Republic, the USA, Israel, South Africa and China*, pp. 189–213. New York: Macmillan Press, 1988.

Brown, R. *The Nature of Social Laws: Machiavelli to Mill.* London: Cambridge University Press, 1984.

Brugger, B. "The Law of Value and the Rule of Law." In B. Brugger, ed., *China: Radicalism to Revisionism, 1962–1979*, pp. 228–48. Totowa, NJ: Barnes & Noble Books, 1981.

Burrow, A. S. "The Chinese Legal System: Structure and Operation." *Journal of the Law Society of Scotland* 26 (1981): 137–41.

Butler, W. "China in the Family of Socialist Legal Systems." *China Now, II* 91 (1980): 11–14.

Butler, W. E., ed. *The Legal System of the Chinese Soviet Republic, 1931–34.* Dobbs Ferry, NY: Transnational Publishers, 1983.

———. *Legislation of the Chinese Soviet Republic (1931–34).* London: University College, Faculty of Law, 1981.

Butterfield, F. *China: Alive in the Bitter Sea.* New York: New York Times Books, 1982.

Buxbaum, D. C. *Traditional and Modern Legal Institutions in Asia and Africa.* Leiden, Netherlands: E. J. Brill, 1967.

Cai, Guicun, Shanghao Rao, and Guixing Huang. "Fujian Sends Criminals to Border Areas for Labor Reform." *Beijing Daily* (*Beijing Ribao*), October 20, 1983, p. 1.

Carpenter, J. J. "Law Enforcement in China." *Journal of California Law Enforcement* 20:1 (1986): 24–27.

"The CCP's Central Committee's Ad Hoc Commission on Comprehensive Mainteinence of Social Order Held First Meeting in Beijing (*Zhong-yang she-hui zhi-an zong-he wei-yuan-hui di-yi-ci hui-yi zai jing zhao-kai*)." *People's Daily* (overseas edition), March 23, 1991.

"Central Disciplinary Committee's Regulation on Disciplinary Penalty against Party Members Who Violated the Party's Disciplines (*Zhong-ji-wei guan-yu gong-chan-dang-yuan wei-fan dang-ji chu-fen de ruo-gan gui-ding*)." *People's Daily* (overseas edition), January 18, 1990.

Chai, W., ed. *Essential Works of Chinese Communism*. New York: Bantam Books, 1972.

Chan, A., S. Rosen, and J. Unger, eds. *On Socialist Democracy and the Chinese Legal System: The Li Yizhe Debates*. New York: M. E. Sharpe, 1985.

Chang, Chen-pang. "Problems of Social Order on the Chinese Mainland." *Issues & Studies* 19:10 (1983): 4–7.

Chang, Chi-yun. "Confucius' Philosophy of Law." *Chinese Culture* 22:3 (1981).

Chang, Chin-tsen. "Li and Law." *Chinese Culture* 2:4 (1960): 1–16.

Chang, Chung-Yuan. "Law and Reason in Chinese Culture." *United Asia* 7 (1955): 225–27.

Chang, D. W. "Government and Crime Control in China: Its Relevance to U.S. Criminal Justice." *Police Studies* 7:2 (1984): 94–111.

Chen, Fu-mei Chang. "On Law in Imperial China." *Harvard Journal of Asiatic Studies* 29 (1969): 274–84.

Chen, P. H. *Chinese Legal Tradition under the Mongols*. Princeton, NJ: Princeton University Press, 1979.

Chen, P. M. *Law and Justice: The Legal System in China, 2400 B.C. to 1960 A.D.* New York: Dunellen Publishing Co., 1973.

Chen, Shouyi. "A Review of Thirty Years of Legal Studies in New China." *Journal of Chinese Law* 2:1 (1988): 181–200.

Chen, Yan. "Chinese Communist Party Expanded Its Membership to 57 Million (zhong-gong dang-yuan dui-wu zhuang-da zong-shu da 5700 duo-wan ming)." *People's Daily* (overseas edition), June 13, 1996.

Chen, Yung-fa. *Making Revolution: The Communist Movement in Eastern and Central China, 1937–1945*. Berkeley: University of California Press, 1986.

Cheng, Shu-ping. *Chinese Communist System of Reform Through Labor*. Taiwan: World Anti-Communist League, China Chapter, Asian People's Anti-Communist League, 1978.

Cheng, Y. "Criminal Procedure in China: Some Comparisons with the English System." *International and Comparative Law Quarterly* 37 (1988): 190–207.

Cheung, Tai Ming. "Big Brother Is Watching." *Far East Economic Review*, November 3, 1988, pp. 24–25.

Ch'ien, Tuan-sheng. "Law and the Administration of Justice." *The Government and Politics of China*, pp. 245–61. Stanford, CA: Stanford University Press, 1950.

China: Daily Report, "Lawbreakers Involved in Riot Sentenced," Foreign Broadcast Information Service (F.B.I.S.), January 7, 1991.

China: Daily Report, F.B.I.S., November 21, 1991, at 11.

China: Facts and Figures. Beijing: Foreign Language Press, 1982.

China Legal Daily (*Zhongguo Fazhi Bao*), May 31, 1985

China Morning Post, September 23, 1989.

China Spring 101 (1991).

"Chinese Legal System." *China Legal Daily* (*Zhongguo Fazhi Bao*), April 16, 1982.

Ching, F. "China Crime Laws, Framed Last Year, Are Often Sidestepped by Authorities." *Wall Street Journal*, July 24, 1980, pp. 2, 20(e), and 24(w).

Chiu, H. "Certain Problems in Recent Law Reform in the People's Republic of China." *Comparative Law Yearbook* 3 (1979): 1–33.

———. "China's Criminal Justice System and the Trial of Pro-Democracy Dissidents." *New York University Journal of International Law and Politics* 24:3 (1992): 1181–1201.

———. *Chinese Attitude toward International Law of Human Rights in the Post-Mao Era.* Baltimore, MD: University of Maryland, School of Law, 1989a.

———. "Chinese Law and Justice: Trends over 3 Decades." *Occasional Papers Series in Contemporary Asian Studies* 7 (1982a): 1–34.

———. "Criminal Punishment in Mainland China: A Study of Some Yunnan Province Documents." *Journal of Criminal Law and Criminology* 68:3 (1977): 374–98.

———. "The 1982 Chinese Constitution and the Rule of Law." *Review of Socialist Law* 11 (1985): 143–60.

———. "Socialist Legalism: Reform and Continuity in Post-Mao People's Republic of China." *Occasional Papers Series in Contemporary Asian Studies* 1 (1982b): 1–35.

———. *The Status of Customary International Law, Treaties and Semi-Official or Unofficial Agreement in Chinese Law.* Baltimore: University of Maryland, School of Law, 1989b.

Chiu, Vermier Y. *Marriage Law and Customs of China.* Hong Kong: Chinese University of Hong Kong, New Asian College, Institute of Advanced Chinese Studies and Research, 1966.

Chow, R. "Violence in the Other Country: Preliminary Remarks on the 'China Crisis,' June 1989." *Radical America* 22:4 (1989): 23–31.

Ch'u, T'ung-tsu. *Confucianization of Chinese Law* (*Zhong-guo fa-lu zhi ru-jia-hua*). Beijing: Beijing University Press, 1948.

———. *Law and Society in Traditional China.* Paris: Mounton & Co., 1965.

Clark, J. P. "Conflict Management Outside the Courtrooms of China." In R. J. Troyer, J. P. Clark, and D. G. Rojek, eds., *Social Control in the People's Republic of China*, pp. 57–69. New York: Praeger, 1989.

Clark, J. P., and S. M. Clark. "Crime in China—As We Saw It." *Justice Quarterly* 2:1 (1985): 103–10.

Cohen, J. A. "China's New Lawyers' Law." *American Bar Association Journal* 66 (1980): 1533–39.

———. "Chinese Criminal Code Symposium: Foreword—China's Criminal Codes." *Journal of Criminal Law and Criminology* 73:1 (1982): 135–37.

———. "Criminal Law: Reflections on the Criminal Process in China." *Journal of Criminal Law and Criminology* 68:3 (1977): 323–55.

———. *The Criminal Process in the People's Republic of China, 1949–1963.* Cambridge, MA: Harvard University Press, 1968.

———. "The Party and the Courts: 1949–1959." *China Quarterly* 38 (1964): 120–57.

———, ed. *Contemporary Chinese Law: Research Problems and Perspectives.* Cambridge, MA: Harvard University Press, 1970.

Collection of Laws, Statutes and Decrees of the People's Republic of China, January–December 1989 (*Zhong-hua ren-ming gong-he-guo fa-gui hui-bian*). Beijing: Law Publishing Co., 1989.

"Concepts of Law in the Chinese Anti-Crime Campaign." *Harvard Law Review* 98 (1985): 1890–1908.

Confucius. *The Analects.* Translated with an Introduction by D. C. Lau. London: Penguin Books, 1979.

Conner, A. E. W. "Anticorruption Legislation: Will More and Better Rules Curb Widespread Corruption?" *East Asian Executive Reports* 11:1 (1989): 8–14.

Constitution of the People's Republic of China, 1954. Beijing: Foreign Language Press, 1954.

"Constitution of the People's Republic of China, September, 1954." In W. Chai, ed., *Essential Works of Chinese Communism,* 2nd ed., pp. 246–96. New York: Bantam Books, 1972.

"Constitution of the People's Republic of China, 1982." In R. H. Folsom and J. H. Minan, eds., *Law in the People's Republic of China,* pp. 945–68. Boston: Martinus Nijhoff Publishers, 1989.

"Counterrevolutionary Statute of the Nationalist Government, March 30, 1927 (*Guo-min zheng-fu fan-ge-ming tiao-li*)." In *New Regulations and Statutes of the Nationalist Government* (*Guo-min zheng-fu xin-fa-lin*), pp. 1–3. Nanjing, China: Guangzhi Bookstore Printing, April 1928.

Creel, H. G. "The Royal Government: Justice." In *The Origins of Statecraft in China,* vol. 1, pp. 161–93. Chicago: University of Chicago Press, 1970.

Criminal Code of Japan. Rutland, VT: C. E. Tuttle, 1954.

The Criminal Law and the Criminal Procedure Law of the People's Republic of China. Beijing: Foreign Languages Press, 1984.

Criminal Law Research Group, Law Institute, Chinese Academy of Social Sciences. "Lectures on the Criminal Law." *Chinese Law and Government* 13:2 (1980): 1–112.

Crockett, G. W., Jr. "More Than a Great Wall Separates American and Chinese Ideals of Justice: Criminal Justice in China." *Judicature* 59:5 (1975): 239–47.

———. "Teaching Criminals a Lesson: A Report on Justice in China." *Judicature* 61:6 (1978): 278–88.

Crockett, G. W., Jr., and M. Gleicher. "Inside China's Prisons." *Judicature* 61:9 (1978): 409–15.

Croghan, N., P. K. Chen, and M. Zhang. "Documents from the Chinese Democratic Movement." *Radical America* 22:4 (1989): 13–21.

Cross, A. R. *Punishment, Prison and the Public.* London: Stevens & Sons, 1971.

Davis, Michael C. "Anglo-American Constitutionalism with Chinese Characteristics." *American Journal of Comparative Law* 36 (1988): 761–81.

Davis, S. B. "Death Penalty and Legal Reform in the PRC." *Journal of Chinese Law* 1:2 (1987): 303–34.

Dawson, C. *Religion and Culture.* Leiden, Netherlands: E. J. Brill, 1948.

de Bary, W. T., W. T. Chan, and B. Watson, eds. *Sources of Chinese Tradition.* New York: Columbia University Press, 1964.

Denenberg, R. V. "Keeping the Peace on Dong Jiadu Street." *Student Lawyer* 16 (1981): 16–32.

Deng, Liquin. "Speech at the National Conference of Legal Propaganda and Education (*Zai quan-guo si-fa xuan-chuan jiao-yu gong-zuo hui-yi shang de jiang-hua*)." In Z. Gan, J. Lin, and H. Shen, eds., *Law Yearbook of China* (*Zhong-guo fa-lü nian-jian*), pp. 665–70. Beijing: Law Publishing Co., 1987.

de Tocqueville, A. *Democracy in America.* Edited by R. D. Heffner. New York: New American Library, 1956.

Ding, Ling. *The Sun Shines over the Sanggan River* (*Tai-yang zhao-zai Sang-gan-he-shang*). Beijing: People's Publishing Co., 1955.

"The Director of a Foreign Trade Bureau Was Dismissed Because of Bribery (*Wai-mao-ju-zhang shou-hui bei-che-zhi*)." *People's Daily* (overseas edition), February 24, 1983.

"The Disciplinary Inspection Committee Issued a Regulation on Handling the Problems in Complaints, Accusations, and Appeals (*Zhong-ji-wei gong-bu guan-yu chu-li jian-ju, kong-gao, shang-su de ruo-gan wen-ti de gui-ding*)." *People's Daily* (overseas edition), September 7, 1988.

"The Disciplinary Organs Seriously Investigates Cases of Violating Party Discipline (*Zhong-ji-wei ren-zhen diao-cha wei-fan dang-ji de an-jian*)." *People's Daily* (overseas edition), June 30, 1990.

Doder, D. "Deng Counts His Corrupt Chickens." *U.S. News & World Report*, November 7, 1988, p. 53.

Dolan, R. E. "Criminal Justice and Public." In R. L. Worden, *China: A Country Study*, pp. 507–40. Washington, DC: U.S. Government Printing Office, 1987.

Dong, Zhongshu. "*Chun-qiu fan-lu*." In *Si-bu bei-yao*. Beijing: China Book Bureau, 1975.

Douglas, Cathleen H. "Crime in Communist China." *Federal Bar Review News* 23 (1976): 302–5.

———. "The Police in the People's Republic of China." *Police Law Quarterly* 6 (1977): 36–40.

Drapkin, I. *Crime and Punishment in the Ancient World*. Toronto: Lexington Books, 1989.

Dutton, M. *Policing and Punishment in China*. New York: Cambridge University Press, 1992.

Duyvendak, J. J. L. *The Book of Lord Shang: A Classic of the Chinese School of Law*. London: A. Probsthain & Co., 1928.

———. "A Literature Renaissance in China." *Acta Orientalia I*. Leiden, Netherlands: E. J. Brill, 1923.

Eberhard, W. *Conquerors and Rulers: Social Forces in Medieval China*. Leiden, Netherlands: E. J. Brill, 1952.

Eberhard, W., K. Gawlikowski, and C. L. Seyschab, eds. *East Asian Civilizations: New Attempts at Understanding Traditions*. Munich: Simon & Magiera Publishers, 1983.

Edwards, R. R. "Formal Law Begins a Comeback in Post-Mao China." *Contemporary China* 2 (1978): 92–102.

———. "The Gang of Four Trial: Chinese Criminal Justice in Practice." *China Law Reporter* 1 (1981): 173–211.

———. "Reflection on Crime and Punishment in China." *Columbia Journal of Transnational Law* 16 (1977): 45–74.

Engel, J. W. "Marriage in the People's Republic of China: Analysis of New Law." *Journal of Marriage and the Family* 46:4 (1984): 955–61.

Engels, F. "Letter to van Patten, 18.4.1883." In M. Cain and A. Hunt, eds., *Marx and Engels on Law*. London: Academic Press, 1979.

Epp, T. D. "The New Code of Criminal Procedure in the People's Republic of China: Protection, Problems, and Predictions." *International Journal of Comparative and Applied Criminal Justice* 8:2 (1984): 43–53.

Epstein, I., ed. "Juvenile Delinquency in China." *Chinese Education* 19:2 (1986).

Evans, W. M. *Law and Sociology*. New York: Free Press of Glencoe, 1962.

Fairbank, J. K. *The Great Chinese Revolution, 1800–1985*. New York: Harper & Row, 1987.

Farmer, E. L. "Social Order in Early Ming China: Some Norms Codified in the Hung-wu Period." In B. E. McKnight, ed., *Law and the State in Traditional East Asia: Six Studies on the Sources of East Asian Law*, pp. 1–35. Honolulu: University of Hawaii Press, 1987.

Felkenes, G. T. "Criminal Justice in the People's Republic of China: A System of Contradictions." *Judicature* 69:6 (1986): 345–52.

Feng, Yu-lan. *A Short History of Chinese Philosophy*. New York: Macmillan, 1948.

Fenwick, C. R. "Crime in Post-Mao China: Toward the Construction of an Integrated Social System Theory." *International Journal of Comparative and Applied Criminal Justice* 11:2 (1987): 177–92.

Finckenauer, J. O. "Juvenile Delinquency in the USSR: Social Structural Explanations." *International Journal of Comparative and Applied Criminal Justice* 12:1 (1988): 73–80.

Finkelstein, David. "The Language of Communist China's Criminal Law." In Jerome A. Cohen, ed., *Contemporary Chinese Law: Research Problems and Perspectives*, pp. 188–219. Cambridge, MA: Harvard University Press, 1970.

Fiss, O. M. "Two Constitutions." In R. H. Folsom and J. H. Minan, eds., *Law in the People's Republic of China*, pp. 61–71. Boston: Martinus Nijhoff Publishers, 1989.

Fogel, D. "China: Trial by the Masses." *Corrections Magazine* 3:4 (1977): 42–44.

Fogel, J. *Recent Japanese Studies of Modern Chinese History*. New York: M. E. Sharpe, 1989.

Folsom, R. H., and J. H. Minan, eds. *Law in the People's Republic of China*. Boston: Martinus Nijhoff Publishers, 1989.

Foster, F. H. "Codification in Post-Mao China." *American Journal of Comparative Law* 30 (1982): 395–430.

Fox, R. G. "Structure of the Criminal Prosecution and Trial Process in the People's Republic of China." *Australian and New Zealand Journal of Criminology* 16 (1983): 133–45.

Fung, V. "China's Campaign to Arrest Immorality Corners Prostitutes and Their Patrons." *The Asian Wall Street Journal Weekly* December 19, 1983.

Gan, Yupai, ed. *Special Edition on Criminal Law* (*Xing-fa-xue zhuan-lun*). Beijing: Beijing University Press, 1989.

Gan, Z., J. Lin, and H. Shen, eds. *Law Yearbook of China* (*Zhong-guo fa-lü nian-jian*). Beijing: Law Publishing Co., 1987.

Gao, Chao, and Z. Jiang, eds. *Selections of Classical Legal Literature* (*Gu-dai wen-xuan*). Beijing: Law Publishing Co., 1989.

Gao, Ming-xuan, ed. *The Birth of the Criminal Law of the People's Republic of China* (*Zhong-hua ren-ming gong-he-guo xing-fa de yun-yu yu dan-sheng*). Beijing: Beijing University Press, 1987.

Gao, Ming-xuan, K. Ma, and G. Gao. *Penal Law* (*Xing-fa xue*). Beijing: Law Publishing Co., 1981.

———. *Penal Law* (*Xing-fa xue*), 2nd ed. Beijing: Law Publishing Co., 1983.

Garbus, M. "Justice without Courts: A Report on China Today." *Judicature* 60 (1977): 395–402.

Gelatt, T. A. "The People's Republic of China and the Presumption of Innocence." *Journal of Criminal Law and Criminology* 73:1 (1982): 259–316.

Gellhorn, W. "China's Quest for Legal Modernity." *Journal of Chinese Law* 1:1 (1987): 1–22.

Gen, L. "Some Characteristics of the Ancient Chinese Law." *Asian Review* 48 (1952): 156–60, 233–40.

Ginsburg, George. "Soviet Sources on the Law of the People's Republic of China." In Jerome A. Cohen, ed., *Contemporary Chinese Law: Research Problems and Perspectives*, pp. 328–58. Cambridge, MA: Harvard University Press, 1970.

Giovannetti, D. "Principle of Analogy in Sino-Soviet Criminal Laws." *Dalhousie Law Journal* 8 (1984): 382–401.

Glendon, M. A., M. W. Gordon, and C. Osakwe. *Comparative Legal Traditions*. St. Paul, MN: West Publishing Co., 1982.

Glueck, S., and E. Glueck. *Unraveling Juvenile Delinquency*. Cambridge, MA: Harvard University Press, 1950.

Goldman, M. *China's Intellectuals.* Cambridge, MA: Harvard University Press, 1981.

Gong, Ming-li. "On Confession (*Zi-shou lun*)." In Yupai Gan, ed., *Criminal Law* (*Xing-fa-xue zhuan-lun*), pp. 370–418. Beijing: Beijing University Press, 1989.

Goodman, E. J. "The People's Court Hears a People Problem." *National Law Journal* 3 (August 18, 1980): 13–19.

Goossen, R. J. "An Introduction to Chinese Law: Does It Exist? What Is It? How Is It Interpreted?" *Osgoode Hall Law Journal* 27:1 (1989): 93–122.

Griffin, Patricia E. *The Chinese Communist Treatment of Counterrevolutionaries, 1924–1949.* Princeton, NJ: Princeton University Press, 1976.

"Guo Luoji, a Well Known Scholar, Charges Li Tieying with Political Persecution (*Guo Luoji kong Li Tieying deng zheng-zhi po-hai*)." *World Journal* (*Shi-jie ri-bao*), February 21, 1992.

"Guo Luoji Sues the National Educational Commission Again." *World Journal* (*Shi-jie ri-bao*), April 15, 1992.

Han shu (History of the former Han Dynasty). Beijing: China Book Bureau, 1962.

Hansen, Ole. "Legality and Lawlessness in China." *Poly Law Review* 6 (1980): 46–52.

Harrison, J. F. "Wrongful Treatment of Prisoners: A Case Study of Ch'ing Legal Practice." *Journal of Asian Studies* 13:2 (1964): 227–44.

Hasskell, M. R., and L. Yablonski. *Juvenile Delinquency.* 3rd ed. Boston: Houghton Mifflin, 1982.

Hebei Law Review (*Hebei Faxue*), no. 2, 1984.

Herbst, K. P. "Book Review: The Chinese Criminal Process: Revolutionary Ideology and Human Rights." *Stanford Law Review* 30 (1978): 469–80.

Hillstrom, Donald. "Criminal Law in China since the Downfall of the Gang of Four." *Bench & Bar of Minnesota* 38 (1981): 35–40.

Hipkin, B. "Law and Modernization in China." In S. Spitzer, ed., *Law and Research.* New York: JAI Press, 1981.

Hirschi, T. *Causes of Delinquency.* Berkeley: University of California Press, 1969.

Houts, M. "The 'New' China's 'Court Doctors': Their Words Are Law!" *Trauma* 22:6 (1981): 1–3.

Hsia, T. *Chinese Culture Revolution.* Translated by G. Onn. New York: McGraw-Hill, 1972.

Hsia, Tao-tai, and C. A. Johnson. *Law Making in the People's Republic of China: Terms, Procedures, Hierarchy, and Interpretation.* Washington, DC: U.S. Government Printing Office, 1986.

Hsu, Immanuel C. Y. *The Rise of Modern China.* 4th ed. New York: Oxford University Press, 1990.

Hu, Qiao-mu. "How Has the Chinese Communist Party Developed Marxism? (*Zhong-guo gong-chan-dang zen-yang fa-zhan le ma-ke-si zhu-yi*)" *People's Daily* (overseas edition), June 25, 1991.

———. "Report to the Second Meeting of the Constitutional Revision Committee on the Draft of Conditional Revision." *People's Daily* (overseas edition), March 1, 1982.

Hulsewé, A. F. P. *Remnants of Ch'in Law.* Leiden, Netherlands: E. J. Brill, 1985.

———. *Remnants of Han Law.* Leiden, Netherlands: E. J. Brill, 1955.

Hunter, E. *Brain-Washing in Red China.* New York: Vanguard Press, 1951.

"Implementation of the Law of Demonstration and Assembly of the PRC in Shanghai." In *Collection of New Laws of the PRC* (*Zhong-hua ren-ming gong-he-guo fa-gui hui-bian*), vol. 1. Beijing: Law Publishing Co., 1990.

Ingraham, B. L. *The Structure of Criminal Procedure: Law and Practice of France, the Soviet Union, China, and the United States.* Westport, CT: Greenwood Press, 1987.

"It Is Worrisome When the Country Does Not Follow the Law. *China Spring* 3 (1991): 37–39.

Jan, Lee-Jan. "Corrections in Taiwan (Republic of China)." *International Journal of Comparative and Applied Criminal Justice* 12:1 (1988): 93–100.

——. "Deterrence as Social Control in the United States and China." *International Journal of Comparative and Applied Criminal Justice* 7:2 (1983): 195–200.

——. "Preventing Juvenile Delinquency in Taiwan." *International Journal of Comparative and Applied Criminal Justice* 10:2 (1986).

Jesen, G. F., and D. G. Rojek. *Delinquency*. Lexington, MA: D. C. Heath, 1980.

Jiefang Ribao, December 5, 1989, in F.B.I.S., January 10, 1990.

Jin, Liang-nian. *Corporal Punishment and Chinese Society* (*Ku-xing yu zhong-guo she-hui*). Hangzhou, China: Zhejiang People's Publication Co., 1991.

Johnson, C. A. *Chinese Law: A Bibliography of Selected English-Language Materials*. Washington, DC: Law Library of Congress, Far Eastern Law Division, 1990.

Johnson, E. H. "Incarceration in the People's Republic of China: Functions and Implications." *International Journal of Comparative and Applied Criminal Justice* 8:2 (1984): 141–49.

——. "Neighborhood Police in the People's Republic of China." *Police Studies* 6:4 (1983–84): 8–12.

——. "The People's Republic of China: Possibilities for Comparative Criminology." *International Journal of Comparative and Applied Criminal Justice* 7:1 (1983): 151–56.

——. "Politics, Power and Prevention: The People's Republic of China Case." *Journal of Criminal Justice* 14 (1986): 449–57.

Johnson, K. A. "The Revolutionary Tradition of Pro-Democracy Students." *Radical America* 22:4 (1989): 7–12.

Johnson, W. "General Principles of the T'ang Code." In W. Johnson, ed., *The T'ang Code*, pp. 14–38. Princeton, NJ: Princeton University Press, 1979.

Jones, M., and G. Ruge. "Crime and Punishment in China: Law and Order Minus Judges, Prosecutors, Defense Lawyers." *Atlas World Press Review*, September 1975, pp. 19–21.

Jones, T. A. "The Evolution of Crime in Industrial and Preindustrial Societies." *Comparative Social Research* 8 (1985): 3–15.

Jones, W. C. "A Possible Model for the Criminal Trial in the People's Republic of China." *American Journal of Comparative Law* 24 (1976): 229–45.

——. "Understanding Chinese Law: Thought Control in Prewar Japan and Crime Prevention in the PRC." *Review of Sociological Law* 3 (1977): 219–26.

——, ed. *Basic Principle of Civil Law in China*. New York: M. E. Sharpe, 1989.

Kaminski, G. "International Law: Robust Plant among the Hundred Flowers of China's Law Reform." *Asian Thought & Society* 7:19 (1982): 3–17.

——. "Visitation of the Law and Court in Action in the PRC: The New Hundred Flowers of the Chinese Legal System." *Asian Thought & Society* 4:2 (1979): 205–21.

Kaplan, H. B. *Deviant Behavior in Defense of Self*. New York: Academic Press, 1980.

Kaplan, H. B., S. S. Martin, and R. J. Johnson. "Self-Rejection and the Explanation of Deviance: Specification of the Structure among Latent Constructs." *American Journal of Sociology* 92 (1986): 384–411.

Kelman, M. *A Guide to Critical Legal Studies*. Cambridge, MA: Harvard University Press, 1987.

Kim, Chin. "The Death Penalty in Traditional China." In C. Kim, ed., *Selected Writings on Asian Law*, pp. 329–57. Littleton, CO: Fred B. Rothman & Co., 1982a.

———. "The 1975 Constitution of the People's Republic of China." In C. Kim, ed., *Selected Writings on Asian Law*, pp. 359–85. Littleton, CO: Fred B. Rothman & Co., 1982b.

———. "The 1978 Constitution of the People's Republic of China." In C. Kim, ed., *Selected Writings on Asian Law*, pp. 395–423. Littleton, CO: Fred B. Rothman & Co., 1982c.

———. "Recent Developments in the Constitutions of Asian Marxist-Socialist States." *Case Western Reserve Journal of International Law* 13 (1981): 483–500.

Kim, Hyung I. *Fundamental Legal Concepts of China and the West: A Comparative Study*. Port Washington, NY: Kennikat Press and National University Publications, 1981.

Klepper, S., and D. Nagin. "The Deterrent Effect of Perceived Certainty and Severity of Punishment Revisited." *Criminology* 27:4 (1989): 721–46.

Klotter, J. C. *Criminal Law*. 2nd ed. Cincinnati, OH: Anderson Publishing Co., 1988.

Koeltl, J. G. "Civil Rights and Liberties in China." *Albany Law Review* 46 (1982): 740–50.

Kracke, E. K., Jr. *Civil Service in Early Sung (Song) China*. Cambridge, MA: Harvard University Press, 1968.

Kristof, N. D. "For China's Congress, How Much Democracy?" *New York Times*, March 19, 1989.

Kruttschnitt, C., L. Heath, and D. A. Ward. "Family Violence, Television Viewing Habits, and Other Adolescent Experiences Related to Violent Criminal Behavior." *Criminology* 24 (1986): 235–67.

Kun, Bela. *Fundamental Laws of the Chinese Soviet Republic*. New York: International Publishers, 1934.

Lan, Mingliang. "China: Recent Achievements in the Development of the Legal System and in the Field of Crime Prevention and the Treatment of Offenders." *Crime Prevention and Criminal Justice* (United Nations) 11 (December 1984): 2–4.

Larson, C. W. "A Peek at Public Safety in Peking." *Police Chief* 45 (1978): 32–33.

"Law and China." *New Yorker*, January 19, 1987, pp. 25–26.

Laws and Regulations of the People's Republic of China. Vol. 1. Hong Kong: Kingsway International Publications Ltd., 1982.

Law Yearbook of China, 1992. Beijing: Press of Law Yearbook of China.

Lawyers Committee on Human Rights. *Criminal Justice with Chinese Characteristics*. New York: Lawyers Committee on Human Rights, 1993.

Lee, D., R. Neff, A. Bonus, and J. Barnathan. "China's Ugly Export Secret: Prison Labor." *Business Week*, April 22, 1991.

Lee, Hsueh-Teng. "The Earlier Concepts of Human Rights and Their Implementations." *Chinese Culture* 23:1 (1982): 47–59.

Lee, Shu-Ching. "Administration and Bureaucracy: The Power Structure in Chinese Society." *Transactions of the Second World Congress of Sociology*. Paris: World Congress of Sociology, 1954.

"Legal Expert, Gao Ming-xuan, Interviewed on Wei Jingsheng Case (*Xing-fa zhuan-ja Gao Mingxuan tan Wei Jingsheng an*)." *World Journal* (*Shi-jie ri-bao*), February 29, 1996.

Leng, Shao-chuan. "Crime and Punishment in Post-Mao China." *China Law Report* 2:1 (1982a): 5–33.

———. "Criminal Justice in Post-Mao China: Some Preliminary Observations." *Journal of Criminal Law and Criminology* 73:1 (1982b): 204–37.

———. *Justice in Communist China*. Dobbs Ferry, NY: Oceana Publications, Inc., 1967.

———. "The Role of Law in the People's Republic of China as Reflecting Mao Tse-Tung's Influence." *Journal of Criminal Law and Criminology* 68:3 (1977): 356–73.

Leng, Shao-chuan, and H. D. Chiu. *Criminal Justice in Post-Mao China: Analysis and Documents*. Albany: State University of New York Press, 1985.

Lenin, V. I. "State and Revolution." In S. S. Hendel, ed., *The Soviet Crucible.* North Scituate, MA: Duxbury Press, 1973.

Lewis, M. E. *Sanctioned Violence in Early China.* Albany: State University of New York Press, 1990.

Li, K. T. *Corrections and Education.* Beijing: Public Publishing Co., 1986.

Li, Lupo. "China Faces Severe Shortage in Judgeships: Urgent Need for Training and Formal Education *(Zhong-guo fa-guan yan-zhong kui-fa mian-lin tiao-zhan: you-guan ren-shi hu-yu da-li jia-qiang pei-yang).*" *People's Daily* (overseas edition), November 18, 1988.

Li, P. "In Search of Justice: Law and Morality in Three Chinese Dramas." In R. W. Wilson, S. L. Greenblatt, and A. A. Wilson, eds., *Moral Behavior in Chinese Society,* pp. 104–25. New York: Praeger, 1981.

Li, Shu-ching. "Administration and Bureaucracy: The Power Structure in Chinese Society." In *Transactions of the Second World Congress of Sociology,* pp. 3–15. London: International Sociological Association, 1954.

Li, T'ien-min. "The Trial of the Lin Piao and Chiang Ch'ing Cliques." *Issues and Studies* 17:6 (1981): 19–26.

Li, V. H. "Law and Penology: System of Reform and Correction." In M. Oksenberg, ed., *China's Developmental Experience,* pp. 144–219. New York: Praeger, 1973.

———. *Law without Lawyers: A Comparative View of Law in China and the United States.* Boulder, CO: Westview Press, 1978.

———. "The Role of Law in Communist China." *China Quarterly* 44 (1970): 66–111.

Li, Z. T. "Lawless Laws and Crimeless Crimes." In A. Chan, S. Rosen, and J. Unger, eds., *On Socialist Democracy and the Chinese Legal System: The Li Yizhe Debates,* pp. 163–76. New York: M. E. Sharpe, 1985.

Liang, Haoren, ed. *Criminal Law (Xing-fa fen-lun).* Beijing: China University of Political Science and Law Press, 1987.

Lifton, R. J. *Thought Reform and the Psychology of Totalism.* Chapel Hill: University of North Carolina Press, 1989.

Lin, Biao. "Report to the Ninth National Congress of the Communist Party of China." N.p., April 1969.

Lin, Chong-pin. "China: The Coming Changes." *The American Enterprise,* January/February 1991, pp. 19–25.

Lin, Yutang. *My Country and My People.* New York: Reynal and Hitchcock, 1935.

———. *The Wisdom of Confucius.* New York: Modern Library, 1966.

"Lin Yun on Counter-Revolutionary Offenses and Capital Punishment." *Beijing Review* 28 (1979): 16–17.

Lipman, J. N., and S. Harrell. *Violence in China: Essays in Culture and Counterculture.* Albany, NY: State University of New York Press, 1990.

Liska, A. E., and M. D. Reed. "Ties to Conventional Institutions and Delinquency: Estimating Reciprocal Effects." *American Sociological Review* 50 (1985): 547–60.

Liu, Hui-Chen Wang. "An Analysis of Chinese Clan Rules: Confucian Theories in Action." In A. F. Wright, ed., *Confucianism and Chinese Civilization,* pp. 16–49. Stanford, CA: Stanford University Press, 1964.

Liu, J. T. C. *Reform in Sung (Song) China.* Cambridge, MA: Harvard University Press, 1968.

Liu, Juan. "Beijing Ribao Article: Qi Beyu, Chi Qun, Lin Chuangtang, and Others Convicted for Actively Joining and Following the Lin Biao, Jiang Qing Counterrevolutionary Clique in Criminal Activities." Joint Publications Research Service, *China Report: Political, Sociological and Military Affairs,* February 10, 1984, no. 84–013, pp. 84–86.

Liu, Nanping. "'*Judicial Review' in China: A Comparative Perspective.*" *Review of Socialist Law* 14:3 (1988): 241–53.

Liu, Qing. "Prison Memoirs." *Chinese Sociology and Anthropology* 15:1–2 (1982/83): 148–81.

Liu, Zhi. *Rehabilitation through Labor in China* (*Lau-dong gai-zao xue*). Beijing: Future Publishing Co., 1986.

Lo, S. K. "Traditional Chinese Philosophy of Life." *Asian Thought & Society* 8:22–23 (1983): 1–8.

Los, M. *Communist Ideology, Law and Crime.* New York: St. Martin's Press, 1988.

Lotveit, T. *Chinese Communism, 1931–34: Experience in Civil Government.* Scandinavian Institute of Asian Studies Monograph Series, no. 16. Lund, Sweden: Studentlitteratar, 1973.

Lowa, Mary Johnson. "People's Law in China." *Juris Doctor* 8 (1978): 11–31.

Lowe, J. D. *The Traditional Chinese Legal Thought.* Berkeley: University of California Press, 1984.

Lu, Yun. "A Day in the Life of the Police." *Beijing Review,* December 16, 1985, pp. 24–26.

Lubman, Stanley B. "Emerging Functions of Formal Legal Institutions in China's Modernization." *China Law Reporter* 2 (1983): 195–265.

———. "Western Scholarship on Chinese Law." In John R. Oldman, ed., *China's Legal Development,* pp. 83–100. New York: M. E. Sharpe, 1986.

Lung, Kwan-hai. "Principles of Government and Social Control." *Journal of the Chinese Society* 13 (1976): 35–46.

Lyerly, R. R., and J. K. Skipper, Jr. "Differential Rates of Rural-Urban Delinquency: A Social Control Approach." *Criminology* 19 (1981): 385–99.

MacCormick, G. *Traditional Chinese Penal Law.* Edinburgh, Scotland: Edinburgh University Press, 1990.

MacFarquhar, C., T. Cheek, and W. Wu, eds. *The Secret Speeches of Chairman Mao.* Cambridge, MA: Harvard University Press, 1989.

MacInnis, D. E. *Religion in China Today: Policy and Practice.* New York: Orbis Books, 1989.

Mackerras, C. *Western Images of China.* Oxford: Oxford University Press, 1989.

Madson, R. "The Politics of Revenge in Rural China during the Cultural Revolution." In J. N. Lipman and S. Harrell, eds., *Violence in China,* pp. 175–202. Albany: State University of New York Press, 1990.

Magnusson, P. "China's Ugly Export Secret: Prison Labor." *Business Week,* April 22, 1991, pp. 42–46.

Mao, Zedong. "The Chinese Revolution and the Chinese Communist Party." In W. T. de Bary, W. T. Chan, and B. Watson, *Sources of Chinese Tradition,* pp. 877–83. New York: Columbia University Press, 1960a.

———. "The Dictatorship of the People's Democracy." In W. T. de Bary, W. T. Chan, and B. Watson, *Sources of Chinese Tradition,* pp. 891–94. New York: Columbia University Press, 1960b.

———. *Mao Zedong Selected Works* (*Mao Zedong xuan-ji*). Vol. 3. Beijing: People's Publishing Co., 1965.

———. *Mao Zedong Selected Works* (*Mao Zedong xuan-ji*). Vol. 5. Beijing: People's Publishing Co., 1970.

———. "On Art and Literature." In W. T. de Bary, W. T. Chan, and B. Watson, *Sources of Chinese Tradition,* pp. 928–33. New York: Columbia University Press, 1960c.

———. "On Contradiction, August, 1937." In W. Chai, ed., *Essential Works of Chinese Communism,* 2nd ed., pp. 75–94. New York: Bantam Books, 1972a.

——. "On the Correct Handling of Contradictions among the People, February, 1957." In W. T. de Bary, W. T. Chan, and B. Watson, *Sources of Chinese Tradition*, pp. 933–41. New York: Columbia University Press, 1960d.

——. "On the Correct Handling of Contradictions among the People, February, 1957." In W. Chai, ed., *Essential Works of Chinese Communism*, 2nd ed., pp. 305–18. New York: Bantam Books, 1972b.

——. "On Ideological Work (Talk at a Conference Attended by Party Cadres from People's Liberation Army Units under the Nanjing Command and from Jiangsu and Anhui Provinces), 19 March 1957." In R. MacFarquhar, T. Cheek, and W. Wu, eds., *The Secret Speeches of Chairman Mao*, pp. 321–50. Cambridge, MA: Harvard University Press, 1989.

——. "On People's Democratic Dictatorship, July, 1949." In W. Chai, ed., *Essential Works of Chinese Communism*, 2nd ed., pp. 231–44. New York: Bantam Books, 1972c.

——. "Report on an Investigation of the Hunan Peasant Movement." In W. T. de Bary, W. T. Chan, and B. Watson, *Sources of Chinese Tradition*, pp. 860–77. New York: Columbia University Press, 1960e.

——. "Report on an Investigation of the Peasant Movement in Hunan, March, 1927." In W. Chai, ed., *Essential Works of Chinese Communism*, 2nd ed., pp. 31–43. New York: Bantam Books, 1972d.

——. "Some Questions Concerning Methods of Leadership, June, 1943." In W. Chai, ed., *Essential Works of Chinese Communism*, 2nd ed., pp. 202–8. New York: Bantam Books, 1972e.

Marger, E. "Turnabout in Prison—The Chinese Way." *China Law Report* 2:1 (1982): 54–56.

Marx, K. "Critique of the Gotha Program." In T. B. Bottomore and M. Rubel, eds., *Karl Marx: Selected Writings in Sociology and Social Philosophy*. Harmondsworth, England: Penguin Books, 1963.

Marx, K., and F. Engels. "Communist Manifesto." In S. Hedel, ed., *The Soviet Crucible*. North Scituate, MA: Duxbury Press, 1973.

McKnight, B. E. *The Quality of Mercy: Amnesties and Traditional Chinese Justice*. Honolulu: University Press of Hawaii, 1981.

Meadows, Thomas Taylor. *The Chinese and Their Rebellions: Viewed in Connection with Their National Philosophy, Ethics, Legislation and Administration*. London: Smith, Elder & Co., 1856.

Meisner, M. J. "The Chinese Rediscovery of Karl Marx: Some Reflection on Post Maoist Chinese Marxism." *Bulletin of Concerned Asian Scholars* 17:3 (1985): 2–16.

——. *Mao's China*. New York: Free Press, 1977.

Menzies, R. J. "Law, Politics, and Madness: On the Pathologization of Deviance." *Canadian Criminology Forum* 2 (Spring 1980): 11–28.

Merryman, J. H. "The Convergence (and Divergence) of the Civil Law and the Common Law." In M. Cappeletti, ed., *New Perspectives for a Common Law of Europe*, pp. 222–27. Boston: Sijithoff Publishing Co., 1978.

Michael, F. *China through the Ages*. London: Westview Press, 1986.

——. "The Role of Law in Traditional, Nationalist and Communist China." *China Quarterly* 3:9 (1962): 124–48.

Migdal, J. S. *Strong Societies and Weak States: State-Society Relations and State Capabilities in the Third World*. Princeton, NJ: Princeton University Press, 1988.

Miles, A. L. "Policing in Nationalist China." *Police Chief* 66:9 (1979): 53–55.

Miller, D. *Social Justice*. Oxford: Oxford University Press, 1979.

Miller, E. E. "Corrections in the People's Republic of China." In American Correctional Association, *International Corrections: An Overview*, Monograph no. II, pp. 65–71. College Park, MD: American Correctional Association, 1987.

———. "Prison Industries in the People's Republic of China." *Prison Journal* 68:2 (1982): 52–57.

Mishiba, Taichiro. *The History of Chinese Penal Law* (*Zhong-guo xing-fa-shi yan-jiu*). Translated from Japanese by Duan Qiu-guan. Beijing: Beijing University Press, 1985.

Moberly, W. *The Ethics of Punishment.* London: Faber and Faber, 1968.

Molm, L. D. "Punishment Power: A Balancing Process in Power-Dependence Relations." *American Journal of Sociology* 94:6 (1989): 1392–1418.

Moody, P. R. *Opposition and Dissent in Contemporary China.* Stanford, CA: Stanford University Press, 1977.

Morris, C. Preface to D. Bodde and C. Morris, *Law in Imperial China.* Philadelphia: University of Pennsylvania Press, 1973.

Moser, M. J. *Law and Social Change in a Chinese Community.* New York: Oceana Publications, 1982.

Munro, R. "Syncretic Sects and Secret Societies: Revival in the 1980s." *Chinese Sociology and Anthropology* 21:4 (1989).

Myren, Richard A. "The Criminal Justice System of China." *Justice Reporter* 2 (1982): 1–8.

Needham, J. "History of Scientific Thought." In J. Needham, ed., *Science and Civilization in China*, vol. II. New York: Cambridge University Press, 1956a.

———. "Human Law and the Laws of Nature in China and the West." In J. Needham, ed., *Science and Civilization in China*, vol. II. New York: Cambridge University Press, 1956b.

Neier, Aryeh. *Crime and Punishment.* New York: Stein and Day Publishers, 1976.

Ni, Zhengmao, Ronggang Yu, Qin Zheng, and Pei Cao. *Four Thousand Years of Chinese Legal Realm* (*Zhong-hua fa-yuan si-qian-nian*). Beijing: Public Publishing Co., 1987.

Nivison, D. S., and A. F. Wright, ed. *Confucianism in Action.* Stanford, CA: Stanford University Press, 1959.

Nye, F. I. *Family Relationships and Delinquent Behavior.* New York: Wiley, 1958.

Ogden, S. *China's Unresolved Issues: Politics, Development, and Culture.* Englewood Cliffs, NJ: Prentice Hall, 1989.

Oksenberg, M., and R. Bush. "China's Political Evolution: 1972–82." *Problems of Communism*, September–October 1982, pp. 1–19.

Oldham, John R., ed. *China's Legal Development.* Armonk, NY: M. E. Sharpe, 1986.

"Organizational Law of the People's Courts of the People's Republic of China (*Zhong-hua ren-min gong-he-guo ren-min fa-yuan zu-zhi-fa*)." In Z. Gan, J. Lin, and H. Shen, eds., *Law Yearbook of China* (*Zhong-guo fa-lü nian-jian*), pp. 137–40. Beijing: Law Publishing Co., 1987.

"Organizational Law of the People's Procurate of the People's Republic of China (*Zhong-hua ren-min gong-he-guo ren-min jian-cha-yuan zu-zhi-fa*)." In Z. Gan, J. Lin, and H. Shen, eds., *Law Yearbook of China* (*Zhong-guo fa-lü nian-jian*), pp. 140–42. Beijing: Law Publishing Co., 1987.

Ostergaard, C. S. "Explaining China's Recent Political Corruption." *Corruption and Reform* 1 (1986): 209–33.

Paragon, D. "Some Firsthand Observations on China's Legal System." *Judicature* 63:10 (1980): 476–84.

Parsons, T. "The Law and Social Control." In W. Evans, ed., *Law and Sociology*, pp. 56–72. New York: Free Press of Glencoe, 1962.

Peng, Zhen. "Report to the Fifth Meeting of the People's Congress on Revising the Draft of the Constitution of the PRC, 11.26.1982 (*Guan-yu zhong-hua ren-min gong-he-guo xian-fa xiu-gai cao-an de bao-gao*)." In *Selected Works of Peng Zhen, 1941–90* (*Peng Zhen wen-xuan, 1941–90*), pp. 435–63. Beijing: People's Publication Co., 1991.

———. "Speech at the Meeting of the Executive Committee of the Provincial, Autonomous Regional and Municipal People's Congress, March 12, 1984 (*Zai sheng shi zi-zhi-qu ren-da chang-wu wei-yuan-hui shang de jiang-hua*)." In Z. Gan, J. Lin, and H. Shen, eds., *Law Yearbook of China* (*Zhong-guo fa-lü nian-jian*), pp. 639–41. Beijing: Law Publishing Co., 1987.

"People's Courts Must Consciously Accept the Party's Leadership and Strengthen Judicial Work to Serve the Reform (*Ren-min fa-yuan yao zi-jue jie-shou dang de ling-dao, jia-qiang shen-pan gong-zuo wei gai-ge kai-fang fu-wu*)." *People's Daily* (overseas edition), January 5, 1990.

People's Daily, August 31, September 20, and October 17, 1989, and October 13, 1990.

People's Republic of China: Administration Atlas. Washington, DC: CIA, 1975.

Pepinsky, H. E. "A Season of Disenchantment: Trends in Chinese Justice Reconsidered." *International Journal of the Sociology of Law* 10 (1982): 277–85.

Pfeffer, Richard M. "Crime and Punishment: China and the United States." In Jerome Alan Cohen, ed., *Contemporary Chinese Law: Research Problems and Perspectives*, pp. 261–81. Cambridge, MA: Harvard University Press, 1970.

Pinard, J. L. "The People's Republic of China: A Bibliography of Selected English-Language Legal Materials." *China Law Reporter* 3 (1985): 46–143.

Platt, A. *The Child Savers.* 2nd ed. Chicago: University of Chicago Press, 1977.

"Population." In *China: Facts and Figures.* Beijing: Foreign Languages Press, 1982.

Pound, R. "Common Law." In E. R. A. Seligman and A. Johnson, eds., *Encyclopaedia of the Social Sciences*, vol. 4, p. 51. New York: Macmillan, 1937.

———. *An Introduction to the Philosophy of Law.* New Haven, CT: Yale University Press, 1922.

"Prime Minister Li Peng's Conversation with Malio Warsckis, President of *Mexican Sun Times*, May 30, 1991 (*Li Peng zong-li wu-yue san-shi-ri hui-jin mo-xi-ge tai-yang-shi-bao zong-jin-li, Ma-lo wa-ke-si shi de tan-hua*)." *People's Daily* (overseas edition), June 15, 1991.

Primoratz, I. *Justifying Legal Punishment.* Atlantic Highlands, NJ: Humanities Press International, Inc., 1989.

"Prosecutory Priority in Next Year: Advancement of Anti-Embezzlement, Corruption, and Bribery (*Zhong-guo ming-nian jian-cha gong-zou zhong-dian: shen-ru fan tan-wu hui-lu*)." *People's Daily* (overseas edition), October 13, 1990.

Pu, J., and Kunpo Zhou. *Introduction to the History of the Chinese Legal System* (*Zhong-guo fa-zhi-shi jian-ming jiao-cheng*). Beijing: Beijing University Press, 1987.

Pusey, James R. "On Liang Qichao's Darwinian 'Morality Revolution,' Mao Zedong's 'Revolutionary Morality,' and China's 'Moral Development.'" *In Richard W. Wilson, S. L. Greenblatt, and A. A. Wilson, eds., Moral Behavior in Chinese Society*, pp. 73–103. New York: Praeger, 1981.

Qu, Tong-zu. *Chinese Law and Chinese Society* (*Zhong-guo fa-lu yu zhong-guo she-hui*). Beijing: China Books Bureau, 1981.

Rahav, G. "Family Relations and Delinquency in Israel." *Criminology* 14 (1976): 259–70.

Reckless, W. C. *The Crime Problem.* 4th ed. New York: Appleton-Century-Crofts, 1967.

———. "A New Theory of Delinquency and Crime." *Federal Probation* 25 (1961): 42–46.

Reckless, W. C., Simon Dinitz, and Barbara Kay. "The Self Component in Potential Delinquency and Potential Nondelinquency." *American Sociological Review* 22 (1957): 566–70.

Reckless, W. C., Simon Dinitz, and Ellen Murry. "Self Concept as an Insulator against Delinquency." *American Sociological Review* 21 (1956): 744–46.

Regney, H. *Four Years in a Red Hell: The Story of Father Rigney*. Chicago: Henry Regney Co., 1956.

Regoli, R. M. "Law and Social Control in China: An Application of Black's Thesis." *Criminal Justice Review* 9:1 (1984): 1–6.

Ren, Jianxin. "Speech to the National Working Convention of the People's Courts, January 4, 1990." *People's Daily* (overseas edition), January 5, 1990.

"Renmin Ribao Article: Commentator on Time Limit of Criminal Procedure." Joint Publications Research Service, *China Report: Political, Sociological and Military Affairs*, July 11, 1984, no. 84–134, pp. K5–K6.

"Renmin Ribao Article: Official in Jilin Executed for Corruption." Joint Publications Research Service, *China Report: Political, Sociological and Military Affairs*, January 25, 1984, no. 84–009, pp. 110–11.

Rescher, N. *Distributive Justice*. New York: Bobbs-Merrill Co., 1966.

"Revision of Criminal Procedure Law and Law of Administrative Penalty (*Zing-chu xing-su liang-fa jiang zuo duo-chu xiu-gai*)." *World Journal* (*Shi-jie ri-bao*), March17, 1996.

"Revision of Criminal Procedure Law at Seventeenth Session of Standing Committee of the 8th National People's Congress (*Ba-jie quan-quo ren-da chang-wei-hui di-shi-qi-ci hui-y shen-yi xing-shi su-song-fa xiu-shang-an deng ba-bu fa-lu cao-an*)." *People's Daily* (overseas edition), December 21, 1995.

Reynolds, Paul D. "The Role of Law in China's Modernization." *Poly Law Review* 6 (1980): 12–20.

Richard, I. A. *Mencius on the Minds*. London: Kegan Paul, 1932.

Rickett, W. Allyn. "The New Constitution and China's Emerging Legal System in Perspective." *Journal of the Royal Asiatic Society of Hong Kong* 22 (1982): 99–117.

———. "Voluntary Surrender and Confession in Chinese Law: The Problem of Continuity." *Journal of Asian Studies* 30 (1971): 797–814.

Rickett, W. Allyn, and A. Rickett. *Prisoners of Liberation*. New ed. San Francisco: China Books, 1981.

Rider, B. A. "White Collar Crime: The Unacceptable Face of Communism." *Company Lawyer* 2:2 (1981): 85–86.

Rodzinski, Witold. *The Walled Kingdom: A History of China from Antiquity to the Present*. New York: Free Press, 1984.

Rojek, D. G. "The Criminal Process in the People's Republic of China." *Justice Quarterly* 2:1 (1985): 118–25.

Rosen, S. "Chinese Women." *Chinese Sociology and Anthropology* 20:3 (1988).

———. "Prosperity, Privatization, and China's Youth." *Problems of Communism*, March–April 1985, pp. 1–29.

———, ed. "The Rehabilitation and Dissolution of 'Li Yizhe.'" *Chinese Law and Government* 14 (1981): 3–121.

Rosenberg, M., C. Schooler, and C. Schoenbach. "Self-Esteem and Adolescent Problems." *American Sociological Review* 54 (1989): 1004–18.

Saich, T. "The Fourth Constitution of the People's Republic of China." *Review of Socialist Law* 2 (1983): 113-24.

Scalapino, Robert A., and George T. Yu. *Modern China and Its Revolutionary Process: Recurrent Challenges to the Traditional Order, 1850–1920.* Berkeley: University of California Press, 1985.

Schatz, B. A., and J. R. Silkenat. "Signals from China's Legal System." *National Law Journal* 2 (1980): 13–14.

Schell, O. "China's Andrei Sakharov." *Atlantic Monthly,* May 1988, pp. 35–52.

Schurmann, F. *Ideology and Organization in Communist China.* Berkeley: University of California Press, 1968.

Schwartz, B. "On Attitudes toward Law in China." In Milton Katz, ed., *Government under Law and the Individuals.* Washington, DC: American Council of Learned Societies, 1957.

———. "Some Polarities in Confucian Thought." In D. S. Nivison and A. F. Wright, eds., *Confucianism in Action,* pp. 49–62. Stanford, CA: Stanford University Press, 1959.

Schwartz, M., and S. Stryker. *Deviance, Selves and Others.* Washington, DC: American Sociological Association, 1970.

Schwartz, M., and Sandra S. Tangri. "A Note on Self-Concept as an Insulator against Delinquency." *American Sociological Review* 30 (1965): 922–26.

Schweisberg, D. R. "China Admits to Torture." *New York Times,* April 30, 1990.

Selden, M. *The Yanan Way in Revolutionary China.* Cambridge, MA: Harvard University Press, 1971.

Separovic, Z. P. "Criminal Justice in Yugoslavia." In E. H. Johnson, ed., *International Handbook of Contemporary Development in Criminology,* pp. 630–59. Westport, CT: Greenwood Press, 1983.

Seymour, J. D. *The Fifth Modernization: China's Human Rights Movement, 1978–79.* Stanfordville, NY: Human Rights Publishing Group, 1980.

Shaffer, L. "Marxism Enters a Confucian Realm: The People's Republic in the Perspective of Chinese History." *Fletcher Forum of World Affairs* 14:1 (1990): 1–9.

Shapiro, F. C. "Letter from Beijing." *New Yorker,* December 28, 1987, pp. 96–103.

Sharan, P. "The Judiciary." In *Political System of China,* pp. 112–24. Meerut, India: Meenakshi Prakashan, 1968.

Shelley, L. "Soviet Justice." *Problems of Communism,* July-August 1985, pp. 69–73.

Shen, Jia-ben. *Historical Inquiry of Penal Law (Li-dai xing-fa kao).* Beijing: China Publications Bureau, 1985.

———. "Prison Inquiry (*Yu-kao*)." In Department of Justice of the People's Republic of China, ed., *Collection of Literature on History of Chinese Penal Institutions (Zhong-guo jian-yu shi-liao hui-bian),* vol. 1, pp. 232–362. Beijing: Public Publishing Co., 1988.

Sheu, Chuen-Jim. "Juvenile Delinquency in the Republic of China: A Chinese Empirical Study of Social Control Theory." *International Journal of Comparative and Applied Criminal Justice* 12:1 (1988): 59–71.

Shiga, Shuzo. "Some Remarks on the Judicial System in China: Historical Development and Characteristics." In D. C. Buxbaum, ed., *Traditional and Modern Legal Institutions in Asia and Africa,* pp. 44–76. Leiden, Netherlands: E. J. Brill, 1967.

"Sichuan Ribao Article: Crackdown on Criminal Activities Urged." Joint Publications Research Service, *China Report: Political, Sociological and Military Affairs,* October 15, 1984, no. 84–068, pp. 140–42.

Silk, M. A. "The Crime of Dissent in China." *Problems of Communism,* July-August 1985, pp. 61–67.

———. "Economic Crime in China." In R. H. Folsom and J. H. Minan, eds., *Law in the People's Republic of China,* pp. 353–59. Boston: Martinus Nijhoff Publishers, 1989.

Simon, R. J. "A Trip to China." *Justice Quarterly* 2:1 (1985): 99–101.

Smith, R. J. *China's Cultural Heritage: The Ching Dynasty, 1644–1912.* Boulder, CO: Westview Press, 1983.

Spence, Jonathan D. *The Search for Modern China.* New York: W. W. Norton & Co., 1990.

Spitzer, S., ed. *Deviance and Control In Chinese Society.* New York: Praeger, 1977.

Stahnke, A. "The Background and Evolution of Party Policy on the Drafting of the Legal Code in Communist China." *American Journal of Comparative Law* 15 (1967): 506–25.

Stanilaus, K. L. "Traditional Chinese Philosophy of Life." *Asian Thought & Society* 8 (1983).

Stark, R., L. Kent, and D. P. Doyle. "Religion and Delinquency: The Ecology of a 'Lost' Relationship." *Journal of Research in Delinquency and Crime* 19 (1982): 4–24.

"The State Department Issued a Regulation on Punishing Embezzlement and Bribery (*Guo-wu-yuan fa-bu tan-wu hui-lu chu-fen gui-ding*)." *People's Daily* (overseas edition), September 18, 1988.

The Statute on Punishing Counterrevolution in the PRC. Beijing: Law Publishing Co., 1951.

Streib, K. K., and V. L. Streib. "Social Control in Traditional International China." *Journal of Comparative and Applied Criminal Justice* 2:2 (1978): 207–18.

Takagi, P., and T. Platt. "Behind the Gilded Ghetto: An Analysis of Race, Class and Crime in Chinatown." *Crime and Social Justice* 9 (1978): 2–25.

Tao, L. S. "Criminal Justice in Communist China (I)." *Issues & Studies* 13:6 (1977a): 15–42.

——. "Criminal Justice in Communist China (II)." *Issues & Studies* 13:7 (1977b): 19–50.

Teiwes, F. C. *Politics & Purge in China: Rectification and the Decline of Party Norms.* New York: M. E. Sharpe, 1979.

Thieme, G. V. "The Debate on the Presumption of Innocence in the People's Republic of China." *Review of Socialist Law* 10 (1984): 277–90.

Tiene, D. "*'People's Trial' in Communist China: An Informal Approach to Criminal Justice.*" *Southwestern Journal of Social Education* 13 (1983): 28–44.

Tifft, L. L. "Reflections on Capital Punishment and the 'Campaign against Crime' in the People's Republic of China." *Justice Quarterly* 2:1 (1985): 127–37.

Timothy, K. "Criminal Justice in China." *International Journal of Law Libraries* 8:3 (1980): 108–15.

Tompkins, P. "The Most Precious Chinese Possession." In P. Tompkins, ed., *The Eunuch and the Virgin*, pp. 31–45. New York: Clarkson N. Potter, 1962.

Townsend, J. R. *Politics of China.* Boston: Little, Brown and Co., 1980.

Troyer, R. J., J. P. Clark, and D. G. Rojek, eds. *Social Control in the People's Republic of China.* New York: Praeger, 1989.

Ts'ao, I. J. H. "The Politico-Criminal Trial in Beijing: Perspective and Prospect." *Asian Thought & Society* 6:16 (1981): 49–62.

Ts'ao, Wen-yen. *The Development of Chinese Law.* Taipei, Taiwan: China Culture Publishing Foundation, 1953.

——. "Equity in Chinese Customary Law." *Chinese Culture* 3:2 (1960): 9–28.

Tseng, Y. H. *Modern Chinese Legal and Political Philosophy.* Shanghai: Commercial Press, 1934.

Tung, Hei Hsiao. *A Great Trial in Chinese History.* Beijing: New World Press, 1981.

Turk, A. T. "Political Deviance and Popular Justice in China: Lessons for the West." In R. J. Troyer, J. P. Clark, and D. G. Rojek, eds., *Social Control in the People's Republic of China*, pp. 34–42. New York: Praeger, 1989.

van der Sprenkel, Sybille. "The Chinese Experience of Law: A Historical Survey." *Poly Law Review* 6 (1980): 5–8.

Vials, Thelma. "Facets of Natural Justice in China." *Poly Law Review* 6 (1980): 38–42.

Vladimirov, P. P. *China's Special Era, 1942–45*. Bombay: Allied Publishers, 1974.

Vogel, E. F. *One Step Ahead in China*. Cambridge, MA: Harvard University Press, 1989.

Vohra, Ranbir. *China's Path to Modernization*. Englewood Cliffs, NJ: Prentice-Hall, 1987.

"Voluntary Surrender—Remission of Penalty: Amphetamine Users Are Facing the Deadline (*Zi-shou mian-xing, xi-an-zhe mian-lin zui-hou-qi-xian*)." *World Journal* (*Shi-jie ri-bao*), February 24, 1992.

Wakeman, F., Jr. "All the Rage in China." *New York Review*, March 2, 1989, pp. 19–21.

Wallacker, B. E. "Han Confucianism and Confucius in Han." In D. T. Roy and T. H. Tsien, eds., *Ancient China: Studies in Early Civilization*, pp. 215–28. Hong Kong: Chinese University Press, 1978.

Wang, Da-ming. "Legal Education Should Focus on Strengthening Citizens' Socialist Consciousness (*Fa-zhi jiao-yu yao zhao-yan yu zeng-qiang she-hui zhu-yi gong-min yi-shi*)." In Z. Gan, J. Lin, and H. Shen, eds., *Law Yearbook of China* (*Zhong-guo fa-lü nian-jian*), pp. 685–91. Beijing: Law Publishing Co., 1987.

Wang, Huai-an, Min Gu, Zhun Lin, and Wan-zhong Sun. *Collection of Laws, Statutes, and Regulations of the People's Republic of China*. Chang Chun, PRC: Jilin People's Publishing Co., 1989.

Wang, James C. F. "China: The Chinese Party's Inner Party Discipline and Democracy." *Asian Thought & Society* 6:17-18 (1981): 248–58.

Wang, Joseph En-pao, ed. *Outlines of Modern Chinese Law*. Arlington, VA: University Publications of America, 1976.

Ward, R. H. "The Police in China." *Justice Quarterly* 2:1 (1985): 111–15.

Ward, R. H., and D. H. Bracey. "Police Training and Professionalism in the People's Republic of China." *Police Chief* 52:5 (1985): 36–38.

Weber, M. *Max Weber on Law in Economics and Society*. New York: Simon and Schuster, 1969.

Wei, H. *Courts and Police in Communist China to 1952*. Lackland Air Force Base, TX: U.S. Air Force Personnel and Training Research Center, 1955.

Wells, L. E. "Theories of Deviance and the Self-Concept." *Social Psychology* 41 (1978): 189–204.

"What Is Behind Crime (*Fan-zui de bei-hou*)?" *People's Daily* (overseas edition), February, 24, 1983b.

White, Theodore H. *China: The Roots of Madness*. New York: Wolper Productions, 1968.

Whyte, M. K. "Corrective Labor Camps in China." *Asian Survey* 13 (1973): 253–69.

———. "The Social System." In F. M. Bunge and R. S. Shinn, eds., *China: A Country Study*, pp. 79–134. Washington, DC: U.S. Government Printing Office, 1981.

Wilson, A. A. "Deviance and Social Control in Chinese Society: An Introductory Essay." In A. A. Wilson, S. L. Greenblatt, and R. W. Wilson, eds., *Deviance and Social Control in Chinese Society*, pp. 1–13. New York: Praeger, 1977.

Wilson, A. A., S. L. Greenblatt, and R. W. Wilson, eds. *Deviance and Social Control in Chinese Society*. New York: Praeger, 1977.

Wilson, Richard W. "Moral Behavior in Chinese Society: A Theoretical Perspective." In R. W. Wilson, S. L. Greenblatt, and A. A. Wilson, eds., *Moral Behavior in Chinese Society*, pp. 1–20. New York: Praeger, 1981.

Woo, Margaret Y. K. "The Right to a Criminal Appeal in the People's Republic of China." *Yale Journal of International Law* 14:118 (1989): 118–60.

Wright, A. F. *Confucianism and Chinese Civilization*. Stanford, CA: Stanford University Press, 1964.

"Writ of Appeal to the Nanjing District Court and Supreme Court of Jiangsu Province by Guo Luoji, March 10, 1992 (*Guo Luoji de shang-su zhuang*)." *China Spring*, May 1992, pp. 44–48.

Wu, Jianfan. "Building New China's Legal System." In John R. Oldham, ed., *China's Legal Development*, pp. 1–40. New York: M. E. Sharpe, 1986.

Wu, John C. H. "Chinese Legal Philosophy: A Brief Historical Survey." *Chinese Culture* 1:4 (1958): 7–48.

———. "Confucius and Chinese Culture." *Journal of the China Society* 14–15 (1979): 17–23.

Wu, Tien-wei. *Lin Biao and the Gang of Four: Contra-Confucianism in Historical and Intellectual Perspective*. Carbondale and Edwardsville: Southern Illinois University Press, 1983.

Xiao, Du. "Judge's Confusion (*Fa-guan de mi-huo*)." *People's Daily* (overseas edition), August 9, 1988.

Xiao, Hongbin. "A Veteran Rural Mediator." *China Constructs*, July 1986, pp. 15–16.

Xiao, Zhu. "The Cultural Revolution and Class Struggle." In J. D. Seymour, ed., *The Fifth Modernization*, pp. 132–37. New York: Human Rights Publishing Group, 1980.

"Xinhua Ribao Article: Nanjing Newspaper Urges Criminals to Turn Themselves In." Joint Publications Research Service, *China Report: Political, Sociological and Military Affairs*, March 7, 1984, no. 84–020, pp. 67–68.

Xiu, J. F., H. K. Shu, M. Z. Shao, and Q. S. Yu, eds. *The System of Rehabilitation through Labor*. Beijing: Public Publishing Co., 1983.

Xu, Jian. "The Principles and Development of Juvenile Justice Administration in the People's Republic of China." *Police Studies* 10:4 (1987): 181–84.

Xu, Yi. "Corruption: Why It Occurs, What's Being Done." *China Constructs*, May 1986, pp. 26–29.

Yan, Jiaqi, and G. Gao. *History of the Ten-Year Cultural Revolution* (*Zhong-guo wen-ge shi-nian-shi*). Beijing: China's Research Publishing Co., 1986.

Yang, Dunxian, and Zhenxiang Zhou. "Study of Counterrevolutionary Crime (*Guan-yu fan-ge-ming-zui ji-ge wen-ti de yan-jiu*)." In Y. Gan, ed., *Special Edition on Criminal Law* (*Xing-fa-xue zhuan-lun*), pp. 475–527. Beijing: Beijing University Press, 1989.

Yang, Hegao. *Shang Yang's Legal Thoughts* (*Shang Yang de fa-lü si-xiang*). Beijing: Public Publishing Co., 1987.

Yang, Hegao, and Qiuguan Duan, eds. *History of Chinese Legal Thought* (*Zhong-guo fa-lü si-xiang shi*). Beijing: Beijing University Press, 1988.

Yang, Hong-Lie. *Evolutionary History of Chinese Law* (*Zhong-guo fa-lü fa-da-shi, Shang, Xia*). Vols. 1 and 2. Beijing: China Book Bureau, 1990.

Yao, Zhaohui. "New Crimes Emerging in the Process of China's Development and the Strategic Policies and Measures to Be Taken." *UNAFEI: Resource Material Series*, no. 30 (December 1986): 53–66.

Ye, Xiao-xin, Wei Qiao, and Peng-sheng Chen, eds. *History of Chinese Legal System* (*Zhong-guo fa-zhi shi*). Beijing: Beijing University Press, 1989.

Yen, Ching-Yueh. *Crime in Relation to Social Change in China*. Chicago: University of Chicago Press, 1934.

Yi, Changxin. "Why Capital Punishment Remains in China." *China Daily*, December 31, 1983, p. 4. Also printed in Joint Publications Research Service, *China Report: Political, Sociological and Military Affairs*, January 25, 1984, no. 84–009, pp. 74–76.

Young, Stephen B. "The Concept of Justice in Pre-Imperial China." In R. W. Wilson, S. L. Greenblatt, and A. A. Wilson, eds., *Moral Behavior in Chinese Society*, pp. 38–72. New York: Praeger, 1981.

Yu, Shutong. "Development of the Juvenile Justice System in China." Paper presented at the Seventh United Nations Congress on the Prevention of Crime and the Treatment of Offenders, Milan, Italy, August 29, 1985.

Yuen, G. "A Cross-Cultural Perspective to Juvenile Offenders in the U.S.: A Chinese Perspective." *International Journal of Comparative and Applied Criminal Justice* 12:1 (1988): 89–100.

Zheng, Henry R. *China's Civil and Commercial Law.* St Paul, MN: Butterworth & Co. (Asia) Pte, 1988.

Zhou, Lipo. *Thunder Storm* (*Bao-feng zhou-yu*). Beijing: People's Publishing Co., 1955.

Zhou, Mi. *History of Chinese Penal Law (Zhong-guo xi-fa shi).* Beijing: Public Publishing Co., 1985.

Zhou, Yan. "On China's Current Class Struggle." *Beijing Review* 25:33 (1982): 17–19.

Zhu, Qiwu. "General Aspects of the Chinese Criminal Code and Code of Criminal Procedure." *UCLA Pacific Basin Law Journal* 2 (1983): 65–75.

Zhuzi jicheng. Beijing: China Book Bureau, 1958.

Zvirbul, V. K. "Criminology, Crime and Justice in the Union of Soviet Socialist Republics." In E. H. Johnson, ed., *International Handbook of Contemporary Developments in Criminology*, pp. 617–28. Westport, CT: Greenwood, 1983.

Index

About the Author

XIN REN is Associate Professor of Criminal Justice at California State University, Sacramento.

ISBN 0-313-29096-2
90000>
EAN
9 780313 290961
HARDCOVER BAR CODE